Journey
Vastness

Ngakpa Chögyam belongs to the White Lineage of Ngakpas (Awareness-spell people) who are predominantly nomadic or mountain-dwelling Lamas. He travelled to the Himalayas in the early 1970s to study; since then he has practised under the personal guidance of several accomplished Masters of Tantra and Dzogchen, completing numerous long solitary retreats. While fulfilling his Lama's instruction to practice in wild and fearful places he survived a terrifying sequence of events in which he realised his shamanic potential.

Since his return from the Himalayas in 1983 (and the publication of *Rainbow of Liberated Energy*) he has taught in Europe and America, and receives many invitations from individuals and organisations who have come to hear of his unique and dynamic approach. He is a healer, qualified teacher and professional counsellor who is regularly invited to speak on radio and contribute to journals and books on psychology and meditation. He now works increasingly with those involved in mainstream psychology and alternative therapy as a spiritual consultant, and is a regular contributor to conferences and seminars in this field.

He is the spiritual guide of 'Sang-ngak-chö-dzong' Tibetan Tantric Periphery: a growing association of apprentices who combine their practice in the White Tradition with working and family lives. An authority on Tantric Symbolism, he is an accomplished Thangka painter and calligrapher whose work appears in a number of books and publications.

Ngakpa Chögyam currently lives in Cardiff with his wife – a feminist psychologist and lecturer who is researching into women and personal power.

The Tibetan Mystic Path

The Tibetan Mystic Path series looks at our lives from the perspective of Tibetan Tantra in a down-to-earth humorous way. It is written to make available powerful teachings that have long been obscured by cultural and academic barriers. Ngakpa Chögyam's work is a bridge between the most magical tradition of Tibetan Buddhism and the everyday realities and pressures of city life. The series is based upon the numerous courses, seminars and talks given by Ngakpa Chögyam since 1983 and reflects his determined interest in enabling people to make real use of Tibetan teachings rather than being over-whelmed or confused by them. For this reason, these books have been written with the intention that no one having read them will be left saying: "So what do I do now?" This series covers subjects that have intrigued and baffled readers since books on Tibet first appeared, and presents them in a way that offers us the possibility of changing our lives.

Journey into Vastness

A Handbook of Tibetan Meditation Techniques

Ngakpa Chögyam

Element Books

BY THE SAME AUTHOR

Great Ocean
An Authorised Biography of the Dalai Lama
with Roger Hicks

Rainbow of Liberated Energy
Working with Emotions through the Colour
and Element Symbolism of Tibetan Tantra

First published 1988 by
Element Books Limited
Longmead, Shaftesbury, Dorset

Printed and bound in Great Britain by
Billings, Hylton Road, Worcester

Designed by Humphrey Stone

Cover photo: Dr. Jean Lorre/Science Photo Library

Cover portrait of author, photography of meditation
and kam-nye postures by Rob Brazier

British Library Cataloguing in Publication Data
Chögyam, Ngakpa
Journey into vastness: a handbook of
Tibetan meditation techniques.
1. Meditation
I. Title
158'.12   BL627

ISBN 1-85230-017-5

Contents

This book is gratefully dedicated to:
His Holiness The Fourteenth Dalai Lama of Tibet

The Twin Incarnations of Nuden Dorje Drophang Lingpa:
The Fabulous and Incomparable Yogi Terton and Scholar
H.H. Dudjom Rinpoche (1904–1987)
The Memory of Whom Will Always Remain Vivid,
and My Spiritual Father H.E. Khordong Terchen Tulku
Chhimed Rigdzin Rinpoche
Who is an Endless Source of Power Clarity and Kindness.

The Great Dzogchen Master – Lama Namkhai Norbu Rinpoche,
and to all The Marvellous Tantric Yogis and Yoginis
from whom I have received Teachings.

May the White Lineage thrive for the sake
of everyone everywhere!

Acknowledgements

It's an immense and difficult pleasure to find myself obliged to so many kind and delightful people. It's impossible to say enough about you, impossible to do you justice and impossible to name you all.

Because some of you will have to await another time and another book, I'd like to start by thanking all those splendid people whose names do not appear – this will be remedied on a future occasion. People are more important than books, but sometimes it takes a book to remind us of that. In this spirit I affectionately acknowledge:

My wonderful wife and friend Fruitbat Cutmore-Smith for opening me to the wisdom of women and to the accommodating spaciousness of my own femininity.

My dear friend Dr David Fontana for his quiet, gentle humour and true light-heartedness. His commitment to the spadework of dismantling the dam between Western psychology and the lineages of liberation has released rivulets of new possibilities for many people. David's own practice has enabled him to dissolve boundaries between different paths and open to the essence of many different presentations of reality. As a Reader in Educational Psychology at Cardiff University his intellectual achievements are prodigious, but his simplicity of expression and uncompromising warmth sparkle through at every turn.

My Vajra-Brother Johannes Frischknecht (Lobsang Phunstog), Director of 'Ri-me Jang-chub Chö-ling' – Institut Für Vajrayana Philosophie, Zurich, Switzerland, for his friendship, enthusiasm and active non-sectarianism. For Johannes, the spirit of Ri-me has always been a lived reality rather than a diplomatic stance. His commitment and dedication along with his humour, carefree kindness and uncontrived humility make him an example of what can be accomplished through practice.

My dear friend of many years, the irrepressible Dr Steve Glascoe, and his wife Sue, for being thoroughly and completely human. Steve has tended my health with exuberance and prescriptions of high-speed humour. Sue has tended our garden and nurtured our digestions with the deftness of a woodland elf. Thank you both for adding so much colour to the world.

My dear brother the 'Psychedelic sky-falling building-society manager', and his wife Jill for my two astonishing nieces Jessica and Ruth – the little Sky-Dancing Ladies.

Norzin Lama (Laxmi), daughter of Khordong Terchen Tulku Chhimed Rigdzin Rinpoche; for being who she is – an extraordinary dakini. Thank you for your directness, brilliance, warmth and open-hearted friendship – and for riding pillion on the 'Angel of Death'.

Dr John Crook for allowing me to turn everything upside down and break most of the rules. John's rich life as a teacher of Ch'an and Zen grows in influence, and his Western Zen retreats have become a formula for life-changing insights. That he invited me to unleash my mirth, mischief and mayhem on his 'Yogins' Retreat' (exploding the Silent Sitting with Ati-yoga Yells) says much for his openness and lack of attachment to familiar form.

Michael Mann of Element Books for encouragement, questions and suggestions. Michael alters very little of my text in spite of its audacity, eccentricity and cavalier treatment of the English language, but what he does alter makes all the difference. Michael's support of my strong wish to break through the conventions of contemporary Tibetan Buddhist writing, requires both courage and an understanding of the subject matter that lies beyond the level of 'information'. Thank you for sharing the intention to make such teachings available to a wider audience. Thank you too, Annie Walton and Michael Froomberg in similar vein.

Revd. James Low (Ngakpa Mikyö Seng-ge) – friend, ally and Vajra-Brother without whose support, encouragement and loyalty at a very difficult time, this book would have suffered considerable delay. James is a rare individual, a Tantric yogi with an acute understanding of Western psychology, whose warmth and free-flowing brilliance should be receiving wide acclaim. I feel honoured to know you. Thank you too, Barbara Terris for your great warmth, hospitality, openness and integrity in a world where those qualities are sometimes inconsistent.

Chloë Goodchild for your Outer, Inner, Secret and Ultimate Voice. Your fruity guffaw, once heard, is never forgotten. Ha! Also Roger Housden for being so quick to recognise that there can be no method to *Being*. Thank you both for your uncomplicated enthusiasm.

Caroline Sherwood, Mistress of Mysteries, friend and *agent provocateur* of roshies, medicine-men and lamas. Thank you for your incandescent laughter.

My apprentices, especially Pete Davis (Ngakchung Ozer Dorje), Su Graves and Brian O'Donovan (Dawa Khandro and Nyima Dorje), Caroline Cram (Dechen Khandro), Andy Hicks (Kunzang Dorje), Patrick Rennison (Jigme Dorje), Jane Whittle (Pema Khandro) and Tony Court (Dorje Pawo), Michael Froomberg (Rigdzin Dorje), Peter Stanford (Dorje Pawo), Babette Le Pataurel (Yeshe Khandro).

Sun Bear for your friendship, humour and good work. I wish there were more people like you in the world. Thank you for the risks you've taken and for your solid earthy wisdom. Thank you for saying that you 'don't believe in any philosophy that doesn't grow corn.' Thank you also to Wabun, Donna Dupree (Singing Pipe-Woman), Casie, Lou, Mary Kay and Aaron DeSabla, Morning Star, Mary Thunder and Horse, Jaya, Jude, Shabari, Auntie Lani Kalama, Amy Lee (She who catches the Rainbows), Brant Secunda, Robin Raindrop and Jospeh Creel Jnr.

I would also like to say thank you to Dr Sue Blackmore, Dr Michael West, Dr Martin Skinner, Dr John Pickering, Stephen Batchelor, John Snelling, Paul Bodenham and Linda Brogan, Penny Arnold, Reg and Sarah Clark, Alf Vial for not conforming, 5 Cram for sensitivity, technical virtuosity and intelligence above and beyond the call of duty, Carol Evans, John and Heather Harvey, Diana and John Lilley, Nancy Benson and Nelly Cartier, Anna Gore-Langton, Jake Lyne deVer, Jill Morely,

Kurt Schaffhauser for being Kurt Schaffhauser, Liz Rose, Ann Rimmer, Sue Parkinson Smith Amber and Lewis Motram, Johanna Van DerSchaft, Sue and Bernard Tagliavini, Kevin Barlow, Vanessa and Len Sinclaire for the Jnana-jive, Michael Hunt and Denise Brock for the dry humour and significantly stunning stitchcraft, Lesley and Jonathan for the fabulous crochéed Ngakpa shawl and the many months it took to complete it, Patrick Graham, Mel and Pete Goodridge for the Da, Richard and Nancy Stockart, Norma Levine, Chrissie Coburn-Krzowska.

Lastly to Francis and Juliet Deas, Mary and Magnus Carter, Lee Bray and to all those who have remained my friends – I cannot express how much I value you.

NGAKPA CHÖGYAM
Roath Cardiff and Monroe New York
June 1987

THE 'CHHI-MED RIG-'DZIN SOCIETY
FOR THE STUDY AND PRACTICE OF VAJRAYANA BUDDHISM
FOLLOWING THE NYINGMAPA LINEAGES OF BYANGTER & KHORDONG

Patron :

H. H. DUDJOM RINPOCHE
SUPREME HEAD OF THE
NYINGMAPA SECT

Founder :

VEN 'CHHI-MED RIG-'DZIN LAMA
KHORDONG TERCHEN TULKU
SANTINIKETAN INDIA

A Foreword to "Journey into Vastness"
  by Ven. Ngakpa Chögyam Ögyen Togden

    It gives me great pleasure to write a note in this work
of "Journey into Vastness" written by the Ven. Ngakpa Chögyam.
I have known Ven. Ngakpa Chögyam over numbers of years and in
that time have been on several occasions to his home and met at
other places to practise meditation together. He has profusely
studied and practised the Tantric Buddhism of Tibet and meditation
in the Nyingma line.

    His first book "Rainbow of Liberated Energy" has established
his masterly contribution in this field, and his present book
"Journey into Vastness" shall once again establish the author's
command over the subject. As a handbook of meditation it covers
Shi-ne, Lha-tong, Nyi-med and Lhundrup practices. Shi-ne is
the ground of meditation and through the subsequent practices,
the concept of an absence of connection between self and other is
liberated in its arising and melts inside the supreme Knowledge.

    His contribution in this book will greatly help the readers.
His present book is of considerable value.

    dated the twentyfourth of October, 1986

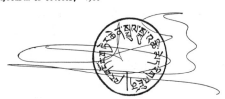

Khordong Terchen Tulku Chhimed Rigdzin Rinpoche

Introduction

There are many good books on meditation, so what makes this one rather special? The answer is that in addition to its admirable clarity and openness it shows a rare understanding of the human mind. The author writes as a man who is already on intimate terms with his readers, who knows in advance the joys and setbacks each of them will encounter on the rewarding, maddening path of meditation. Like a wise friend, he stands at one's shoulder, prompting, helping, encouraging, chuckling; full of patience and of the confidence that everyone can succeed provided they give it a little time and patience. He wastes no words on describing exalted states, beautific visions, blinding illuminations. Meditation, he assures us, is first and foremost a way of Sitting with yourself and realising your own true nature. Easy? Of course. Difficult? Of Course. And in an odd kind of way beyond both easy and difficult. Read Ngakpa Chögyam's book, Sit and meditate with him, and you'll see what I mean.

So how has Ngakpa Chögyam come by his understanding of the human mind? The answer to that is simple. By studying himself. He writes and teaches as a man who has had long, first-hand experience of each of the things about which he writes, and of using them in the exploration of his own being. First-hand experience gained in the setting both of the East where the ideas and techniques he describes originated, and in the West, where he was born and raised and where he now lives. For Ngakpa Chögyam is one of a very rare breed. A highly educated Westerner (he holds a first-class honours degree in Art) who has followed the rigorous training of an ordained Nyingma Lama, with its long solitary retreats, under the direction of teachers who embody the authentic traditions of Tibet. Co-author of the authorised biography of His Holiness the Dalai Lama, Ngakpa

Chögyam has absorbed the Nyingma tradition of Tibetan Buddhism into his bones while still remaining enough of a Westerner to be able to offer aspects of that tradition to Westerners in a form which they can understand and which has direct relevance to their daily lives. Like most Buddhist Schools (and in marked contrast to Western psychology) the Nyingma tradition holds that the way towards a true knowledge of the mind is first to turn one's focus of awareness inwards, and to know oneself. Only then is one ready to start studying and teaching others. This Ngakpa Chögyam has done, hence the wisdom and the sound good sense contained in this book.

But have no fear. Ngakpa Chögyam isn't asking you to throw everything up and go and live in the Himalayas (though if you wanted to do that he would tell you how to go about it), or to abandon your personal spiritual traditions and beliefs in favour of his own. He isn't out to 'convert' anyone, or to get the better of them in a philosophical or theological argument. His task is to help you live your life in a fuller, richer (and at the same time simpler) way, to free yourself from some of the more painful demands of your ego, and to realise the vast and joyous potential of your own being. And if that isn't a worthwhile task for any writer to undertake, I'm not sure what is.

In spite of the obvious benefit to the West of having teachers like Ngakpa Chögyam working amongst us, I am nevertheless sometimes asked why we should bother ourselves with Eastern ideas. Haven't we in the West spiritual and psychological traditions enough of our own, without bothering ourselves with other people's? Certainly we have, and very powerful many of them are too. But in the West we've made two fundamental mistakes in our approaches to our own traditions. In the first place we separated out spirituality and psychology (soul and mind) instead of seeing them as vital to each other. And in the second place we've neglected and forgotten many of the techniques like meditation which help personal growth in these two areas. By and large this isn't true of the East. Though we must be careful not to blind ourselves to their shortcomings. Eastern traditions work on the admirable premises that we can't understand human beings unless we see them as a whole, and that we can't fully assist their development unless we have a personal psychotherapy of techniques which each person can practice for him or herself.

Acceptable as this answer is to many people, others quite reasonably still have reservations. In particular those trained in Western psychology and in Western psychotherapy question whether Eastern traditions are sufficiently scientific in their approach. Science (particularly behavioural science) has its drawbacks, but it does at least attempt to introduce precision and a degree of objectivity into matters. The Western scientist tries to produce results that can be clearly demonstrated and readily generalised, and he or she has a deep suspicion that when you strip away the colourful language, Eastern traditions may have nothing much to offer except vague sentiments and clever showmanship. Even those scientists who take a more charitable view argue that Eastern spiritual and psychological techniques *may* work for *some* people *some* of the time, but at such an impossibly subjective level, that there is no way in which they can be put to scientific test. Nor can we establish precisely what it is about these techniques that actually works – an essential step if this 'active ingredient' is to be extracted and made available in the instant, painless form so attractive to the modern Western mind!

Such reservations cannot be lightly brushed aside. Indeed to do so would render any rapprochement between Western and Eastern thought even more difficult than currently it is. Western scientists do have a right to ask Eastern traditions for their credentials, and do have a right to speak out against the loopholes in these credentials through which the misguided and the credulous can be lured by the unscrupulous. Similarly Eastern thinkers and practitioners have a right to question the authenticity of Western approaches, and to speak out against the narrowness of the paradigms which underpin them. Only through such a process of mutual examination in an atmosphere of respect and trust can we arrive at the understanding which will allow these two distinct systems of thought and belief to inform and enrich each other.

Inevitably a process of this kind depends upon individuals who are prepared to be open enough, and persevering enough, to study both systems and build the necessary bridges between them. In this sense, we live in fortunate times. Modern methods of travel and of communication mean that East and West can touch each other as never before. The tragic events surrounding recent Tibetan history have also released a stream of Tibetan teachers ready and willing to share their wisdom with Westerners. Unprecedented opportunities exist for Westerners to study Tibetan thought in some detail, and to re-examine their own ideas and practices within the light of it. And thankfully many Westerners, including psychologists and therapists, have been quick to grasp these opportunities. Things don't seem to work quite so well the other way around though. For various reasons, there aren't that many Tibetan teachers who have studied Western thought at first-hand, and who are courageous enough to modify aspects of their own traditions in the light of this thought. And to modify them in such a way that these traditions become appropriate to the social and cultural imperatives of the West.

Which brings me back to Ngakpa Chögyam and his book. I have already said that Ngakpa Chögyam is a highly educated Westerner who has followed at first-hand the rigorous training of a Tibetan Lama. But he is more than that. He is a man who, after completing this training and returning to the West to teach, then set about mastering the teaching of Western psychologists so that he could not only speak to them in their own language but attempt such modifications to his traditional presentation as might seem necessary. In recent years he has worked increasingly with Western psychologists, therapists and medical practitioners – addressing academic conferences, running joint workshops, taking initiatives in opening up extensive new areas of dialogue and debate. And in so doing helping generate not only a new basis for understanding, but also a creative flow of new ideas which has profound implications for the future.

But in emphasizing the work Ngakpa Chögyam is doing to bring Tibetan and Western psychology closer together, don't let me give the impression he is advocating some vague East-West compromise, lacking the strength of either tradition. His aim is to present his school of Tibetan Buddhism in a form that makes sense to those from a quite different cultural and historical background, but he has no intention in so doing of losing any of its essential essence. This was symbolized for me particularly at a major international conference organised by the British Psychological Society. The Society is more used to sober lounge suits and ties (and their female sartorial equivalents) in its invited speakers than the robes of a Tibetan Lama. Yet, nothing daunted, Ngakpa Chögyam moved amongst us each day in the full costume of an ordained Nyingma, contriving all the time to look more natural and more at home than anyone. The centre each day of a large, attentive group of Western academics and therapists, he tirelessly and patiently defined and re-defined the extraordinarily intricate complexities of Tibetan psychology until he was sure everyone had fully understood and was in a position to see the links between it and their own thinking.

The popularity of the intensive series of workshops that he mounted at the Conference, together with the close attention with which everyone attended to his keynote address to the whole gathering, were further proof of how successfully he achieved his aims. But perhaps the best symbol of Ngakpa Chögyam co-operating with Western thought without losing any of his Tibetan essence was the sight of him, festooned with electrodes and wires, calmly Sitting in deep meditation wrapped in robes whose style hasn't changed for centuries. As the scientists gathered around their equipment to study Ngakpa Chögyam's brain waves, the picture of Western technology meeting Tibetan age-old wisdom was perfect.

So in Ngakpa Chögyam we have an innovator who yet remains true to the root teachings from which his innovations take their meaning. But that doesn't, of course, make him immune to criticism. Criticism has a habit of following innovation, just as night follows day, and there are those embedded in tradition who feel Ngakpa Chögyam is travelling too far and too fast, just as there are those in the West who think that we psychologists who interest ourselves in Eastern theory and practice are becoming far too mystical and directionless. Time alone will tell whether these criticisms are justified or not. Just as time alone will tell whether those Western medical scientists who marvel over the unusual brain rhythms produced by Ngakpa Chögyam when in deep meditation, are on to something of great significance to the study of the human mind or not. And just as time will tell whether the counselling and psycho-therapeutic techniques based upon the interface between Tibetan Tantric psychology and Western methodology which Ngakpa Chögyam is pioneering in his own counselling practice represent a major advance or not.

But enough of this. Even if I had no interest in the Tibetan traditions and the men and women who teach them, I would still as a psychologist find it my duty to study Ngakpa Chögyam. To study him in order to find out what makes him such a happy and positive person – what makes him so warm and compassionate with everyone, so kind and unselfish, as much at peace with himself peeling potatoes in his kitchen in Cardiff as he is tramping in the Himalayas. It would have been my duty because whatever his secret it needs to be made available to others. Happily much of that secret is spelt out for us in this book, and in one of Ngakpa Chögyam's previous books *Rainbow of Liberated Energy*. The reader will have to decide for him or herself what to make of this secret. It offers no simple answers. It offers no shortcuts. The more one gets to grips with it, the more one has the feeling that its 'active ingredient' just isn't the kind of thing that can be conveniently packaged and taken by the ounce. Hence no doubt the word 'Journey' in the title. Journeys have a habit of taking a long time and of making certain demands upon the traveller. But they also have a habit of changing the scenery around you, and perhaps even changing something inside yourself. So read this book and see what happens. I can guarantee one thing – in the author you'll have the best of travelling companions.

DAVID FONTANA B.A., M.Ed., Ph.D., F.B.Psychol.S.
University College Cardiff

Opening

The opening pages of a book should give a *taste* of its *Essence*. You'll know from the first few sentences if this book is for you or not. Either something will speak to you, or there'll be little purpose in persevering.

Meditation is simple – *so simple* that there ought to be no need at all for this book to have been written. There should be no need for anyone to read such a book. Why should there be a handbook for showing us how to *be what we actually are?*

Meditation is simple – *so simple* that with our incredible complexity we can't approach it directly: we need words, explanations, metaphors and symbols. It should be possible just to say: 'Be Here and Now!'. That should be enough. But from our artificially complicated perspective it leaves many questions unanswered, and seems to create all kinds of new questions. We're so used to the relentless censorship that our intellect imposes on our perception that the instruction: 'Be Here and Now!' sounds vaguely incomprehensible.

Meditation enables us to side-step the bureaucracy of our rigid intellectual processes and experience ourselves *directly*. But before we side-step intellect, we need to feed it a little – we need to give it some *real food* to work on. We need to direct our intellectual appetite away from the processed abstractions of philosophical junk-food, and take a good healthy bite at the reality of what we are. This is where our use of the intellect stops being a game and starts to become a valuable tool which prompts us to *look directly into the nature of mind*. This is known as the development of *View*.

View is the collected experience of three thousand years of meditation practice in which a very great number of people have discovered the same thing. *View* comprises the 'mechanical functioning' of unenlightenment and the nature of the enlightened state in so far as it can be expressed or pointed at by words, symbols and direct transmission. The View, which concerns the nature of mind, has become (in the Tibetan tradition) as pragmatic as the art of lighting a fire. No one has ever got colder sitting in front of a fire. No one has ever succeeded in making a fire using pebbles and river-water. When we know how to allow a fire to spring into being we don't need to remember the exact wording of the instruction booklet – we just create fire. As soon as we integrate the View, the View disappears and becomes knowledge. Knowledge is like breathing – we don't have to remember how to breathe. So View is a way of using intellect to transcend intellect. To this end, View must always be tested in the laboratory of our own experience. This is the creative use of intellect in which we confront the day-to-day sensation of what we are.

Because our intellect is in essence a genuine faculty, it can become untangled. *Journey into Vastness* is an exploration of how we are as 'beings tangled in complexities', and of how we are as 'beings becoming untangled'. We are going to explore what are known in the Tibetan tradition as View, Meditation and Action. View provokes or incites our natural intelligence. Meditation opens our realisation of the View. Action is the Pure Appropriateness of our spontaneity in the state of Realisation.

Meditation enables us to *find out for ourselves* – so this book wasn't written to be kept for ever. There's no Great Wisdom in the following pages that's worth remembering beyond our discovery of what we actually are. It's deliciously and painfully amusing that we're all our own greatest teachers. It's deliciously amusing because sometimes everything seems to unfold spontaneously – we seem to flow with circumstances. It's painfully amusing because the irony of our situation makes its own point and sometimes we can't help but notice it.

In some ways, this book sets out to stand conventional logic on its head, but that doesn't mean that there's no place for intelligent reasoning in our lives. We merely need to unlearn the habit of compulsively attaching ourselves to the conditioned patterns of our intellect. The reach and range of 'reasoning-mind' is quite small and although it's capable of remarkable feats, it can't give us access to *all* the answers. It's not a cerebral American Express card. There are unimaginable vistas beyond the 'reasoning-mind', to which intellect has no visa, and this is something that must be experienced *directly* – or missed completely.

We've probably all realised that 'thinking' isn't a particularly efficient way of dealing with emotional pain. If we think about our emotional pain we just end up with our thoughts running in dizzying circles. Thinking about emotionally painful experiences only seems to make matters worse – it never seems to bring us nearer to an understanding of what we're going through. Thinking about our pain is only 'thinking around it', that is to say thinking about the circumstances that surround the pain. We never think about the pain itself because we'd have to enter into the language of pain and that might seem to be the most terrible thing in the world. Thought isn't capable of bringing us to understanding the nature of our pain – we can only *investigate* with the non-conceptual observation of meditation. Thoughts just create a barrier between us and the actual experience of 'pain'.

We're probably all quite familiar with the way that circular thoughts keep us awake at night, even when our greatest wish is that we could get to sleep. So, we seem to be addicted to the process of thought, and as with any kind of addiction we need to examine 'the damage done'. This book is an exploration of 'the damage done' and a handbook of methods for freeing ourselves. The basic method of meditation in the Tibetan system is called Shi-ne (pronounced shee-nay) and is found in all systems of Tibetan practice as well as in all schools of Buddhism. The Japanese call it 'Zazen' and the Cherokees call it 'Listening', but whatever it's called, it's about *stilling* our continual internal dialogue – the mental gossip that gets between us and direct perception of anything.

So, Shi-ne is our *treatment* for our addiction to thought patterns.

If we decide to enter into this treatment, the first thing we may find is that it can be boring, irritating, frustrating and deadly tedious. This is because the practice of Shi-ne is 'going without our fix' and the experience has some slight similarity to the 'cold-turkey' experienced by a heroin addict. This kind of comparison may sound a little extreme, but to anyone who has ever entered into the practice with commitment it will seem fairly apt as a description of some of the worst moments. Thought attachment withdrawal symptoms aren't always so delightful, and can make us want to give up almost as soon as we've got started. But the ghastly alternative is to resign ourselves to the world of living as 'thought attachment junkies', and that world (which is a distortion of our Natural Being) is actually much more distressing.

Unlike the dreadful discomfort and distress of heroin withdrawal symptoms however, thought attachment withdrawal symptoms are a fertile field of self-discovery. Whatever we feel when we practise Shi-ne is a fundamental expression of *how we are*. When we confront ourselves in this way (through the practice of Shi-ne) we are brought face to face with our underlying insecurity, fear, loneliness, vulnerability and bewilderment. These underlying tensions distort our Being whether we practice Shi-ne or not, so to avoid the practice of Shi-ne is not really an answer – we have little choice in this situation.

Maybe we could look at it another way. Say we get an electricity bill: we can either do something about it or we can poke it under the doormat and pretend we never got it. Whichever we do, we'll either end up paying or getting disconnected.

If we find ourselves in the midst of a battle, then whether we face the enemy or not the chances are that we'll catch a bullet. But at least if we face the enemy we can gain the measure of the situation.

Like all analogies these only hint at the meaning and we should not elaborate on them too much. If we ask too many 'intellectual' questions about analogies the best of them fall to pieces.

So, to practice Shi-ne is to work directly with how we are and to begin to live our lives rather than letting our lives live us. To practice Shi-ne is to get back into the driver's seat – to open our eyes and *see* the world. With our eyes Open we realise that we no longer have to play blind man's buff with our emotions.

The clarity that spontaneously arises from the Discovery of Space within our practice of Shi-ne shows us that loosening our attachment to the thought process enables us to experience thought itself more intimately. We become able to experience the *colour, tone* and *texture* of thought because we develop the experience of Space in which we can *see* thought in its Spatial context. We become transparent to ourselves, our motivation becomes simpler – a natural compassion arises that doesn't need to be forced or fabricated. We get a *real taste of freedom.*

I'm writing this book not just for those interested in the Tibetan Path, but for as wide an audience as possible within the range of those who are open to interest. These methods are part of the heritage of our world and belong equally to everyone who feels a connection with them.

You don't have to be a practitioner of the Tibetan Mystic Path in order to practise Shin-ne, because its method doesn't depend on accepting any kind of dogma or philosophy. *Journey into Vastness* does describe a View, but it's one that has to be validated through experience.

I know from my own experience that the methods outlined in the following chapters can make a real difference to anyone's life. They have been the most powerful catalyst of growth and change in my life, and my deep affection and appreciation for my lamas continually prompts me to do whatever I can to make these methods available to anyone who could benefit from them.

Although I practise within the Tibetan tradition, and the methods outlined are from that tradition, most of them are open to anyone whatever path they follow. As far as the simple practice of Shi-ne is concerned, belief in Buddhism is not required, nor for that matter is the need to believe in anything. For those specifically interested in the Tibetan Mystic Path (who are not already working with a Lama) I would like to advise that they seek instruction from a Lama at some stage, as working completely on your own is difficult for most people.

Until you find yourself working with a teacher of whatever

tradition, you will be working on your own. It's not necessarily a bad thing to be working on your own, because ultimately that's where we all are anyway. So use Shi-ne to gain an understanding of what you are, so that when you have the opportunity to meet a teacher you will have some experiential questions to ask that come from you. Don't be too quick to exchange old beliefs for new ones, even if they are part of the Buddhist View. Buddhism isn't structured to promote belief in itself – it's essentially an experiential science that encourages us to test everything. The Buddha made a point of stressing that people shouldn't accept what he was saying just because he said it, but that they should test it rigorously against their own experience. The Buddha never asked anyone to sell their integrity for a set of spiritual props, but to sell their limitations and discover themselves on their Journey into Vastness.

Ga – Opening

PART ONE

Lhag – beyond

1
Meditation *isn't*

Strange as it may seem, it's important to look quite carefully at what meditation isn't, before we think about participating in what it is.

Even if we've got no preconceptions to clear away about what meditation may or may not be – our own complicated perception tends to breed misconceptions. It's as if the field of our perceptions were some kind of cognitive 'culture-chamber' – because often no sooner have we been introduced to the idea of meditation than all sorts of ideas proliferate like growths all over it. Our understanding of meditation becomes infected or encumbered by unhelpful perceptual goitres. In the late 1950s and early 1960s when the Tibetan refugees poured out of Tibet over the Himalayas into India and Nepal, they fell prey to every kind of disease imaginable. Many older Tibetans died and many infants never made it to adulthood – the scale of human suffering was appalling. The reason for this awful catastrophe (apart from the tragedy of their motherland being invaded by the Chinese) was that Tibet was a very high plateau with a cool, dry climate, but India was hot and damp. They did have diseases in Tibet, but nothing in comparison to the wealth of illnesses offered on the other side of the Himalayas. The Tibetans had very little immunity to these new illnesses, and so they fell victim to them in large numbers.

This chapter then is about developing immunity to the diseases of distraction, distortion and complication.

There are many methods that go under the name of meditation and it's specifically for this reason that I won't be using the word again very often. When I do, it will be as a 'cover term' or when I'm discussing different techniques within the range of Tibetan meditative systems. When I introduce specific methods I'll use specific terms, and the first of these terms if Shi-ne, which means: remaining uninvolved.

A number of years ago when Lama Chhimed Rigdzin Rinpoche visited my home in Cardiff we talked at length about the mechanism of Understanding. We were drinking tea at the time and so he used the most immediate analogy: 'Understanding is a special art – like receiving a bowl of tea. If your bowl is full you can receive no more tea. To receive fresh tea you must first drain or empty your bowl. Sometimes you must also clean your bowl, otherwise the stale residue of old tea will pollute the fresh tea. If we do not have a clean bowl, others will be saying that this tea is very good – they will be enjoying its taste, but we will not think it is so good. We would rather not drink it.' I think that this little story explains itself: we must be open to what we hear or read, and we must not let our prejudices get in the way of the possibility of our understanding.

Meditation is an English word. It has been seized upon to translate a fair few words from a variety of Eastern languages. So we can't assume that it will mean the same thing to everyone. In the light of this linguistic problem, it should be understood that Shi-ne is in no way part of the hotch-potch of self-hypnosis and fantasy exercises that are also termed 'meditation', whatever the value of these exercises.

It would be completely wrong to suggest that Shi-ne is 'The True Meditation' and that other forms of practice that carry the name meditation have nothing to do with meditation. There are many different techniques from many different systems, but their purposes aren't necessarily identical. For this reason it's important not to become confused by imagining that advice which applies to one system of 'meditation' can be applied to another. We can become intoxicated through imbibing spirits, wine or beer – but if we mix them – we get the worst kind of hangover.

There's a misconception that has arisen in recent years that 'meditation' can be some kind of therapy or relaxation technique – a way of winding down after a tense or exhausting day at the office, factory of wherever. This may well be true of some techniques known as 'meditation', but it's not true of Shi-ne. Although the *fruit* of Shi-ne is the most profound relaxation of *mind, voice* and *body*, the path of Shi-ne cannot honestly be described as something you'd look forward to after a hard day's grind.

But relaxation *is* important, and knowing how to relax is a vital part of being able to enter into the practice of Shi-ne. Within the Tibetan system there are numerous exercises which are designed to relax the entire body-mind – these exercises are called Kum-nye and you will find some exercises of this type in Chapter 4, 'Gestures of Being', which deals specifically with physical posture, and how to find yourself both physically relaxed and alert.

The Path of Shi-ne is a continuing *personal experiment* in which we're bound to come up against a fair number of difficulties and obstacles. So Shi-ne, from the point of view of our unenlightenment, is something to be avoided. Unenlightenment is continually struggling to preserve itself, and so any attempt to undermine that process will seem like a threat of some kind.

Meditation to some people may be synonymous with prayer, but Shi-ne isn't prayer. It may well be that what some people call prayer is in fact no different from Shi-ne. But as the word is commonly understood, prayer and Shi-ne are intrinsically different processes.

Shi-ne isn't a state of introspection or trance in which we've 'gone deeply into ourselves'. Shi-ne isn't about cutting off from the external world or escaping from the external conditions of our lives. Shi-ne isn't some sort of emotional anaesthetic or some way of convincing ourselves that: 'It's all just fine – really!'

If someone says that they're practising Shi-ne, and that they're really enjoying it – then I'm afraid that I become deeply suspicious. I become even more suspicious if they've just started, because although Shi-ne has many benefits as a practice – they're by no means immediate unless we're already quite extraordinary people. For most of us, unfortunately, the practice of Shi-ne is either about working with drowsiness, with unremitting 'thought-stories' or boredom.

I'm aware that I'm making the practice of Shi-ne sound very uninviting. This is deliberate. However, I also wish to convey my great enthusiasm for this practice – but that is a much more subtle task, and one that needs to be approached with greater honesty than we commonly expect.

If mountaineers wrote books about the joys of climbing Cho-mo-lung-ma (Everest), but said nothing about the pain involved or the bitter cold and danger we'd have to endure – they'd be doing us no favours. If they just regaled us with tales of what an amazing trip it was, and how it was just about *the* peak experience (without discussing problems such as vertigo and altitude sickness, and the degree of physical fitness required) they'd be selling us short.

If someone tells us that becoming a great concert pianist is the bee's knees but plays pianissimo on the theme of the hours and hours of practice, day in day out for years – then they're setting us up for failure. If they say nothing about the frustration and tedium of playing scales and arpeggios, and the difficulties involved in making the left and right hands perform different activities – they're just priming us for disappointment and loss of interest.

It's for this reason that it's not really such bad news to hear the 'bad news' first. I've read and heard too many 'full-colour glossies' on 'meditation' that would have you imagine that it's just like rolling off a log or that it's the best thing since sliced bread – but all that 'soft soap' or 'hard sell' is little different from detergent ads.

I've talked to quite a number of people on courses I've given over the years, and had to spend a fair amount of time attempting to untie the conceptual knots with which people have confused themselves in their approach to Shi-ne. I've sometimes asked groups of people (some of whom have practised Shi-ne for years) what the purpose of this practice is, and how it functioned. The answers have nearly always been vague and tentative – mostly regurgitations of the full-colour glossy 'meditation' presentations. But this atmosphere of misunderstanding and fumbling in the dark has made it possible for me to put together the ground plan of *Journey into Vastness*, and for this I'm grateful. Answering persistently confused questions has continually put me on the spot, continually made me explain the same thing in many different ways. From these experiences it became obvious that someone should write something to portray a clear account of Shi-ne and the practices that lie beyond it.

So, let's forget the full-colour glossy accounts we've heard and read. If we practice Shi-ne we're not going to 'groove with the cosmic now', in fact we shouldn't really 'expect' anything at all. Anything we expect is hardly likely to manifest and if it does it will probably have little connection with the destination that the practice of Shi-ne has lined up for us. The first time we Sit is bound to be a big disappointment. We can't expect to Sit at the piano for the first time and have brilliant improvisation cascade from our fingertips – it's just not like that. And after all: why should we expect the practice of Shi-ne to be any easier than playing a musical instrument? Why should it involve the development of any less 'skill' than the most difficult of human endeavours? But Shi-ne isn't the most difficult practice in the world, nor is it the easiest – merely the simplest and most available to anyone. The difficulty or ease of Shi-ne is entirely dependent on the rigidity or otherwise of our conditioning. But however we happen to be, we can all become more open and less inhibited by our set patterns of perception and response. Anyone interested enough to be reading this has the right qualifications to begin practising Shi-ne, and has the possibility of discovering what all Enlightened Beings have discovered.

So, to begin with there is boredom, and after that there's some more boredom. Unless we're prepared to work with our boredom – to Sit through our boredom as a continuing project, there's no way we can practise Shi-ne. But strangely, Shi-ne is the only means by which we can come to an understanding of boredom. With the practice of Shi-ne in fact, our boredom can ultimately become very interesting! Shi-ne enables us to find the frontiers of our boredom, and cross over into an infinitely wider horizon that includes the energy of boredom as part of its rich landscape. Once we've developed our practice of Shi-ne, boredom is no longer boredom but a wellspring of nourishment – a rolling wave of energy.

So from the point of view of Shi-ne, boredom marks the beginning of our Realisation. Without boredom there can be no possibility of Discovery in our practice of Shi-ne. If we avoid the experience of boredom, we also avoid the opportunity of entering a new *dimension of Being*. Boredom is a defence mechanism of our unenlightenment – it manifests whenever we're close to suspecting that we're not as solid, continuous, separate, permanent, and clearly defined as we thought we were. Boredom is the officious little sign put up by the petty tyrant in us, and reads: 'DO NOT UNDER ANY CIRCUMSTANCES GO BEYOND THIS POINT ON PAIN OF NOT ENJOYING IT!'

Now many people who have begun to practise will want to give up at this point and from a conventional standpoint who could blame them? But from the viewpoint of Shi-ne this is just the point at which something interesting could happen. If we take notice of the sign and obey its imperative we'll return within the boundaries of our conditioning, but if we pursue the practice of Shi-ne we may well 'trespass' into our own Vastness. The method of Shi-ne encourages us to question authority and transgress the laws of our fixed limitations.

Our sense of comfort is a dreadful dictator – unenlightenment is strictly autocratic and under such an authoritarian regime we have no freedom or personal responsibility.

A long time ago when people had very different ideas about the world to those we have today, they really believed that if they sailed too far into the west they'd fall off the edge of the earth. To test out the edge of the earth, even on the most convincing mathematics, must have taken considerable courage.

So, when our boredom starts to read like the sign that says: 'DO NOT GO PAST THIS POINT OR YOU WILL SAIL OFF THE EDGE OF THE EARTH!' we need to arouse some healthy suspicion – we need to challenge the red tape of our conditioning a little. When we practise Shi-ne we have to look boredom square in the face and Sit with it – we have to stare it out. We have to put theory (or View) into practice in order to realise that boredom isn't the end of the world but the beginning of a *new world*. It's not the same old tune on a tape loop but a *symphony*, something we've never heard before – but only because we didn't know how to listen.

Shi-ne isn't 'thinking about things'. No matter how profound a concept or point of view may be; and no matter how deeply it moves us or to what spiritual elevation it takes us – 'thinking about it' is *not* the practice of Shi-ne. Such contemplation may well have great benefits and may inspire us to live a 'better' life, but this is *not* the practice of Shi-ne.

Someone may say that they're going off to practise Shi-ne. Let's say they've gone off to some quiet room, and that they're Sitting there with their eyes closed. Say we creep up on them very quietly in our stockinged feet and when we get close enough make a loud 'Crack!' with two pieces of wood – what happens then? If this person leaps up in the air with a terrified yell, then whatever else it is they imagine they're doing – it's *not* Shi-ne.   On numerous occasions I've seen people jump in the air quite a while after hearing a loud noise. I've watched them flinch a little as their nervous system reacts to the noise, then a fraction of a moment later after the flinch has passed them jump up with a cry of fear or surprise. This time-lapse is very interesting, because people will almost always insist that they leaped up immediately they heard the sound. The interval of time is actually a period of high-speed thinking, but we're so often oblivious to the mechanisms of our own mental processes that they become invisible to us.

The person who gets interrupted in practice to take an urgent telephone call for someone else and reacts angrily to having been interrupted has missed the point completely.

So, Shi-ne is *not*: prayer; relaxation; dreaming; drowsing; entrancement; directed or guided thinking; contemplation; thoughtless blankness; introspection; or any other state that isn't Precisely and Completely Here and Now.

If while we're Sitting, someone quietly asks us a question we should be able to answer quite normally. If we're Sitting and someone whispers in our ear: 'Where did you leave your shoes before you came in here to Sit?'. we should be able to answer immediately: 'Outside the door by the heater.' If we say 'What –

sorry – pardon, who, what did you say?!?' – yes, you guessed it: we're not practising Shi-ne.

So, what is Shi-ne? Well, there's an old Tibetan saying that runs something along these lines:

> *'Meditation* isn't
> Getting used to – *is.'*

This obviously needs some explanation.

Gang-mo – laughter

2
Getting used to – *is*

"Meditation isn't,
Getting used to – is."

Before I explain what this means; you need to develop some experience of your own. Once you have your own experience to go on you won't be a total stranger to the kind of material that we're going to look at. So it's important at this point that you begin to Sit in order to find out just what practice means in your own experience.

This is a handbook, so let's take it one page at a time – one exercise at a time. Even if you've had some experience of practice the following exercises may well prove interesting – stemming as they do from lesser-known origins.

This is a handbook, so it's designed to be used in conjunction with practical exercises geared to take you to the level of experience. Reading ahead will be of no help. Reading ahead will only feed you with ideas before you've been able to make discoveries for yourself. Reading ahead will just rob you of unique opportunities to gain your own first-hand experience without being pre-empted.

This is a handbook so let's get down to something practical. Let's participate in the practice before we go any further with explanations.

---

first exercise

Sit comfortably somewhere quiet with your eyes closed / try to Sit reasonably upright / if thoughts come – let them come / if thoughts go – let them go / if you find yourself involved in a stream of discursive thoughts and you notice what is happening, don't be upset or annoyed – just let go of your involvement / keep letting go of your involvement / remain uninvolved / just let go / keep letting go / just let be / keep letting be / whatever happens – let it be as it is / keep letting it be as it is / if you feel good – don't cling to the sensation of the thoughts that surround it / if you feel bad – don't reject the sensation or the thoughts that surround it / especially if you feel nothing at all – don't drift into numbness and lack of Presence / remain alert /

Try this for ten minutes or so / see how it goes / if you've already gained some experience in practice and you're able to sit for longer – sit for as long as you'd usually sit / if you're used to Sitting with your eyes partially open, then continue in that practice / see how it goes /

first exercise – follow-up

So, now you've Sat for a while – you've had some sort of experience, and now you have a memory of that. Write down as much as you can of what remains in your memory. Keep a notebook specifically for the purpose, and keep a record of your impressions after each new exercise.

You've made a good start. Whatever happened, whatever you felt, was part of your own experience. What you experienced was the *play* of your own Energy. It was a good start.

These are some of the things that you may have thought after the exercise: that was easier than I thought / that was a complete and utter waste of time / I enjoyed that / I felt stupid / I felt relaxed / I didn't really understand what I was supposed to be doing / it was quite pleasant / I didn't see the point of it – it seemed a useless thing to be doing / I fell asleep / I felt quite agitated / what am I supposed to make of this?

Whatever you thought or felt, it was useful, and it provides you with valuable insights into how you see the world. The success of the exercise lies in remaining honest with yourself. Success isn't dependent on having a 'wonderful peaceful experience', but on being honest and being prepared to question the construction of your own reasoning.

In terms of the exercise being either easier or more difficult than you thought, you're working with expectations, and can ask yourself 'What exactly did I expect?', and if you've never Sat before, then, 'What exactly did I base my expectations upon?'

If you thought that your experience was a waste of time, you could ask yourself: 'What do I mean by wasting time?' You could also ask yourself whether it is actually possible to 'waste time'. The idea of wasting time suggests that unless you're occupied in some way that fulfils certain criteria, your time is 'wasted'. You could then ask: 'What are my criteria for evaluating the use of my time?' If we consider that *Just Being* is a waste of time, then we're devaluing the most fundamental aspect of what we are, and this is something we should consider quite carefully.

If you enjoyed the exercise, what was it that you enjoyed? How do you define or recognise the sensation of enjoyment?

If you felt 'self-conscious', you could ask yourself: 'What does that say about me? What sort of image do I have of myself that jars with Simply Sitting and Being?'

If you felt relaxed you could investigate what you personally define as relaxation and what 'signals' enable you to recognise when you're relaxed.

If you didn't understand what you were supposed to be doing, then you probably expected to be engaged in an exercise that accorded with certain guidelines with which you may be more familiar. You could question these guidelines, and ask yourself: 'How did I acquire these guidelines? and when did I learn to accept my definition of what comprises an exercise?'

If you didn't see the point of the exercise, you could examine what constitutes 'usefulness' and 'uselessness'. You could ask yourself: 'In what context of value judgements is this exercise "useful" or "useless"?'

There are as many questions to ask yourself as there are

possible reactions to this exercise.

So, there is a time for using your intellectual capacities and a time for working without them. The intellect functions perfectly within its own parameters, and the practice of Sitting can show us the limitations of those parameters – in this way *View* and *meditation* encourage each other. Maybe you'd like to think now, about the questions that have been raised. Maybe you'd like to repeat the first exercise a couple of times; but if you do – don't take your questions or answers in with you, put them aside. When we Sit we just Sit. When we question, we avoid trying to establish firm conclusions.

Learning how to say 'I don't know' is one of the most profound lessons any of us can learn. Try not to take the whole thing *too* seriously – it can often be quite amusing!

Try the first exercise at least two or three times more before you go on.

second and third exercises

If at the time of reading this book you're undergoing stress, worry, anxiety, emotional pain, bereavement or any other kind of personal crisis, then the second and third exercises should be omitted. They're not in any way 'risky' as exercises, but a fairly calm, relaxed state of mind is preferable in terms of maximising their experiential value.

second exercise

Sit comfortably somewhere quiet with your eyes closed or partially open / Sit reasonably upright / whatever thoughts arise – block them / cut them off immediately / whatever thoughts are in your mind – force them out / remain without thought / continue to remain without thought /

Try this exercise for ten minutes or so – see how it goes / if you already have some experience of practice, try this exercise for as long as you would usually find comfortable – see how it goes / continue to the third exercise after what seems to you to be a comfortable rest / try to experience both exercises on the same day / the closer these two exercises are to each other the better / engage in this exercise before reading the instructions for the third exercise /

third exercise

Sit very comfortably somewhere quiet with your eyes closed or partially open / try to sit reasonably upright / think continuously and actively about anything you like / try not to allow any space at all between thoughts / if you become aware of the slightest gap in your thought process – fill it as quickly as possible and try to ensure that no further gaps occur / fill your mind with as many thoughts as you can / avoid investigating your visual surroundings with stimulus / avoid going to sleep /

Try this for between thirty minutes and an hour – see how it goes / if you already have some experience of practice and are used to remaining still for long periods of time, try this exercise for at least an hour – longer if possible /

second and third exercise follow-up

Now you've had two very different experiences. Write down as much as you can remember of them both. Take a look at how they were different, but also at how they were similar. You've learned a valuable lesson here, but what do you think it is?

Write up your commentary on the experiences of exercises two and three before continuing to read this chapter, and then review these commentaries again at the end of this follow-up section.

Let me fill you in on the origins of the second and third exercises. In Tibet there were various different kinds of practitioner. There were the monks and nuns who lived mainly in Gompas (places of meditation – monasteries) and when most people think about Tibet it's the monastic orders that usually spring immediately to mind. But there were other types of practitioner, both men and women who lived in small farming communities or in nomadic encampments on the Chang-thang – the wide, rolling northern grasslands of Tibet. Some were wanderers, Chodpas, who roamed from place to place with little else but a bell, thigh-bone trumpet and the large Chod-drum whose slow resonant 'heart' beat choreographs the energy of their practice. Some were recluses who lived high in the mountains, and many of these were Re-pas who wore either simple, white lightweight cotton robes or nothing at all, in the tradition of their practice of Tu-mo, the Inner Heat, that is the speciality of the Re-pas. Some were Todgens (accomplished yogis) or Ngakpas, either married householders or people who spent most of their lives in retreat.

Many of these Lamas were great Masters surrounded by groups of pupils all living at a discreet distance, and absorbed in the practices their teacher had set for them. The mountain retreat places used by these Lamas and their pupils were usually built into caves. Some were very simple, and probably not much shelter from the wind and snow, but some were quite comfortable. Some caves were more like little houses, with wooden flooring, windows and more than one room – ideal places to spend many days, weeks, months or years in retreat. Access to these places was usually quite difficult and food supplies sometimes ran out, but such was the life of the Gomchens (Great Meditation Masters). It certainly wasn't the easiest of lives, but the Gomchens often had spectacular powers that enabled them to endure all kinds of privations that would polish most of us off.

The fame of such Lamas often inspired those with mystic leanings to go and seek instruction and apprenticeship.

Now let us suppose that you are such a person seeking

advanced instruction (and you may well be), and that you wish to approach such a Lama. I'll paint a picture of what it might be like to meet with such a person, and maybe from that you'll find out some more about the two exercises you've just experienced.

Imagine you're living in Tibet. You've heard all about the Lamas who live in the mountains close to your home, and for years you've felt a bit restless, dissatisfied with what you've been doing. You've had the idea in your mind of setting out on a serious quest to find out just what could be possible for you if you could really enter into practice under the guidance of a wonder-working Lama in the mountains. Maybe you've been a monk or a nun at the small monastery near your village and maybe you have a 'need' for 'something' that doesn't seem to be happening. So, one day, after weighing up all the pros and cons, after looking very carefully at your life, you decide to go and visit the astrologer and Mo-pa (diviner). Maybe you've had some dreams that seem auspicious, and maybe various omens have indicated that this is the time for change. The Mo-pa tells you that your plan will go well but that it will not be without difficulty, and the astrologer gives you a good day to set off on your travels. So you go to see the Abbot of the largest local monastery because he is noted for his clairvoyance and ask for advice as to where you should go. He looks at you with a smile and asks you a few questions as to what your practice has been. You explain what you've been engaged in and he seems satisfied that your intentions are appropriate. So he gives you the directions and off you go.

It's a long and difficult journey up into the mountains, but you feel very free. You take your shelter where you can (usually under a tree wrapped in your chuba coat and blanket) and maybe for the first time you're able just to lie and look up at the stars. Your small campfire keeps you warm and somehow everything seems delightful – apart that is from the uncertainty in your mind as to how you'll be received. The Abbot has given you no assurances that this Lama will accept you and you've heard that getting to be the apprentice of one of these Gomchens is not necessarily that easy. You've heard that the method of such Lamas is to welcome some aspiring practitioners and to turn others away without a word of explanation – why there are some who'll just throw stones at you from a distance, so that you don't even get close enough to pay your respects. Some of these Gomchens are known to be Crazy-Wisdom Masters and they can behave in almost any way – but there's one thing that you're quite sure of: they're reputed to give the kind of teachings that lead to swift Realisation.

But you've also heard that the Swift Path is very strenuous, difficult and sometimes even dangerous. Sometimes such Lamas make great demands of their apprentices! With a mixture of excitement and trepidation you wonder what's in store for you. You wonder if you're going to be able to cope with the experiences that lie ahead of you – after all, the Mo-pa did say that it was not going to be easy. Maybe you'll find that you're 'not up to it' and you'll get sent away with your tail between your legs, unable either to pursue your wishes or to return to the life you used to lead. What if you failed? – you might not be able to settle to anything, always torn between what could have been possible and what you have become. Your mind is full of strange ideas, images and distorted facts. Your mind races with the stories you've heard, and you're so keyed up with your imaginings that you almost tingle with apprehension. It's a bewildering experience, and somehow it seems to have become a great adventure even before you've got there.

Anyhow, that's how it was for me when I first stuck out my thumb on the M5 trying to get a lift to Scotland in order to find a teacher. I didn't have to sleep rough on the way, and the scenery wasn't quite as inspiring – but the mental journey was pretty much the same.

Finally after a number of days you approach the end of the last valley and begin to climb upward closer to the feet of the snowy peaks. You're soon among the spectacular ragged forms of the mountains, and the track becomes more and more of an obstacle course – strewn with rocks and stones and cut by cascading rivulets of mountain melt-water.

It's wonderful just to be up amongst these mountains, and your spirits lift more the higher you climb. But suddenly you hear a yell that stops you in your tracks – it's quite far off, but it makes your scalp tingle. You begin to walk very carefully looking around you and after a while you start to see or imagine you see the tiny forms of people in the distance sitting among the rocks. As you get closer you're able to pick out a few men and women – they're practising physical exercises of some sort in the open air. You've certainly never seen anyone doing anything like this before and you're full of curiosity. It is these people who let out the occasional piercing yells.

All at once you notice that a short distance away someone is sitting, and seems to be waiting for you. You realise that your approach has been observed. You're greeted with a smile from a very strange-looking person indeed. He has long tousled hair and the remains of his monastic costume are bleached pink by the sun. He stands up and comes over to you – you feel a bit timid, but somehow you know it's going to be all right. This person has a remarkable Presence, apart from his strikingly wild appearance he looks very fresh and bright – very awake. He seems to be taking in every detail of what you are quite exactly. He seems to notice each movement you make and every intonation of your voice as you speak. You feel that you couldn't hide anything from a person like this even if you had the inclination. Maybe he's the Gomchen; but 'No' he laughs at the idea. He laughs in a kindly way so as not to make you feel foolish or embarrassed. He tells you that the Gomchenma (for this Lama is a woman) has been expecting you for some weeks and that you're to follow him to his cave where you'll be able to refresh yourself.

The other apprentices all seem to have more or less the same quality of Being and they all laugh quite frequently, often very loudly. They might laugh at almost anything: the sun peeping out from behind a cloud or the way that a squirrel scampers up a pine tree. Their sense of humour is a little disorientating, but it's also somewhat infectious and has a way of putting you at your ease. The apprentices practise and work – some fetch wood, some carry water and some cook. They take care with whatever they're doing and the sounds of Awareness-spells are often on their lips.

Some are in retreat and have food taken to them; some are returning from journeys into the mountains to collect herbs for medicinal purposes; some are setting off to visit Powerful Places for practice and others are preparing to enter retreat.

They all seem to have a singular brightness in their eyes – their gaze is unblinking but unstrained. You ask lots of questions but don't get quite as many answers as you'd like – some things, you're told, will have to wait until you meet the Gomchenma. You've never really met people like this before and all your usual ways of responding have to be put aside. You wonder what the Gomchenma can be like when all her apprentices are so extraordinary – so perceptive, immediate and carefree.

Finally the day arrives when you're called for, and by now you feel very shy and your stomach certainly isn't feeling quite as it should.

Now, these Lamas can be young, middle-aged, old or ancient; gentle, severe, irascible or wrathful; hilarious, wry, serious or solemn; garrulous, impassive, inscrutable or aloof; handsomely dressed, simply clad, in rags or nothing at all. You wonder what the Gomchenma will look like and how she will be, because her apprentices have given nothing away at all. But when finally you meet her, she eludes most of these possibilities yet seems to contain many of them. You're not at all sure what to say, but she greets you with a warm smile and waves aside your formal greeting. She looks at you very intently but says nothing for a long time. She already seems to know all about you, either from her own Clarity or from what her apprentices have told her. You want to ask all your questions at once, but you're given to understand that this isn't the time for questions. She has instructions to give you and they're fairly cryptic: 'Tomorrow you should go to the cave, below the outcrop of rock, over there. You should Sit from dawn to dusk and have no thoughts. Use any method you wish to banish thought. When the day is over, come and tell me how you got on.' She smiles again and it seems as if it's time for you to go. She gives you a blessing and you leave.

You ask the apprentices about the instructions you've been given but as far as they're concerned, that is something private between you and the Gomchenma – they don't want to hear about it or make any comment. They do, however, confirm that the Gomchenma has taken you as an apprentice. They seem genuinely pleased by this, which in itself is wonderfully encouraging, but they give nothing away no matter how much you ask. So far, nothing that has happened is anything like you thought it would be – it's somehow disappointing, yet somehow better than you could possibly have imagined.

Once accepted as an apprentice you can expect anything to happen – such Lamas can be highly unorthodox in their teaching methods and there are no reference points against which you can check up on what is happening to you.

So, as the next day dawns you go and Sit in your cave. You make yourself comfortable and wait for your thoughts to settle. You think that maybe if you just Sit for long enough it'll happen. But nothing of the sort happens; instead – everything happens! Your mind is crowded with thought, and you panic at the thought of not succeeding in what you've been instructed to do. You try to force thoughts out of your mind, you tense yourself – you try to will your thoughts away, but that just becomes another thought! You shout out: 'Go away' but the words echo in the cave and further thoughts create a counterpoint to the echoes in your mind-stream. You jump up and down, you hold your breath, you shake your head – but nothing seems to work. Your mind is full of the wish to get rid of thought, but there's no getting rid of *that* thought. It's paradoxical and completely frustrating – you've never known such a continual bombardment of thoughts in your life!

So, at the end of the day you climb back up the track very dispirited by your failure, and you wonder what the Gomchenma is going to say to you. You wonder whether you're going to be dismissed as unfit for teaching. But no, the Gomchenma bursts out laughing at the tale of your mental and physical antics and says: 'Very good! Very good! You've tried really hard and done well! Tomorrow you should go back to the cave and Sit from dawn till dusk having nothing but thoughts. Think of anything you like all day long, but allow no gaps to occur between thought!'

So off you go, thinking: 'Well that'll be easy, I'm bound to succeed at that if today's been anything to go by! I seem to be full of thought most of the time quite naturally and without the slightest effort!'

So the next day at dawn you go back to the cave with some sense of confidence. But when you've been there for a while, you discover that things aren't seeming to go in quite the way you imagined they would. You sit down and several pleasant subjects spring to mind, so you think about them. You make various speculations and follow them through, but after a while it's not so easy anymore. You start getting low on things to think about and even get a little bit bored by the process. You wonder where the delight has gone that you used to find in pondering and just letting your mind drift from subject to subject. You used to be able to day-dream for hours at a time but here in this cave you begin to notice that the *fabric* of your thought is starting to get distinctly patchy. The things that you usually like to think about don't really seem to be so fantastically interesting anymore, and although you really try to infuse some new life into them – it doesn't work out very well. Most of the things you decide to think about seem pretty hollow after a while; they get to be a bit thin on meaning. It starts to become really quite unsettling when even the most important aspects of your life cease to be able to hold your attention for long. You root around desperately for something new to think about or some new angle on an old issue – but that scheme falls through as well. You love to walk in the mountains and explore the area – it would be much easier to think if you were doing that, but you've got to sit in this damned cave. As comfortable as the cave is, it's about as fascinating as those unaccountable bits of fluff that occasionally turn up in your navel. So what happens then? Maybe you try conjuring up sexual fantasies – they used to voluptuate into your mind so easily, but now your imagination doesn't seem to arouse anything sufficiently interesting or provocative to stimulate you – even a little!

Eventually you get to the point where *gaps* in the thought

process become impossible to avoid, and long before the day is over you have to jerk yourself out of longer and longer periods of blankness.

At the end of the day you feel pretty wretched. You've failed again. You can't even do what you were once perfectly used to doing. You're fairly sure that the Gomchenma will tell you to pack your bag and send you off down the hill to try elsewhere. But when you tell her your story she looks quite pleased – she nods her head and smiles as you tell your tale of woe and when you've finished, bursts out laughing again. Then she congratulates you saying: 'Good! Wonderful! Now you know how to practise perfectly!'

You're naturally completely bewildered by this, and think to yourself: 'I can't believe this – what on earth can it mean? I'm more confused now than when I first arrived!' But the Gomchenma has taught you very well indeed – you've learnt the most valuable lesson in the best possible way, and it's a lesson that you'll never forget. Something inside you tells you that all is not quite as it seems. You start to find the situation quite funny as well – but when the hilarity has passed, the Gomchenma explains to you exactly what it is that you have learnt.

What do you think it is?

Now the conclusion of the story I've just recounted may sound rather odd, and indeed it is – very odd.

Sometimes someone has to focus our experience for us. If we think about a transparency, sitting in a slide projector that hasn't been focused – what can we say about that? Well, we can say that all the information is there but that we won't know what to make of it until it's focused. Once the transparency is in focus, we can remember the blurred shapes that we saw and we say: 'Of course, I should have known! that was my backyard with Uncle Harry and Aunty Mabel eating their ice-creams.'

Sometimes if we've had the right experiences and we're in the right place at the right time with the right person – then just a few words will change our lives. This is an important method of teaching. When the Gomchenma in the story taught her pupil in that particular way, she was setting the apprentice up to have all the necessary experience to understand exactly what she was going to say. It's a very powerful moment when we realise that 'we've known it all along!' In order for us to understand anything in the fullest sense, the circumstances have to be appropriate. In the right circumstances a few simple words will *pull together* what seemed at first to be confusion, and facilitate remarkable new Realisations.

The apprentice in our story had no idea why the Gomchenma was laughing; no idea why she was pleased by her apprentice's apparent failure; and no idea what could possibly have been learnt from those experiences. A fine old game!

It is sometimes quite an insight to realise that we can be learning something incredibly significant without even knowing what is going on. It's uniquely helpful to work with a Teacher, and I hope that this book encourages you to find such a person.

In our story the Gomchenma was teaching her apprentice that *you cannot force the mind*. Atempting to force thought out merely results in thoughts proliferating like crazy. Attempting to force thought to be continuous merely results in the disintegration of the thought-flow. When she said to her apprentice: 'Good! Wonderful! Now you know how to practise perfectly!' she meant that her apprentice had the knowledge that it was useless to try to force the mind, and that to practise perfectly was to proceed without force.

If we try to force thought in – the mind rebels. If we try to force thought out – the mind rebels. This is why in the practice of Shi-ne, and indeed in all other practices, *we let go and let Be*. We don't encourage thought, but neither do we block it. We treat the process of thought very gently; we let thoughts come and we let thoughts go. Shi-ne means 'remaining uninvolved'. If thoughts come, we let them come – if they go, we let them go. If thoughts are there we let them be there – we don't add to them or protract them in any way. If thoughts leave, we don't detain them – we treat them as welcome but transient guests. We treat thoughts rather like a fire that has served its purpose – we just stop adding fuel. If we stop fuelling our thoughts with our active involvement in them – they settle and we enter into a calm state.

The exercises we've been discussing are rather shorter than the dawn-till-dusk exercises I've portrayed in the story of the Gomchenma and her apprentice, because it's not possible to re-create the environment in which such teaching methods were possible. But if we get some idea from experimenting with these exercises even for short periods of time, we should *Know* that if we want to work with Mind and our attachment to the thought process we'll have to use some method other than coercion.

So, we come back to our old Tibetan saying:

> *'Meditation* isn't,
> *Getting used to – is.'*

When it's said that *'Meditation* isn't,' what is meant is that *meditation is not* a method of doing, but a method of *not-doing*. We're not involving ourselves in doing anything, we're not instigating anything, we're not imposing anything, we're not adding anything, we're not elaborating on anything – we're *Just Being*. There's this fruit drink you can get called 'Just Juice'. The name is supposed to let us know that nothing's been added and nothing's been taken away – that's just how our practice should be: *Just Being*. We simply maintain our alertness and our *motiveless observation*.

When it's said that *'Getting used to – is,'* what is meant is that this practice comprises simply *'Getting used to'* Being.

We're acclimatising ourselves to how we actually are.

We're almost completely unused to our own Enlightenment, so our practice is a way of *'Getting used to'* it. In terms of our deep-rooted attachment to thought, we're *'Getting used to'* non-referentiality. We're *'Getting used to'* Being *Referenceless*.

It would be a good idea at this point to take a look at exactly what's meant by Being *Referenceless*; but without developing further experience of Sitting, such explanations might become a little bit 'heady'. The approach that I'm going to take in this book will be one that you've already met with in this chapter – the method of our imaginary Gomchenma. This approach introduces method first and explanation afterwards. This means that by the time you get the explanation (the theory) it should make *immediate experiential sense*. So let's make a start with the basic methods of Shi-ne.

If you already have some experience of Shi-ne or Za-zen, and find yourself itching to explore the idea of Being *Referenceless*, you could nip forwards to Chapters 9-12. I would recommend, however, that whatever your experience of Sitting, it would be helpful not to skip this initial material altogether because you may well find something new in it due to the nature of the approach that I've adopted. Methods of Shi-ne differ, depending on their origins in the different Buddhist systems, and the method that I'm presenting here is closely related to the Dzogchen system of Sem-de: the *Series of Mind*. In order to follow through I recommend that it's worth running through all the exercises – whatever your experience in order that you'll really come to Know that *'Meditation* isn't,' and that *'Getting used to* – is.'

PART TWO

Dranglak – simplicity

3
Just Sitting

When we begin our practice of Shi-ne, we need to *know* how to Sit.

Our *bodies* know how to Sit – but we have forgotten. Our *bodies* can Sit perfectly but they've been confused by the patterns of our lives and the ambiguities of our wishes and conditioning. The ways in which we conceptualise and the styles of conditioning we've accepted have got in the way of our *body-knowledge*. Our bodies have forgotten how to Sit, so if we are to enter into practice – we need to remind them of the comfort and ease of their *natural posture*.

Many of the problems we encounter in our lives arise as a result of 'body-amnesia', and this in turn disturbs our equilibrium. Mind and body are intimately interrelated and any imbalance in one is reflected in the other. So, when we are out of balance with ourselves it becomes (at times) a monumental effort just to Sit and Be. We find the simplicity of Sitting an almost impossible battle against restlessness, irritation and drowsiness. And so, in order for our practice of Shi-ne to develop we need to encourage our *body-knowledge* – our bodies need to *remember* their natural equipoise and balance.

It may come as quite a surprise that our concepts about ourselves and the world get in the way of how our bodies function. We may ask ourselves: 'How can the way in which I think affect my ability to Sit naturally?'. The answer is not actually quite so 'deep' or complicated as you might expect. Let's look at a concrete example of how concept directly affects our deportment.

Skiing is an interesting example of the debilitating intrusion of rigid concept into the field of physical activity. When skiing, we are always taught that we should keep our weight forward in order to pressurise the front edges of our skis. The reason for this is that it enables us to stay in control. When the fronts of our skis are pressurised, their edges carve the snow and we're able to steer ourselves simply by transferring our weight from one foot to the other. Unless our front ski edges are carving we're not steering, and if we're not steering . . .

Out on the snow, although we understand intellectually exactly what to do, somehow the whole idea of leaning forward into the slope starts to seem suicidal. So when we get the feeling that we're going too fast, instead of getting our weight forward to slow ourselves down as we take a traverse, we lean backwards, and before we know it we've wiped-out in an ignominious heap, with young children whizzing past us as if it were the simplest thing in the world.

The problem here is that we're not *listening* to what our bodies are telling us, we're 'listening' to our fear – which is actually a counterfeit cocktail of abstractions. Most people wipe-out through fear rather than there being anything inherently dangerous presenting itself to them.

In order to learn how to ski, we have to learn to *listen* to the messages that our bodies are giving us rather than 'listening' to the incessant chatter of cerebral anxiety that usually shouts down all other sensory input. The theories of skiing that we learn were not there before the first person skied. The first skier had to learn those things from experience – from being in touch with *body-knowledge*. Leaning backwards on skis (for those of you who've never tried it) is rather like worrying about the speed you're travelling in a car, and deciding to let go of the steering wheel whilst stamping on the accelerator!

So when we decide that we want to practice Shi-ne we have to look at the conceptual picture we have of Sitting.

Now there are many ideas about Sitting that come from various sources. Some people say that the lotus posture is vitally important if you want to get anywhere with meditation – and in one sense they may be quite correct. I wouldn't like to say that it isn't a very important posture – but it's not the only one. I think that people are aware that there are other ways of Sitting, but many still have the idea that these other ways aren't as 'spiritual', that they're merely for those who aren't up to the lotus posture. I would like to discredit this idea completely. The lotus posture definitely has certain powerful characteristics, but it's not the 'ultimate' posture – because there is *no* ultimate posture. Lotus posture is highly respected by many traditions of Buddhism, and to some it is the perfect posture – but to others it is one of a number of postures. In this book you'll find a number of different Sitting postures, all of which can be used depending on how we happen to find ourselves.

The most important thing to remember is that when it comes to Sitting *we should be comfortable*. I feel as if I ought to say that again, so I will, because it's very important – more important even than the famous lotus posture, so here it goes: The most important thing to remember is that when it comes to Sitting *we should be comfortable*.

The main barrier to comfortable Sitting is the idea that we need to have backrests or things to lean on. People tend to have all sorts of ideas about comfort that often inhibit *natural comfort and ease* – and the part of our bodies that usually gets the worst treatment from these ideas is the spine.

Learning to be comfortable is an *art* – an art in which we're encouraging our body-knowledge. Being comfortable is important because it's no help at all if our bodies (and specifically our backs) are causing us painful distraction. So it's important that we learn to Sit in such a way as not to be distracted by our physical posture. This doesn't mean that we should lose all awareness of our bodies and disappear into some 'heady' region in which we're removed from the blood, flesh, sinew, skin and bone of what are. We're not attempting to leave the body behind as if it were some kind of 'non-spiritual' dross. Patriarchal religious disciplines have been slandering the earthiness of our existence for too long, and it's important to shed any residue of this conditioning in ourselves. Our bodies and our world are an important part of our *Mystic Journey* – spirituality doesn't mean that Enlightenment entails becoming a 'spirit'.

So, down to Sitting. The crucial factors are that the spine

should Sit naturally and that we should be relaxed.

The first picture in the next chapter shows my wife Sitting on an ordinary chair. A good upright chair can be very good for Sitting as long as it keeps the thighs and spine at ninety degrees to each other. Using a chair of this type should not be considered as merely a concession to age. Anyone can Sit in a chair no matter what age – the position is as worthy as any other. Although any padded upright chair is good, the ideal chair for Sitting is the 'kneeling-stool' type chair – which is the next in the sequence. As you'll notice, this chair combines both Sitting and kneeling and offers 'no visible support' for the back. I say 'no visible support', because when Sitting/kneeling on this kind of chair the body is positioned in such a way that the spine supports itself very comfortably. This kind of chair is a remarkable replacement for any chair, especially chairs that are used for desk-work and typing. These chairs prevent back-pain developing and improve our general posture. They weren't designed as meditation chairs, but they may as well have been – due to the fact that they allow the spine to settle in its most natural position. When the spine is in its natural position it just Sits there – there is no effort at all involved in Sitting upright, which is ideal for the practice of Shi-ne. Sometimes people who suffer with back-pain find Sitting in Shi-ne rather difficult, but a chair of this kind where the natural spine posture occurs without effort makes good posture in Sitting possible for anyone (other than in certain exceptional circumstances).

But it's not always possible to have a chair on which to Sit, especially if we are travelling, out in the countryside, or in a group. It is important that we look at the traditional postures for practice, because they are valuable and also because they give us a broader range of options. The traditional postures are also part of the rich Tibetan Yogic heritage which this book sets out to portray. Furthermore, as this book caters also for those who have some experience of Buddhism and the Tibetan traditions as well as those who are discovering them for the first time, readers will have to experiment on an individual basis in order to find out what lies within the scope of their own capacities.

Most of the more advanced material comes at the end of the book but the sequence of pictures and explanations of Sitting postures contains physical positions that may be difficult for the beginner. I hesitate to be too specific about the capacity of 'beginners' because we all come to this practice with our own beginningless histories of experience, and there is no telling how quickly any of us will adapt. You may take to it like a fish to water or like a fish to a sun-baked stone.

Let's take a look at Sitting on the ground. This is the most ancient way of Sitting, and it takes us back to the dawn of human history. When we Sit on the ground we are linked to the most ancient of all lineages. There is something very basic and solid about direct contact with the earth – and even if we're Sitting in a high-rise tower block or in a skyscraper apartment, the floor level is always the *earth* in the *Dimension of our Experience*. Contact with the earth has always been important in shamanic cultures – the Hopi (North American Indians) still cut the seat out of their Levi jeans in order to have nothing between them and the earth when they Sit.

So, Sitting on the ground has a special quality about it. This doesn't make it the best way to Sit – it just means that there's a unique quality to it that we can experience. This is a personal thing and you'll have to experience what this means for yourself – it's your experiment. From my experience of Sitting, the *grounded* quality of Sitting at floor level is most valuable in facilitating stability and equilibrium. At times when I have sat and practised on the beach, I've made use of the sand in order to make myself comfortable. Supported by the sand in that way there was no feeling of discomfort at all from the usual pressure points such as the knees and ankles. When the water is warm enough it is also possible to Sit partially submerged in the sea, which has the effect of pleasantly reducing the weight of the body.

Now most people who begin to practise meditation immediately assume that they should Sit with their legs crossed. Unfortunately this can almost be guaranteed to make people feel that Shi-ne is not for them. There almost seems to be a conspiracy of silence about Sitting that creates an atmosphere of confusion. We may hear people say that if we can't Sit in lotus posture, it is acceptable just to Sit with our legs crossed. We could be unwittingly led to assume from this, that Sitting with our legs crossed is easy – but we'd be sadly mistaken. Without guidance, the cross-legged posture can be very uncomfortable indeed and could lead to increasing frustration at our apparent lack of ability to Sit for anything beyond ten to fifteen minutes. So, if you've tried Sitting cross-legged and have found it to be one of the most uncomfortable things that you've ever done – *there's nothing unusual about you!*

It *is* possible to Sit comfortably in the cross-legged posture, but there are certain features to the posture that must become part of the body-knowledge that we're rediscovering. If you just Sit on a cushion and cross your legs, your body is invariably going to become a painful distraction. Let's look at what happens to the body in this position. Sitting on a cushion with our legs crossed will cause our knees to be higher than our hips, and this causes two distinct problems. Firstly, the alignment of the legs makes the pelvis tilt backward and create an unstable seat for the spine. In practical terms this means that when we Sit in this way – one of two things must happen: either we'll slouch forward and get backache (and drowsiness), or we'll try to straighten our backs. The constant effort involved in keeping the back straight will also give us backache but it will be combined with tension and fatigue. Even if we lean against a wall (which is regarded as very unseemly in the Tibetan tradition) the same problems will arise, albeit to a lesser extent. Secondly, the effect of our knees being higher than our hips gives us intense pins and needles. If we ignore our legs 'going to sleep' then we'll experience profound difficulty in trying to stand up again at the end of our Sitting session until we've gone through several minutes of physical distress. This posture is very unstable and will be one of the worst obstacles to practice you'll encounter as you set out on this path.

So, in order to adjust your posture to eliminate such problems you'll need to raise your buttocks high enough from the ground to allow your knees to fall below the level of your hips. Yes – it's that simple.

In the Tibetan yogic tradition it is suggested that a wooden block should be used even for the lotus posture. This isn't quite as austere as it sounds, because the block can be upholstered with a scrap of thick-piled carpet (most carpet shops have off-cuts for sale). The purpose behind using a wooden block is that it cannot squash down – it gives you a guaranteed minimum height from the ground. No matter how many cushions you use to raise yourself off the ground they'll always squash down after a while; and if you use too many you'll just find that they slip on each other and end up spreading out, which can involve you in spending most of your Sitting session readjusting them. The wooden block is the ideal solution, as it gives you a constant height that you can gauge to suit the personal requirements of your ideal Sitting posture.

The dimensions of the wooden block are traditionally based on the measurement of the clenched fist from the tip of the knuckle of the bent thumb to the edge of the hand at the little finger. The measurement of the block that I use is 108 mm. The dimensions of the block are: one measure high, by one measure wide, by two measures long. You may find that you want to make the block a bit higher, so you'll have to experiment with that until you instinctively feel that you've got it right for your own use.

A recent alternative is to double the dimensions of the block and make it instead out of dense industrial foam. But it's a good idea to upholster the foam with some heavy-duty fabric because foam has the tendency to disintegrate with use (and with the almost irresistible temptation to pick little bits off it).

So, whether you've got yourself a foam or wooden block, you can start to Sit. This is where your practice begins. There is something timeless about the moment when we realise that this is how it's always going to be if we're to develop this practice. This block is going to become very familiar – it's going to become part of our lives, and that's quite an important thought. It's a very special, very ordinary moment that will vanish if we try to make anything of it. It's the Beginning of our Practice.

Chag – gesture

4

Gestures of Being

The posture for Practice is a Gesture of Being – a crystallisation of the *Mind-Body* in the present moment.

The postures in this chapter are a selection of very ancient and rather recent ways of Sitting. These postures have not been graded here in terms of classifications such as 'beginners postures' or 'advanced postures' because the prime consideration in all these postures is that the body is at ease, and that the spine *Sits naturally* (see chapter three). Some postures are not as immediately comfortable to assume as others but that does not necessarily mean that you will not find them of value, given time and physical familiarisation. The postures aren't graded in terms of ease or difficulty because we are all different, and anyhow, with such definitions there's always the possible inference to be drawn that: 'if it's difficult, it must be spiritually preferable'. I have no intention in this book of setting up a hierarchy of postures that divides the 'wimps' from the astringently zealous.

My suggestion is: to try these postures – to experiment with them fully and find out which suit your body. You may find that a few of them suit you, or that only one of them suits you. You may find that you can Sit in one of them for longer than others – but don't let that discovery lead you to discard postures that seem workable only for short periods of time. Some of these postures will need some practice if you are not used to Sitting still for long periods of time, or if you are completely unused to Sitting on the floor. It's good to have a range of postures at your disposal in order that you can alter your position during longer sessions of Sitting or in retreat. But however you Sit will eventually cause some kind of discomfort, so it's valuable to be able to alternate between postures that put the stress on different parts of your legs.

Try adopting some of these postures whilst reading, talking with friends or watching the television, in order to physically acclimatise yourself to them. Once you've got used to your set of preferred postures in this manner, you'll find that Practice seems less physically alien, and there'll be one less obstacle to Sitting.

kum-nye

Kum-nye is a method of massaging the *Psychic-body* through massaging and moving the physical body. These methods facilitate a sense of deep physical relaxation and wholesomeness of being which can be developed in conjunction with the *relaxation* of the emotions, perceptions and the *relaxation* of our entire Being.

Loose lightweight clothing should be worn during these exercises, and nothing should be worn on the feet. Constrictive garments such as brassieres should not be worn, no matter how slack or 'comfortable' they may appear to be. You may choose to dispense with clothing altogether (if the temperature is conducive) as these exercises are designed to put you in touch with your body (at outer, inner, secret and ultimate levels). The state of *having a body* can be finely and sensitively appreciated through the Practice of Kum-nye, and we can learn to allow tension and stress to *melt* into the accomodating Spaciousness of what we are.

In these three exercises (there are a great many more), sensation is being developed as a focus of our experiencing. By this means we can discover that the source of our own healing lies within the unlimited yet unexplored treasury of our own Being. Our body vibrates with Energy that we can allow to well up and surge in limitless patterns through the expanse of what we are.

These exercises are named after the vulture, which in Tibet is regarded as a very special bird. Some people have come to regard the vulture only as a scavenger, but that is to view this magnificent bird from an élitist societal perspective. From a perspective in which mendicancy is not scorned, the vulture is seen as a supremely relaxed bird. In the Native American culture the vulture is known as the Peace Eagle and honoured as a powerful being. In Tibet the vulture was a bird who never killed but who waited with patience until its dinner had breathed its last.

It is the vultures in Tibet who make air burial possible – they are the birds who carry our jettisoned physical form into the sky and manifestly symbolise our entry into Intangible Dimensions of Being. The Great Adept who began the line of which Ngakchang Yeshe Dorje Rinpoche is the present incarnation, was said to have had the capacity to take the form of a great white vulture when it suited his purpose: that of entering into the *dimension* of the *sky* and *Integrating* with the Air Element. My Root Teacher Chhimed Rigdzin Rinpoche occasionally wears three vulture feathers in his top-knot when he performs certain rites. With him, this is symbolic of his being the Mind emanation of Padmasambhava the Great Magician and second Buddha who disseminated the Tantric Teachings in Tibet. The use of birds' and animals' names in the descriptions of these exercises derives from Tibet's ancient Shamanic traditions and portrays the way we can learn from every aspect of the phenomenal world. If you really want to learn how to stretch and yawn with perfection, just watch a cat – it will be your best Teacher!

It is important in these exercises to allow feelings and sensations to develop in their own way – encouraged by the Presence of your Awareness. Avoid any inclination to manipulate what you are experiencing apart from allowing sensation to become more and more expansive. Remain Present in your Awareness of whatever arises as a sensation or feeling, but don't try to own your experiences as if you could possess or be dispossessed of what is intrinsically there. There is nothing to lose or gain – only a whole new world to experience. Pleasure or relaxation is always lost when we attempt to capture it and hold it tight. The art of relaxation is simply to let all experiences flow unhindered – just allow them to become deeper, wider and more pervasive. Allow your Awareness to pervade your entire body so that it is not 'you' observing 'yourself', but *You-Yourself* – undivided.

Discover that you are every part of you – that you are pervaded by the Awareness that is *what you are*. These exercises are valuable before sessions of meditation, especially if the meditation is *Simply* a continuation of the Kum-nye exercise (into what ever form of Practice you usually engage in).

These exercises can also be used if you have no wish to follow the Path of the four Naljors as presented in this book. These exercises are an invaluable means of reducing stress and tension in everyday life, and create a lively and intimate sense of feeling real and present in the world.

vulture resting on the wind

This exercise is useful for *softening* the cramped sensation of rigid orientation and loosening the sense of solidity that make it difficult to relax or settle into meditation.

Stand comfortably with your knees slightly bent and putting your weight onto the balls of your feet / breathe softly and evenly / soften the focus of your eyes – but keep them wide open / very very slowly raise your arms until your finger-tips reach the height of your shoulders / allow your elbows to hang down a little so that there is no strain at all in your arms / with palms facing downwards – begin to shake your fingers (begin very very gently and increase slowly until you feel you've reached a point where you don't want to increase the movement any further) / allow the shaking of your fingers to move your hands from side to side / allow the movement of your hands to loosen out your wrists / allow the shaking to ripple gently throughout your arms / allow these rippling movements to loosen out your shoulders / begin to move your head very slowly from side to side as if you were scanning the horizon / as you get used to the 'side to side movement' – slowly let your head hang forwards in gradual stages as your head moves from side to side / when you feel that you want to give it a rest – lie down on the ground in the corpse position (on your back with your hands palms up by your sides) / throughout the exercise – notice the sensations that arise and allow them to become expansive / when you lie down continue to enter into the sensations that arise and expand / allow yourself to melt into the expansiveness of the sensations you have generated /

Repeat this exercise five times or as many times as feels comfortable.

preening vulture

This exercise is useful for opening out the claustrophobic constrictions of stress and tension. It helps to melt the tightness that makes it difficult to gain sufficient rest.

Kneel comfortably / place your hands gently just above your hips / hold your waist very lightly between your thumb (extended backwards) and your other fingers (extended forwards) resting on your stomach / breath softly and evenly / soften the focus of your eyes – but leave them wide open / begin to rotate your elbows – tracing counter-clockwise circles with them in the vertical plane (take the clockwise or counter-clockwise cue from your right arm) / allow all your fingers apart from your index fingers and thumbs to 'ride up' from your waist as you rotate your elbows / allow your shoulders to rise and fall as your elbows trace the circles / when these movements begin to flow comfortably and naturally – begin to trace a clockwise circle in the vertical plane with your head / make all these movements very softly and gently / do not cause yourself any strain or discomfort at all / imagine that your nose and elbows are tracing circles whose diameters are no more than three to four inches / when you've done this for a minute or two (or as long as feels comfortable) pause and absorb your attention in the sensations and feelings that have arisen as a result of the exercise / begin the movements again, but reverse the directions / alternate the

directions with pauses in between for as long as it feels
comfortable / if you feel dizzy – pause and begin again a little
more slowly and gently / after ten minutes or so, lie down and
enter into the sensation as before /

rising vulture

This exercise is useful for unwinding tension in the chest and for
re-vitalisation. It is helpful with nervous exhaustion especially
when the stomach area tightens and makes relaxation difficult to
enter into.

Stand comfortably with your feet at least two feet apart /
breathe softly and evenly / soften the focus of your eyes – but
keep them wide open / with your hands placed gently on your
lower stomach (you will need to remove all upper garments for
this exercise and loosen your trousers or skirt so that your entire
stomach area is free) / begin to 'smooth' your stomach as lightly
as you can whilst retaining full hand contact (as the exercise is
repeated increase the hand pressure until a vigorous massage is
reached) / move the right hand in a clockwise direction and the
left hand in a counter clockwise direction (reversing this
movement each time the exercise is repeated) / once you begin to
enter into the feelings and sensations that arise – very slowly
begin to 'inch' your hands upward in a spiralling fashion
(covering as much of your stomach and chest as you can reach by
this means) / until you reach your shoulders / once your hands
reach your shoulders and can rise no further – allow your hands
to lose contact with your body, tracing wider and wider circles
upward and outward until your arms reach full stretch / co-
ordinate this 'wider and wider circling' with deeper and deeper
breathing, increasing the depth of the breath as the circles grow
wider / once your arms have reached full stretch – begin to slowly
diminish the circles (without making contact with your chest or
stomach until your hands come to rest on your lower stomach
(where they started) / pause for a moment and enter into the

feelings and sensations that have arisen and begin again /
continue for as long as it feels comfortable, then lie down and
enter into the sensation as before / if your sense of balance is good
you can expand this exercise by rising up onto tip-toe when your
arms are at full stretch /

1. Sitting in a supportive chair that allows an upright position. Cushions behind the back may have to be used to prevent slumping.

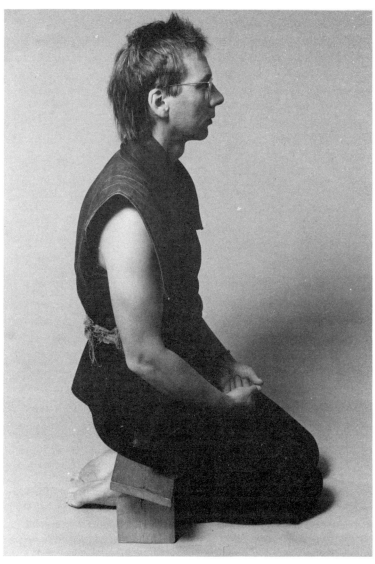

2. Kneeling on a slanting meditation bench. (side view)

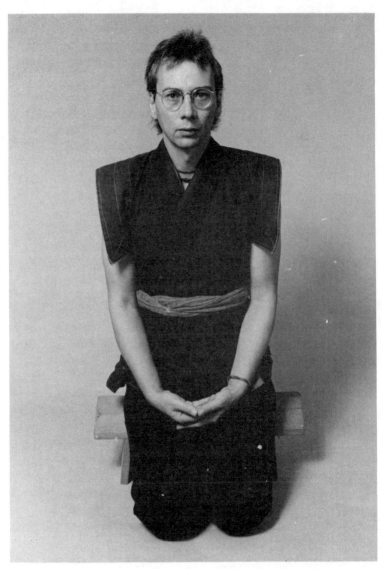

3. Kneeling on a slanting meditation bench. (front view)

4. Sitting with knees spread on a slanting meditation bench.

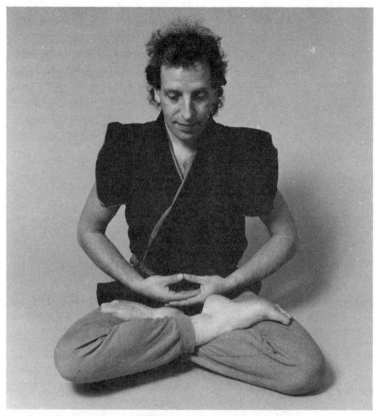

5. Lotus posture.

The lotus posture is very useful in that it needs no physical props. It has seven principal points that ensure physical and mental equipoise (if the posture can be comfortably maintained), these are as follows:

1. Legs: intertwined / each foot placed sole-upward on the thigh of the opposite leg.

2. Arms: relaxed / hanging slightly away from the body / hands resting in the lap / the left hand cradles the right hand / the thumbs are touching /

3. Spine: in its natural position (see chapter three)

4. Eyes: Partially open to let a little light enter / downward gaze /

5. Mouth: jaw relaxed / teeth slightly apart / lips lightly together /

6. Tongue: tip touching palate behind upper teeth /

7. Head: bent slightly forwards /

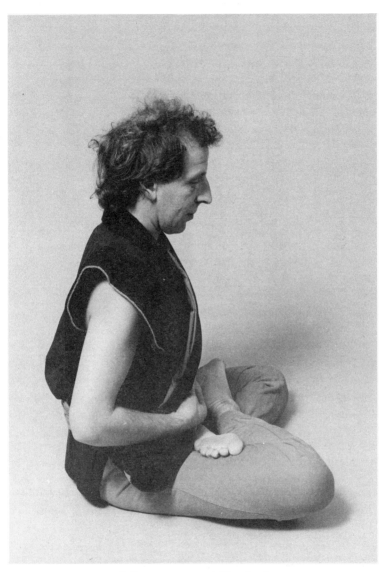

6. Lotus posture. (side view)

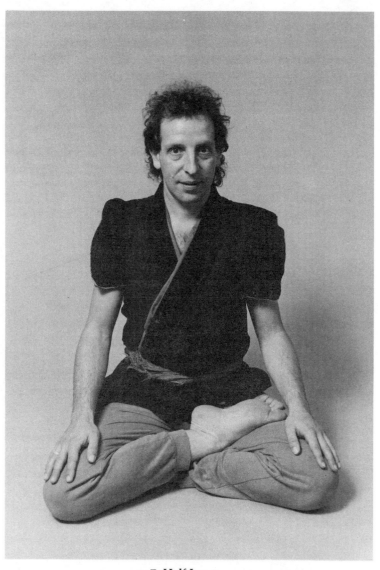
7. Half Lotus.
A more relaxed version of the 'full lotus' but if it is adopted in such a
way that one knee hovers in the air – it is a very unbalanced posture
and best avoided.

8. Magician posture.
A 'laid-back' version of the Lotus posture in which is popular among Yogis. The hands are in the gesture of 'Mind in Relaxation'.

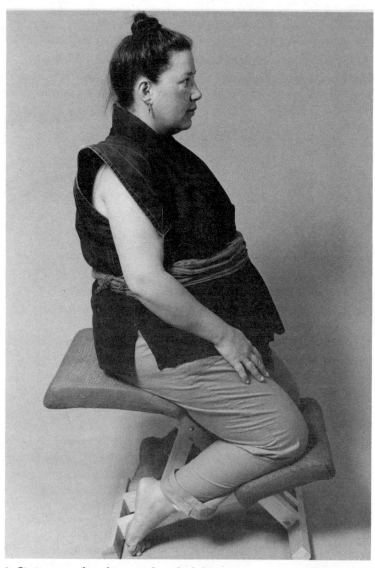

9. Sitting on a 'kneeling stool' – ideal during pregnancy (as shown here at 39 weeks), for the elderly, or those lacking suppleness at any age. (side view)

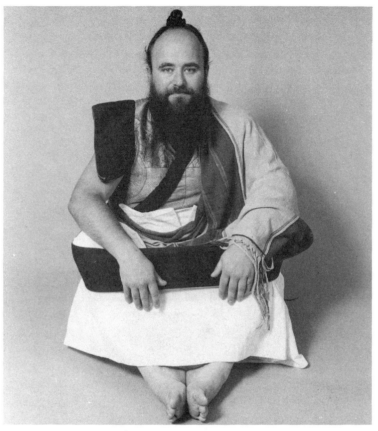

10. Sitting with the support of a Gom-tag. (front view)
This posture is a derivation of a posture described in the practice of the Dzogchen Long-de. Although the method of Dzogchen Long-de is not given in this book in its complete yogic form, this derivation of one of its postures is very useful as a method of Sitting. The strap is made of a good thick material (preferably sewn together in several layers). The measurement of the strap (for its entire circumference) is twice the distance from the middle of your chest to your outstretched finger tips. Alternatively: twice the circumference of your head (as you would measure for a hat) and two hand breadths (which can be obtained by doubling a piece of string – wrapping it around your head and grasping it between your two fists in front of your forehead). The strap needs to be the width of your hand and thick enough not to concerting under stress.

11. Sitting with the support of a Gom-tag. (side view)

12. Vulture Resting on the Wind.

13. Preening Vulture.

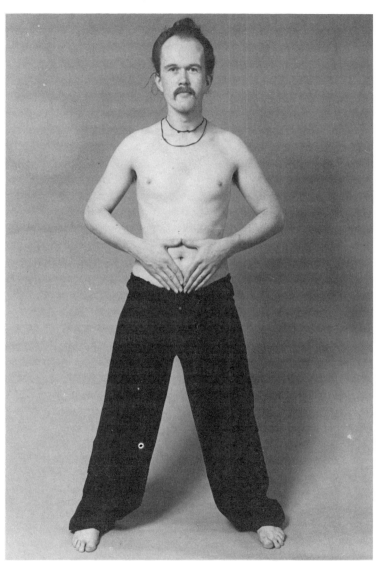

14. Rising Vulture.

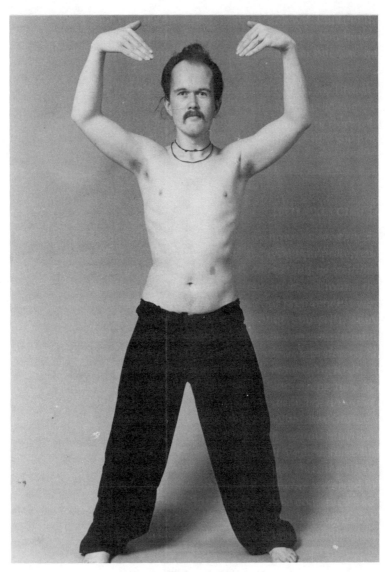

15. Rising Vulture

Lham – now

5
Time without Content

The pressures of work and the dramas of our social lives can sometimes make us long to be quiet and 'do nothing' for a while. Yet often when we find that space, all we want to do is set about filling it again. The wish to find space and the wish to fill space alternate in our lives, and mostly when we have one we seem to want to get back to the other. This is our human condition, it is a very strange thing, and maybe even stranger that so few people ever want to account for it. It would seem that we have unreal expectations of both 'doing' and 'not doing' that make it impossible to accept or reject either – we just bounce between them.

Our relationships with activity and inactivity are nearly always rebound relationships and so we never approach them freshly or from a position of freedom. We could learn a lot from looking at our histories of romantic liaisons, in terms of what they would show us about how we relate in other ways. If we look at rebound relationships and then look at how we pick one book up and put another one down, we will see certain similarities. If we look at how we move from one activity to another, or from activity to inactivity and back again – we will see that we are always carrying the baggage of previous impressions. We cling to the idea of the perfect relationship, but it only seems perfect until the moment we enter into it. In our relationship with 'doing' and 'not doing', we see them as polarised and live in the artificial tension that appears to exist between them. But 'doing' and 'not doing' are aspects of Being, and from the perspective of Being the *taste* of 'doing' and 'not doing' are identical. It's only from the distorted perspective of 'doing or not doing' that the problem of opposites arises. Our lives seem generally dominated by 'doing' – so much in fact, that 'not doing' is usually only ever a fleeting experience.

The need for 'not doing' manifests in us all the time even though we continually reject it. Whenever we find the *space of not doing*, our definition of who we are starts to blur and melt, which signals us to project ourselves into 'activity' in order that we can feel as if we know who we are.

'Not doing' *is*, however, part of our culture even though we might not recognise it described in such a way. Sitting in front of an open log-fire smoking a pipe is a fairly time-honoured approximation of 'not doing'. Sunbathing is a more widespread kind of 'not doing' popular among younger people. Fishing is also a kind of 'not doing', because not everybody who fishes is primarily concerned with catching fish – as Lama Sogyal Rinpoche once remarked 'If the fish is unsporting enough to allow itself to be caught, the fisherman could find himself (how do you say?) . . . somewhat inconvenienced.'

When I was a little boy I used to Sit sometimes and stare at nothing in particular. It used to make my poor old father quite annoyed. 'What are you doing?' he'd bark, and I'd say: 'I'm thinking,' hoping of course that he wouldn't ask me what I'd been thinking about. For some reason I had the impression that to say that I was thinking was a reasonable thing to be doing, but I was wrong. He'd say: 'Why don't you play properly or do something useful!' I had no answer to that, so I'd apologise as best I could in a confused kind of way and head off for the woods. I was very lucky to have woods behind our house when I was young, and I'd often go there to be on my own. I would Sit by the stream and watch the endless sparkling patterns of the flowing water. The sound of the trickling water would completely absorb me and often I'd be late home for a further scolding. If I ever sat and stared at home, I had to be quite alert in order to catch the sound of my father's approaching footsteps. I knew that if I let my vigilance slip I'd get caught out, so in the end I got quite good at seizing a toy the moment before he entered the room.

I must have been a bit too slow sometimes, because once I overheard my father in the kitchen saying: 'There's something wrong with that boy, he's not normal!' I had a quiet grin about that, but it did make me wonder what it was like to be normal. But then my school years started and I found out all about normality, and a distressing business it was to be sure – life became a lot more complicated. I lost contact with my Silence and it was only years later that my Tibetan teachers showed me how to re-establish my practice of Sitting. But by that time, it was no longer so easy to Sit, I had become very complicated and so what should have been easy and simple had become quite complicated and difficult. Sitting had become fraught with personal difficulties – the kind you may already have started to experience in the previous exercises.

Today, the memories of my childhood that are the most clear to me are those connected with my silent Sitting. I spent a lot of time in the woods on my own – there was an old yew tree that I used to climb in order to Sit in the crook of its branches. I used to call it the 'Music Tree', because several of its branches had been sawn off, and could be tapped with a stick to make sounds. It was a little bit like a living xylophone, and the silent spaces left by the disappearance of the notes were magical moments for me – I used to think of them as the 'spaces behind the stars' that I used to gaze at from my bedroom window when I was supposed to be asleep. The memory of the 'Music Tree' was triggered when I was first invited to teach on one of Dr John Crook's Zen retreats in Mid Wales. The clacking of the Zen wooden fish – the repeated sound, suddenly interrupted leaving a moment of time with no content.

'Not doing' isn't easy. Before engaging in the exercises in this book, you may have thought of 'not doing' as simply not doing anything – as if it were as simple as that. But when we try to let go of activity as a deliberate exercise, we realise it's not quite as relaxing as we may have expected.

Time without content seems alien and uncomfortable. What we usually describe as 'doing nothing' is actually just as much of an activity as anything else that we do. The kind of 'doing nothing' we're used to, is just a time in which there is no recognisable social or 'personally productive' content – content of other descriptions, however, is very rarely lacking.

It may come as a surprise to discover that from the viewpoint of Shi-ne there is little difference between 'worthwhile' and 'worthless' activity – they're both fuelled by compulsion. Our attachment to activity of any kind – no matter how deliberate or random, creative or destructive, organised or disorganised, makes both activities compulsive. As long as we act through compulsion it's not possible to have a real relationship with life.

Because *unexcused* letting go (of all activity) is something very unusual for us, we need some way of *almost doing nothing*. In the Buddhist traditions the most popular method of doing nothing is to *follow the breath with wordless observation*.

There are various ways to follow the breath, but the way I'm going to describe is linked to the Dzogchen system. Shi-ne isn't itself a practice of Dzogchen, but this particular way of practising Shi-ne is an approach to the practice of Dzogchen. Within this approach, Shi-ne is the first of the Four Naljors which culminates in Dzogchen – the Great Completeness, in which the practice itself *is* Enlightenment. We'll look at what this means in Chapter 14, 'Beyond Practice', but for now, we'll look at Shi-ne and how we can proceed with it as a daily practice.

Among the many systems of following the breath, differing levels of *attention* are employed. Some systems advocate concentrating on the rise and fall of the abdomen in conjunction with the breath, whilst others recommend fixing the concentration on the sensation of breath at the entrance to the nostrils. These methods have a tangible orientation in their focus on the breath, and you may like to employ these methods if you find the methods in this chapter too intangible or abstract.

The method I will be presenting involves the merest attention on breath. This attention is described as *finding the Presence of Awareness in the movement of the breath*.

Finding the Presence of our Awareness in the movement of our breath is a particular way of describing this technique. The words I've used are quite important because they indicate a state which is not conditioned by dualistic considerations. So, we're not concentrating, we're not watching or even observing. There is Awareness; and that Awareness is *present* in the movement of the breath. You could say that the Awareness and the movement of the breath are indivisible.

Breath is important throughout the different schools of Buddhism as a focus of practice. We use breath because it is subtle – because it is only just tangible. Breath can almost be imperceptible, but if we have it we're alive and if we haven't we're dead. Apart from the Visualised focus of Awareness-Beings in the practice of Tantra, and yet more subtle practices of Dzogchen, breath is the most subtle focus of attention available to us, and yet one which is always with us.

In one sense breath is very boring. It's there all the time, coming and going like the endless lapping of the sea – it's almost impersonal. But in another sense, breath is vitally interesting and personal. The point I would like to make is that from the perspective of Shi-ne practice, the interest value of breath can be just another way of distracting ourselves from *Simply Being*. The interest value of breath can be just another excuse to define ourselves by engaging in some kind of 'doing'. When we Sit the interest value of breath is no concern of ours – we're using it as the merest tangible focus. In the practice of Shi-ne we find ourselves *immersed* in the experience of breath, but not to such a degree that we cut off to the context of where we are.

We could think of breath as being like the line that connects an astronaut to a spaceship – it's our life-line but not the subject of our fascination; because there's the Vastness of Space into which we can gaze.

---

fourth exercise

Sit in a comfortable position with your eyes partially open / make sure that your knees, pelvis and spine are aligned according to the instructions in Chapter 3, and that you adopt one of the postures in Chapter 4 / find the Presence of your Awareness in the movement of your breath / silently count each exhalation up to twenty-one / having arrived at twenty-one – reverse the count and return to one / repeat this exercise for the duration of your

Sitting / if you find that you become lost in a 'thought-story' and realise that you have stopped counting your outbreaths – return to number one and begin the process again /

Try this for fifteen minutes or so – see how it goes / if you've already gained some experience in practice and you're able to Sit for longer periods of time – then Sit for as long as you would normally Sit / see how it goes /

fourth exercise follow-up

So now you've experienced an initial exercise in *Shi-ne with form*. Maybe you preferred this approach to the first exercise which is called *Shi-ne without form*. Maybe you preferred the first exercise and found the fourth exercise undesirable in some way. Your preference is worth noting because it will tell you something about yourself. Think about the following questions and see what comes up from them in the light of your experience.

1 If you preferred Shi-ne with form, was it because it gave you something to do, or was it because you felt that you had learnt something new about yourself by the end of it? What other feedback do you have?
2 What has Shi-ne with form shown you about yourself and how you function?
3 If you preferred Shi-ne with form, was it because it seemed less threatening or because it seemed less abstract?
4 If you preferred Shi-ne without form was it because it seemed less contrived and artificial or because it seemed more restful and less taxing in some way.
5 What has Shi-ne without form shown you about yourself and how you function?

Write down as much as you can about these two kinds of experience before reading on. Try to repeat exercises 1 and 4 several times in order to examine your impressions of these two techniques and how they function in relation to your experience.

Shi-ne without form is a stage beyond Shi-ne with form. It is a method without focus – when we practise in this way, we just remain naturally as we are. There is no focus of attention with this method, and so it is not often suitable for those without experience of lessening attachment to the thought process through other means. You may wonder in view of this why Shi-ne without form was introduced as the first exercise. The answer is that often the *beginner's mind* is more open to insights than the mind of someone who has started to develop ideas on a subject, and so the initial experience is an important one – one that may well have been quite powerful.

Although the exercises in this book are presented in a linear fashion, there is no saying where it would be better for a beginner to start. Having gone through all the exercises in this book you may well find that you are most suited to the last technique you practise. What is most likely is that you will learn to relate to these exercises as a bag of implements for working with how you happen to find yourself at any given time. It is valuable to have a range of techniques with which to approach Shi-ne, because you will need to accommodate the fluctuations in your energies from day to day. Even within the same day you will find that your energy changes – one moment you may feel quite sleepy and the next you may unaccountably liven up. You will find that your capacity to enter into practice will differ and you will need to be able to cope with these changes in an informed way.

The method of counting your outbreaths up to twenty-one may seem rather contrived and artificial as a technique, or it may seem as if it enables you to have some sense of attachment, but its purpose is precise and has little to do with either of these ideas. You may have found that this technique has taught you something interesting about yourself. It will have taught you that (unless you are rare in your ability to concentrate) you are not able to count your out-breaths up to twenty-one without considerable and somewhat 'determined letting go'. This will have been something very interesting to have learnt, because it opens up the question of how much concentrative ability we may have at other times. We're usually not quite so alerted to lapses of our attention in our ordinary daily activities, so these lapses and wanderings are never so apparent. It's usually only when we're engaged in high-risk activities that we have some idea that a moment's distraction could well be the last moment of our lives. This is why such concentration is so exhausting and why high-speed racing drivers could do well to practise a little Shi-ne in their lives. When we try to keep our attention from wandering off while we Sit, we can notice quite well how weak our concentration can be. But with this practice of counting we can develop our ability to stay with whatever we are doing and find the Presence of our Awareness there. Once we have developed the ability to maintain our attention and have established some confidence in that – we can let go of the counting.

The value of counting is that it splits our commitment to involvement with the thought process. We have the breath, the counting and the arising thoughts. So in this three-way split, the arising thoughts get less than half of our available attention.

The method of counting is a barometer of our ability to settle into our practice of Sitting. This means that the method of counting shouldn't be relegated to the position of a mere introductory exercise – it has a value for a long time as a means of showing us exactly where we are. We may well have entered into formless practice, but because of our life circumstances we may find that we are in a condition that lends itself more favourably to counting or working with the breath. We have to be prepared to use every practice at our disposal as our condition indicates. If in our practice we can't get beyond the count of five then we know that to have engaged in some more advanced type of practice would have been a waste of time. So if we begin every practice session with a count of twenty-one, we will always know what condition we happen to be in so that we can proceed to make the best possible use of our time.

The method of reversing the count on reaching twenty-one is to prevent the counting becoming a weird little chant that operates on 'auto-pilot' while you're off having fun or fear in some thought-story fantasy. Once you've run backwards and forwards a few times through this counting method you can move on to the fifth exercise. But if you find that with the fifth exercise you go off into prolonged day-dreams, do not hesitate to return to the fourth exercise.

Another thing you may have noticed in your practice of counting was that you became annoyed with yourself when you found yourself unable to perform what may have seemed to you to have been a fairly simple function. You may even have taken your annoyance to be a worthy feeling on the basis that you *should* be annoyed at apparent lack of success. This sort of rationale is part of a societal conditioning that we would do better to relinquish. Righteous indignation at 'failure' isn't in any way helpful in the practice of Shi-ne – we must start with acceptance. We must accept ourselves just as we are. Even if we feel that we need to change how we are to match some sort of 'Buddhist Ideal' of how we should be, we can't change in that way through non-acceptance of what we are in the moment. If we don't accept how we are, how can we ever find a realistic starting-point. So wherever you start is where you start – that place is unique to you and it is what you possess as the basic material of your practice.

There is no such thing as a 'bad' or 'unsatisfactory' practice session. If we feel that our practice has not come up to our expectations then we have learnt that we have had expectations. When we Sit we should have no expectations – expectations just get in the way and provide subtle definitons of existence that we can relate to rather than *just Sitting*. Being able to have some sense of equanimity in the face of our fluctuating capacity to enter into practice is quite important. The need to see progress or improvement in whatever we are doing is very ingrained in us all, and at first it may seem very strange to attempt to throw off ideas of wanting to get somewhere. It is paradoxical, but although the purpose of practice is very important to us as human beings, we must be *purposeless* in our Shi-ne. Any sense of purpose that we entertain whilst engaged in Shi-ne will mean that we are not really practising Shi-ne.

fifth exercise

Sit in a posture of comfort and alertness with your eyes partially open / find the Presence of your Awareness in the movement of your breath / if you find that you have wandered off into thought-stories – return to Presence of Awareness in the movement of your breath / avoid indulging in annoyance or frustrated internal dialogue on discovering that you have wandered off into 'thought-stories', no matter how many times it happens / as soon as you realise that you have lost your Presence – you have regained your Presence, so just continue in that Presence without comment or judgement / whatever thoughts come – let them come / whatever thoughts go – let them go / allow your Awareness to ride on the movement of the breath / allow yourself to Become the breath / avoid drifting into sleepy non-presence /

Try this for twenty minutes – see how it goes / if you're used to Sitting for longer, Sit for longer / see how it goes /

fifth exercise follow-up

The fifth exercise style of Shi-ne is one which you'll be working on for quite some time – it will be your regular daily practice. How did it feel to let go of the count? Did you find yourself getting irritated by your continual wanderings into thought-stories? Write down your feelings and perceptions so that you can look them up later and check what kind of changes take place as you continue in your practice. The changes will be very subtle, but try not to look for them while you are Sitting – the time to do that is when you read through your notes from time to time.

Remember that the method of counting can be reintroduced at any point in your practice. You may need to begin counting in the middle of a practice session in which you've let go of the count.

Try to develop a sense of what is needed and when. There is no point at all in doggedly pursuing a technique when it's not suited to the energy of how you are in the moment. If you're constantly wandering off into thought-stories for five minutes or so at a time you may as well begin to count again until you've stabilised yourself sufficiently. Please don't fall foul of the idea that this is a retrogressive measure, or involve yourself in ideas of achievement or under-achievement – there's no yardstick by which you're being measured. Progress is much more closely linked to knowing what you need to be employing as a method at any one time. Being able to co-ordinate your knowledge of method, and your sensitivity to how you happen to be is central to the development of practice.

Try to remember that when you catch yourself having gone off into a thought-story, this should not be a cause for being disheartened. You shouldn't be disheartened because the moment in which you wake up to what is happening is a moment of *re-emerging Presence*. These are actually your most successful moments and certainly no cause for despondency. These moments of re-emerging Presence are sudden *awakenings* to where you are and what you're engaged in. If you've spent twenty minutes continually catching yourself wandering off into thought-stories – it hasn't been a 'waste of time', you haven't failed. In reality you have had many moments of re-emerging Presence.

It is important to *encourage* this re-emerging Presence by *letting go*, by completely relaxing as soon as you *wake up* to where you are. By practising in this way our re-emerging Presence becomes a Sparkle – an illuminating experience that opens itself to glimpses of Vastness. This Sparkle of re-emergent Presence is in itself the essence of Sitting, and finding the Presence of our Awareness in that Sparkle *is* Being – *Here and Now*.

This fifth exercise should be practised repeatedly after each chapter up until Chapter 10. If your only experience of practice comes from this book, try to leave as much practice-space between chapters as you can, or you will find the experiential nature of subsequent chapters could be difficult to comprehend.

This will also be true for those who aren't totally new to Shi-ne (or similar practices), but who don't have a great deal of sustained practice behind them. There can be no rule about this, because we're all intrinsically Open to understanding anything, but if by reading on you find yourself getting lost – it would be better to gain more Sitting experience before reading on. It may also help to re-read previous chapters in order to clarify points that have become unclear – it's your experiment, so allow yourself to use this handbook in as flexible a way as is appropriate for you. Follow the approach that your experience suggests and don't worry how long it takes to get to the end of the book.

Ra-ro – intoxication

6

Being Here and Now

When we Sit and practise, we come *face to face* with the raw dynamics of how we are. It's a unique experience, and one that's not always wildly comfortable. When we participate in the practice of Shi-ne, we're bound to meet up with things that we don't particularly like about ourselves; and although it's not always exactly a laugh a minute – a new acceptance of how we are begins to develop.

This is our embarkation point. Everything that we discover when we Sit is what we are, and the entire caboodle is the cargo we've 'decided' to carry.

Once we've sat for a certain length of time, we'll know that *this is what we are.* There'll be nothing lurking in our 'depths' that could possibly dismay us, because we'll have dropped the twenty-four-hour floor-show of entertainments that had made us strangers to ourselves. Once we've sat through the continuing theatrical performance of hiding from ourselves – there'll be nothing left to distress us, but often that can take longer than we'd like. The process of opening to the *fact* of how we happen to be can take days, weeks, months, or maybe even years – just how long is impossible to say, because we're all different. We each have our individual capacity for Realisation, and we each have our own histories of experience on which to draw.

If we're able to Sit through the range of our unacknowledged negative feelings we'll become very solid and grounded as people. This could be described as our first attainment – being able to acknowledge the range of permutations that comprise our response to existence.

So, initially Shi-ne is *'Getting used to'* the *fact* of our existence.

In the Silent Space of Shi-ne, the fantasies and illusions we have about ourselves die of hunger. They get starved out, very simply, because we stop feeding them with the energy of our involvement. This could seem to be a bit of a shame, and to some extent I suppose that it is – because fantasy can be fun. Now this may well shock some people, especially those who have already become involved with the practice of meditation in the Buddhist tradition. We're often instructed to let go of 'fantasy' in order to find 'reality', but in the Divisionlessness of Enlightened Mind the concepts of fantasy and reality have no meaning. I'm not saying this because I'm trying to advocate fantasy, but rather because I don't think that a puritanical attitude is conducive to a *Life-way* grounded in the experience of Practice. Imagination only becomes a problem if we continually indulge in it as an escape from Being Here and Now.

Imagination can be either active or passive. Passive imagination is day-dreaming – a state in which we're not present, not even in the day-dream. This is a drowsy, vague state of being that scarcely leaves us with a memory of what we have been day-dreaming about. Active imagination, however, is a state of being present – it's a creative capacity that we can use as a resource for self-healing, *Visionary Discovery* and artistic creativity.

In terms of fantasy and imagination, all art relies on emptiness. A painting relies on an empty plane. A sculpture relies on empty space. Music relies on silent space. Literature relies on an absence of ideas, themes, descriptions and meanings. If we are to Realise the Art of Freedom and discover our creative potential, we need to rely on the experience of our intrinsic Vibrant Emptiness – the Beginningless Ground of what we are.

The gateway to this experience is the practice of Shi-ne – our method of returning to the white canvas of Being. With Shi-ne we are disengaging from the process of imagination and fantasies of any kind – that's the nature of the practice. We're being completely unmanipulative and uninfluenced by anything. Working with Active Imagination will come later, when we've connected with the Spaciousness of our Being.

So, the experience of Shi-ne may be uncomfortable – an experience we'd rather avoid because it puts us on the spot. When we Sit in this way, we locate ourselves acutely in time and space.

We know that in a certain sense we have limited our options. We know that while we're practising Shi-ne we are where we are, just where we Sit. We know that this is where we're going to be for as long as we've decided to Sit. It's as if the world has stopped – as if time has suddenly stood still. At one moment there's a film running – an epic, a comedy or a melodrama – then suddenly it freezes on a frame of YOU, Sitting in a room. Suddenly there's no movement to distract you from this image. You see every detail of it as it is, and that can be very disconcerting if you've never seen yourself like that before. Not everybody likes to see pictures of themselves, and we're probably all familiar with at least a few people who always say: 'No, don't take a picture of me – I'm not photogenic,' and then pull some grotesque grimace just to prove the point. But what does this strange attitude actually signify? The word 'photogenic' describes a temperament or attitude rather than a physical condition. No one is either photogenic or not photogenic in appearance – only in personality. We either feel comfortable in our own skins or we don't. The camera may occasionally catch unfortunate quirks of expression, but they're also what we are; they're not someone else – that's for sure! Hiding from cameras doesn't stop us looking the way we do, and hiding from confrontation with what we are doesn't stop us being what we are. If we avoid Sitting we'll avoid direct confrontation with ourselves, but we can't avoid the painful frothing patterns of frustration that bubble up in our lives when circumstances dictate. It would appear that if we practise Shi-ne, *we* start to live our lives, and if we don't, *our lives* continue to live us. In some ways, Shi-ne is the moment the shutter is pressed. The shutter mechanism exposes the film to our reflected light, and that's the picture that we get. That's us at that moment. Maybe we like it, and maybe we don't – but it's how we are whether we like it or not.

So when we Sit and practise Shi-ne, we experience ourselves at that point in time. We can try to obliterate that point in time by mentally reliving the past, by projecting possible future events, or by sinking into an oblivious drowse. But we can also Sit and *Be what we are* in that moment. We can Sit and *aimlessly* observe our present mind-moment arising from the death of our previous mind-moment. This is called *Being Here and Now*.

Whenever I talk about *Being Here and Now* it may be that what I'm saying gets to sound a bit magical and mysterious, and maybe people get confused. Maybe you think: 'Where am I if I'm not here and now?', and this is a very good question – a question that I propose to answer. In a sense I've already answered this question in previous chapters, but often questions answered at the level of intellectual reasoning just remain there – and all we're left with is some kind of abstract notion to which we find difficulty in relating. The problem with any kind of intellectual analysis is that unless we can integrate its meaning at an experiential level – it just remains an abstraction that ceases even to hold our intellectual interest. Answers to questions of this kind have to make tangible sense in terms of our everyday experience or else we can't really make much of them. So, I think it's important to take a look at an *echo* of Here and Now that exists either as a memory or as a continuing reality in most people's lives. Let's look at intoxication.

Alcohol is one of life's naturally occurring conceptual scramblers. You can see its effects on warm autumn afternoons when the bird-pecked fruit hangs heavy and over-ripe on drooping orchard branches. The fruit has begun to rot around the pecked holes, and the juice of the fruit begins to ferment through contact with the natural air-borne yeasts. The buzzing of the wasps sounds strangely slurred; and yes, you're right – they're drunk. Their flight patterns get distinctly erratic, and who knows what becomes of them – I've not watched them that long, or hung around to offer them cups of black coffee. Being drunk, or even being slightly tipsy is a condition that many of us will at least remember – so let's take a look at that state of mind.

Without going too deeply into the chemical effects of alcohol on the brain and the central nervous system, we can make a number of interesting observtions. Whether what we want is 'Dutch courage' or the drowning of our sorrows, there's nothing in the alcohol itself that supplies these things. Alcohol contains no pre-packaged easily assimilated human qualities or abilities.

Alcohol disinhibits us and whatever manifests, is part of how we happen to be rather than part of the alcohol. One of the main things that inhibits us, is our fear of the consequences of whatever it is that we're doing here and now. That fear can only arise when we have a strong connection with *past-time* and *future-time*. When we are less connected with past and future time, we become less inhibited and that's just what alcohol does for us. Alcohol blurs our sense of anywhere else and any other time. Alcohol doesn't enable us to find ourselves Here and Now (in the sense we've discussed within the practice of Shi-ne), but there are certain similarities which, when considered, may click with us in trying to understand the real Here and Now.

The unreal here and now produced by alcohol is one of tunnel-vision. Our alcoholic here and now is often such a tiny little space and time, that we completely lack any semblance of Panoramic Awareness. When the capacity of Panoramic Awareness is sufficiently blunted, we become oblivious to anything outside our immediate surroundings. We tend to be insensitive to anything else that may be taking place beyond the immediate range of our senses. We could be in a restaurant with some friends being very uninhibited indeed. We could be fluently regaling them with some highly lurid tale in magnificent style – there's nothing so terrible about that. But if we're talking so loudly that we're offending everyone else in the place, then our lack of inhibition exists only at a price. If we get asked to leave or if the people we're with are embarrassed by our performance then obviously something has been missing from our repertoire of perceptions. We may not have wanted to offend people, but we were unaware of the wider panorama of our situation. The attraction we find in alcohol is that it *does* echo something of our Beginningless Enlightened Nature – even though we might not realise that this is what we were looking for when we opened the bottle.

When people drink alcohol they relax. We spend a lot of our waking lives in varying states of stiffness and tension, and alcohol is a popular means of gaining some sense of relief from that habit. When we drink, we notice that we become physically loose – our bodies feel easier to be with. We're looking at the effects of mild intoxication, of course, rather than the full-blown effects of inebriation in which the body seems unable to comply accurately with any of our intentions. This is a condition in which whatever awareness we have has become completely blasted, and has little to recommend it apart from its anaesthetic value. Pleasure is not exactly a commonplace experience in our lives. It's often difficult to be happy, because we carry a burden of hopes and fears with us that apply to other situations than the ones in which we find ourselves. This is why so many people have to intoxicate themselves in order to experience some sort of happiness, and why parties usually only get off the ground when everybody has had a few drinks.

I'm neither criticising alcohol nor am I advocating it – I'm merely commenting on how we are as people and how we function. I'm illustrating the fact that relaxation and spontaneity are inhibited by not living in the Here and Now. When we don't live in the Here and Now, it becomes difficult to relax, and we relapse into con-strictedness – unable to flow with the nature of what is unfolding around us. Not living in the Here and Now insulates us from the immediacy and potency of where we are and it becomes easy to misconstrue what is happening in our situation.

The chemically induced 'here and now' not only affects our minds, but also our bodies. If we think about the physical mishaps that can befall us, and the differences that intoxication can make to the severity of our injuries – we can observe that concepts have a considerable effect on us according to our circumstances. Sometimes we can take quite a small tumble and hurt ourselves quite badly as a consequence. At other times, in an intoxicated state, people can survive quite alarming accidents and remain relatively unscathed. (This is probably just as well of course, because we're far more likely to have accidents as a result of being drunk anyway.) It would seem to be a question of how stiff and nervous we are, and it seems clear that intoxication cuts through that stiffness and nervousness to a certain extent by inhibiting conceptualisation. It's well known that if the body falls when in a relaxed state, it sustains less injuries as a result. This isn't a recommendation of intoxication as a safeguard against injury, especially if we happen to be driving, but a presentation of how we are – an aspect of life as we commonly experience it.

The only *real* way to relax that is of any long-term benefit, is to relax the rigidity of our mental patterning – to learn how to live in the Here and Now rather than in the 'there and when'.

There are many aspects of life that carry *echoes* or *reflections* of our Beginningless Enlightened State. Alcoholic intoxication is one such aspect of life which is why we've spent some time looking at it. I am aware that discussing aspects of the intoxicated state as echoes of the Enlightened State may cause offence to some people who adhere to the concept of renunciation, but to a certain extent causing offence is an occupational hazard if you place no limit on the analogies at your disposal. Anyone who feels uncomfortable about this could do well to consider the words of Drukpa Kunley the Illustrious Crazy Wisdom Master of Tibet:

> The mountains are thick with trees
> But firewood by the hearth is scarce.
> A torrential river passes by
> But there is no water for chang.*
> The village is plentiful with barley
> But there's no offer of a tipple.
> The bazaar is jostling with young ladies
> But little chance of getting laid.
> Spiritual Traditions flourish everywhere
> But Awareness and Kindness are rare.

Among the different Tibetan Traditions there is a noticeable ambivalence on the subject of alcohol. I think that it is well known that alcohol is forbidden to the monastic orders within Buddhism in general, but it is less well know that this prohibition doesn't exist within the non-monastic Tantric or Ngakpa order known in Tibet as the White Sangha. In order to avoid misunderstanding, one must be aware of the basis of these different approaches. There is no *essential* contradiction between

*Chang is the famous Tibetan barley beer.

them, because both approaches are valid and completely workable within their own frames of reference. There is no right and wrong here, only two methods that operate in different ways and which are designed for different kinds of people.

The monastic order adhere to the rules and principles of the Sutric Path. The rules are called the Vinaya and were developed by Buddha Sakyamuni in order that communities of people who lived and practised together should be able to do so without unnecessary problems and complications. These rules are based on Renunciation, which is the functioning principle of the Sutras. The Tantric Path, however, functions in terms of Trans-formation and so its methods are different. The nuns and monks who practise Tantra within the Tibetan system, do so within the external discipline of the Vinaya. But the White Sangha are not necessarily limited by the rules of the Vinaya unless they choose through Awareness of their condition to make use of its precepts as methods of practice. Within the White Sangha, alcohol is taken with Awareness and its effects are transformed into energy. This does not constitute, as some people may imagine, the excuse to get rip-roaring drunk. Drinking with Awareness is a delicate procedure, and one which employs the means of utilising life-circumstances as the Path. This doesn't mean that Tantric practitioners drink every day or even every week – often they will only do so twice a month on the days that are special to Buddha Padmasambhava, and even then often only in small quantities. The quantity that any particular practitioner will drink will depend on personal capacity for transformation. Obviously if your capacity is low, then your consumption will need to match that or you will just damage yourself. Naturally, what we have here is a question of personal responsibility and personal Awareness, but everyone has their own way of relating to this kind of method.

I remember once when I was with Lama Chhimed Rigdzin Rinpoche preparing to participate in the Visualisation and Awareness-spell Practice of Buddha Padmasambhava, he suggested that I should drink a tot of brandy with him: 'To encourage the Presence and Realisation of becoming Padmasambhava'.

Most Practitioners of the White Lineages drink in moderation, but there are some Lamas who have been famous for their abilities to drink medically impossible quantities of alcohol and remain apparently unaffected. Lama Sangchen Dorje Rinpoche was such a Ngakpa, and there is a most remarkable story told about him that comes down to me through Chhimed Rigdzin Rinpoche. Chhimed Rigdzin Rinpoche met Sangchen Dorje Rinpoche (already advanced in years) when he was a young incarnation wandering in the Himalayas and was most impressed by him. Chhimed Rigdzin Rinpoche is himself very moderate indeed (though not through lack of capacity) so this story is all the more significant.

Sangchen Dorje Rinpoche was a great Dzogchen Master who lived mainly in Sikkim, but who like many such Adepts wandered between Sikkim, Tibet and Bhutan practising rites in remote and hidden places. He was known to be a Wonder-worker – a Lama who could control the weather, making it rain or shine at will. He was one of those extraordinary, wild-looking Ngakpas rarely seen today, and he had what I can only describe as having the air of being from some other world. Unfortunately I was born too late to meet this Lama – I have only ever seen a photograph of him, but none the less, the image of him is as clear in my mind as if I'd actually met him. Unlike my own Teachers, who have either top-knots, plaits or buns, Sangchen Dorje Rinpoche wore the many yards of his hair coiled up on top of his head, surmounted by further coils of braided yak hair to keep his tresses in place. In the photograph the Lama's strange Ngakpa hat is worn at a rakish angle, which, according to Chhimed Rigdzin Rinpoche, was his custom. He wore a simple, homespun, white cotton chuba-coat, and the red, blue and white striped shawl that such masters wear. He had a silvery trailing beard rare among Tibetans and from his ears hung the spiral conch-shell earrings that the great Tantric Adepts wear.

The look in his eyes is one of Fearless Presence and Penetrating Insight – I was so impressed by the picture that I asked Chhimed Rigdzin Rinpoche if he knew who this lama was and this is one of the stories he told me.

Sangchen Dorje Rinpoche's name had become known to the Chögyal (Spiritual King) of Sikkim, and he had become very eager to receive a teaching from this Ngakpa to whom apparently very little was impossible – it was said that he could walk on water! The Chögyal was very curious as to what kind of teaching this extraordinary Master would give, and so he invited him to his palace and entertained him most royally. The Chögyal requested a Teaching of Dzogchen (the Great Completion) which is the most profound and direct teaching within any system of Buddhism, and was both amazed and deeply moved by Sangchen Dorje Rinpoche's explanations. As part of the hospitality the Chögyal lavished on the Lama, he offered some of his prized Scotch Whisky, to which the Lama showed marked appreciation. Indian spirits are notoriously lacking in many of the qualities that go to making drinking imported whisky a pleasure. But this was no ordinary whisky, it was the very best whisky that money could buy, due to the fact that the Chögyal had it imported from Scotland himself. Naturally the whisky was very precious to the Chögyal, but such was his respect for the Lama that he presented him with a number of bottles at his departure from the palace. After this the Chögyal took to visiting Sangchen Dorje Rinpoche and whenever he visited a bottle of whisky would be part of the present given in appreciation of the audience. As the Chögyal's devotion towards his Lama increased, so did the gifts of whisky, until a bottle a day was being delivered whether he visited or not. This did not quite amount to 365 bottles a year because Sangchen Dorje Rinpoche would sometimes be travelling in Bhutan, but by the time the Chögyal died, seven bottles a day were being delivered. During that time Sangchen Dorje apparently stopped eating and drinking, and lived only on whisky. This truly terrifying volume of spirit was observed to have no noticeable effect on him whatsoever – he was able completely to transform what he drank and *distil* the Essence into personal power.

The world is full of stories about the impossible becoming possible, and most of them – like this one, are told of people and places long ago. But lest you imagine that these things only happened in the past, I have quite a collection of other stories in similar vein, a few of which I'd like to regale you with.

The first story comes to me through Dr John Crook – a teacher of Zen and Ch'an meditation, but also a fairly hard-headed and respectable Reader in Psychology at Bristol University. The story is of his meeting with Khamtag Rinpoche and their wilderness journey together in Ladakh. During this breath-taking journey, Khamtag Rinpoche would occasionally break the day's walking by taking John's breath away in a somewhat different fashion – he'd pass round bowls of the fiery Ara, a rather vivid and volatile local spirit. Khamtag Rinpoche's attendant, who always made sure that they travelled well-supplied, would always drink a little with his Lama, but would soon be the worse for wear. John, a little more canny, offered his Ara surreptitiously to the Sa-dag (local earth spirits) after he'd had enough, and remained able enough to save the attendant from disappearing in one of the fast-flowing rivers they had to cross. But Khamtag Rinpoche showed very little effect other than a rosy glow. He explained that the way to avoid becoming drunk and suffering ill effects was always to stop drinking before you got a headache – except with Khamtag Rinpoche, that point never seemed to arrive.

As to my own experience, I have sat drinking with Könchog Rinpoche, a great Tantric Master and Practitioner of Dorje Tröllo who lives in Tso Pema. The experience was very similar to Dr John Crook's story, apart from the fact that as an Initiated Tantric Practitioner there was no way I could consider stealthily decanting my glass and thereby refusing what such a Lama had offered me.

After a long night of animated discussion between Lama Sonam Zangpo, Könchog Rinpoche and myself in which several bottles of 'Old Monk' Indian rum disappeared, we went off to bed at a quarter to three in the morning only to have to get up again for the Buddha Padmasambhava rites that started at five. Könchog Rinpoche was in conspicuously cheerful mood and robust good health, while I was feeling decidedly fragile to put it mildly. I can't speak for Lama Sonam Zangpo apart from saying that he seemed to handle it better than I did. Later in the day when we were engaged in the meditative dances which celebrate the birth of Buddha Padmasambhava, Lama Sonam Zangpo and I were requested to accompany Könchog Rinpoche on the rolmo (wrathful-cymbals) in the Tantric ensemble that co-ordinated the movements of the shamanic dancers as they enacted the nature of the eight manifestations of Buddha Padmasambhava. The rolmo make an indescribable sound (having the qualities of both bell and drum) that have surprising effects on the psycho-physical organism in 'ordinary consciousness' – but in my delicate state it became an experience that I am unable to forget. I put it down to the Presence and Influence of Könchog Rinpoche and remain profoundly grateful to him for his complete and unobstructed kindness.

There is much that I could say about that experience but suffice it to say that all sense of time vanished. Although we were engaged in the performance of that mystic music for five hours, it seemed both far longer and much shorter at the same time. While it continued, and while we continued in it, it seemed as if I'd never done anything but play these rolmo along with Könchog Rinpoche. Once it was over it seemed almost as if it had taken little more than a second. I felt so completely energised by the experience that Lama Sonam Zangpo and I made the hard two-hour climb up to Buddha Padmasambhava Cave high above Tso Pema. We returned much later in pitch blackness, drawn by the glimmering lights of Könchog Rinpoche's monastery which reflected in phantom forms on the rippling surface of the Lotus Lake. How we got down the mountainside almost blind was a mystery to me at that time, but now I see it as being the conclusion of Könchog Rinpoche's teaching on the nature of Being Here and Now.

Lhod – relaxation

7
Time, Place and Person

In order to enter into Practice – in order to make Sitting part of your life, you'll need to observe how you are and how you structure your day. You'll need to look at how you use your time and how you feel at different periods throughout the day. This is quite personal – we're all different, and there's no set formula that suits everyone. If I were to give some kind of rigid rule about the best time to Sit, then it might be excellent for some but possibly even counter-productive for others. The most important thing is that you discover for yourself how to use your time in the most skilful way.

As a general principle: first thing in the morning is an excellent time for Sitting, but if you're one of those people who come alive at night, and feel like hell in the morning – this advice may well be rather off-putting. Two possible alternatives arise if you're a semi-nocturnal person: either you can readjust your body-clock (gently, gradually and over the course of a few months) or you can accept how you are and discover your own best time. It is worth trying to adjust your body-clock, because being mis-aligned with the natural cycle of darkness and light tends to deplete the life-force. Being awake in too many hours of darkness and sleeping during too many light hours puts our energies out of balance and can lead to depression and irritability – a fact worth bearing in mind if you work night-shifts. We actually *need* to see full-spectrum sunlight in order to remain lively and *bright*. If you are a night-worker it's a good idea to obtain full-spectrum lighting in your home so that you don't suffer too much light-deprivation. But whatever, you must respect how you are and work with that rather than attempting to force yourself too much. If it's too difficult to Sit early in the morning, then you'll probably get very little out of it. If you get very little out of your

Sitting you'll probably give it up, so it's better to Sit when you feel fresh and alert.

Sitting first thing in the morning is usually advocated because it's a unique juncture in our daily stream of experience. The time when we wake up is quite special because although we may well have been conceptualising like crazy in the dream-state, at least we've had a break from the habitual patterns of our waking-conceptuality. At the point of waking, there's no accumulation of 'today's conceptual patterns' – it's a space between two long tracts of crowdedness. If we can *Be* in this Space: that *in itself* is meditation. Allowing this sense of Spaciousness to become increasingly expansive, is something that happens more naturally on waking.

But getting up in the morning is not always so easy for many people. One of the chief difficulties of getting up is the blurring that occurs in the transition between waking and getting out of bed. Once we find ourselves in that blurred state it is very likely to become protracted unless we have some very pressing cause to rouse ourselves. This blurring seems a very comfortable state to be in, and I'm sure that a lot of people reading this will find it difficult to accept that remaining in that state is undesirable. Usually when I talk about this blurred drowsing in negative terms, people become rather anxious and summon up all kinds of defences. People often say 'But I need that time in order to feel fully rested', to which I could reply, 'That's like saying that you need to remain as tense as you are in order to relax.' People are often quite surprised when I say that this blurred drowse is in fact most unrestful, and that it leaves us bereft of the freshness we could experience by waking and getting up in a sharper, clearer and more distinct way.

The *only* way to get up skilfully is to get up immediately on waking. Gradual waking up drains our energy and often leaves us feeling as if we could use another night's sleep. It's in this blurred drowse that we get the most bizarre and frustrating dreams – dreams that are continually disturbed by figments of wakefulness. Dream consciousness intrudes on waking consciousness and waking consciousness intrudes on dream consciousness. We keep trying to return to interrupted dreams in order to 'finish them off' satisfactorily – but some new dream cuts in instead; only to get clipped at some equally awkward and disquieting juncture. It's as if someone had picked up a whole string of bits from the film-splicing and editing floor and taped them all together in no particular order. This disjointed jumble of illusory unease, is the interface caused by the lap-dissolve between sleep and wakefulness. In this meandering state our energy gets dissipated in trying to resolve the hybrid issues caused by the jostling of two different patterns of consciousness. Dream-rationality and waking rationality conflict in this blurred drowsing and distort each other's modes of meaning – and unless we have a high degree of Awareness in which we can observe these modes as equally illusory, we just stir up waves of confusion and end of feeling wasted.

If you've ever woken up 'too early' in the morning and decided to go back to sleep again, you'll have some idea of what is meant by skilful and unskilful waking. The first time you wake up you feel really bright and alert – you feel rested and able to start the day with some enthusiasm. But having decided 'it's too early', and having gone back to sleep again – the second waking is a whole different story. This second waking is invariably a bleary affair, with none of the freshness of the initial waking. Instead of feeling even more rested after the extra sleep, you just feel wrecked. I'm fairly confident that most people will have had this sort of experience at least a few times in their lives and will be able to relate to what I'm saying. But if you can't remember such an experience, maybe you'll notice it when it happens in the future. Once you've had this kind of experience, and you've got up 'too early' instead of going back to sleep, it will completely alter how you feel about sleep and the need for rest.

The best way to wake up is to get out of bed as soon as your eyes open. A saying from the Zen tradition has it that we should leap out of bed in the morning as if it were full of poisonous snakes! Although I wouldn't personally recommend such a violent practice – I would recommend leaving your bed immediately on regaining consciousness. If you wake up in this way you'll avoid the draining experience of befuddling yourself between sleep and wakefulness, and feel the fresher for it.

It is possible to get up without an alarm clock, and indeed it's a good idea to gain that kind of ability. This is something that many 'ordinary' or 'mystically disinterested' people do without making much of a song and dance about it. They just think of it as 'self-discipline'. I'm not so happy about the term 'self-discipline', nor am I enthusiastic about the 'up at six for a cold shower' approach, even though it could be quite beneficial for the right person under the right circumstances. Learning to wake up when you need to wake up in order to get to work on time is very useful from the point of view of retaining Awareness within sleep-consciousness. But if you find that you're always over-sleeping and need to use an alarm clock - that's fine. Many people use alarm clocks, even those who've practised regularly for a number of years. But if you own a repeater alarm (the kind that wakes you up at five-minute intervals for twenty minutes, and then at one-minute intervals for ten minutes until you get up) and you can't avoid the temptation to use it - there is only one thing to do: take it into the street or garden and beat it with a stone until it's unrecognisable. If you show any mercy you're lost. The only thing to do is to get hold of an ordinary alarm clock, the sort that rings continuously until you turn it off. If you put the alarm clock in such a position that you have to get out of bed to switch it off, you've virtually won the battle. That's all there is to getting up. The repeater alarm may seem a wonderful device but it's utterly insidious - a cause of exhaustion, fatigue and confusion.

If you need nine hours sleep a night, rather than eight hours or seven hours - it won't help you at all to get one hour less sleep than you need and take up the other hour with 'repeater-alarm-woolly-sock-psychosis'. If you need nine hours sleep, it's better to take nine hours uninterrupted sleep, and then get up immediately the bell rings. Setting your alarm for six and then drowsing until seven will not make you feel more rested, even though it might seem a more gentle process. The 'gentleness' of drowsing your way into waking consciousness is totally illusory, because drowsing-consciousness is full of disturbed patterns - fractured clips of unsequential mini-dramas that have no satisfactory end, and this is by no means either gentle or useful.

Buddhist practice from whatever tradition is geared towards *waking up*, and so linking the practice of *waking* from the 'sleep' of misapprehension with waking from our nightly sleep is a powerful *coincidence* in the development of our practice. Anything we can do to enhance our presence and alertness is valuable. A quick facial wash and vigorous rub dry can be most helpful first thing in the morning, but it's good to leave as little time as you can between waking and Sitting. If it's cold it's a good idea to wrap yourself in a warm blanket rather than turning up the heating, because Sitting in a stuffy overheated room will make you drowsy and might even send you off to sleep again. Many people find it good to have a blanket or meditation wrap that they keep specifically for their Practice, and which they use for no other purpose. Maroon or red is a good colour for such a wrap, because according to the tradition, it's the colour of energy. Using that colour and connecting with it through our visual faculties is a method of creating conducive circumstances for the development of energy at the level of practice. But this is also an individual thing, and there is no limit to the variety of wraps you could make according to your own personal tradition of meaningfulness. The more care and sensitivity you put into your practice equipment, the more it will generate the *feel* of the time when *you* can Sit and Be. The wrap, like the block, cushion or stool, will become very familiar to you as you continue in your practice. The care with which you handle these things and pack them away after use will also become part of your practice. Objects treated in this way will become valuable *supports* for practice in their own right, and when using them, we will find ourselves more able to enter into the spirit of practice.

The practice robes, clothes, possessions and ritual equipment of Tibetan Masters are highly regarded as being *saturated* with the *atmosphere* or personal energy of those Lamas. Sometimes in special circumstances, teachers will give their closest pupils such things in order to advance their practice. It is a great honour and inspiration to wear anything given by your teacher, and having been given a Yogi-shawl (worn by one of my Teachers during his three-year solitary retreat) I can say that it helped me (or inspired me to help myself) through many difficult times in my own retreats. I feel very privileged indeed to have been given robes and ritual equipment by several great Masters, to whose Kindness and Generosity I am endlessly indebted. My Root Teacher Chhimed Rigdzin Rinpoche recently sent me a pair of Tibetan sunglasses that had been his in Tibet as an inheritance of his previous incarnation. Tibetan sunglasses were rather rare in Tibet, inasmuch as they were not made of glass – but of rock-crystal. They are rimless in design, connected by bronze lotus-shapes and twin-jointed sides that terminate in dark amber discs that fold behind the ears. They came to me in a remarkable copper and Chinese Lizard skin case of some antiquity. Together they are great treasures to me. His Holiness Dudjom Rinpoche, Head of the Nyingma School spoke of such sunglasses once when he was giving a teaching in England – he said that in Tibet his glasses had cost him three good horses! Certainly to make lenses like those from crystal must require a high degree of craftsmanship and take an inordinate length of time to cut, shape, grind and polish in a country without the kind of technology we have in the West today. Being able to wear Chhimed Rigdzin Rinpoche's glasses whilst engaging in open-eyed meditative sky-gazing, is a wonderful inspiration as well as being of considerable mundane value.

My eyes are very sensitive to sunlight, and the crystal lenses which are said to *cool* the eyes are large enough to shield my eyes completely from any uncomfortable intensity.

It's good to Sit for a length of time that you can manage every day. Don't be tempted to Sit for longer than you are really able. If you do, you'll just end up finding excuses for not Sitting every day, and then you'll feel as if you've failed. It's important to develop confidence rather than fabricating the sense of incompetence and failure. So go at your own speed. Don't worry if other people tell you they're Sitting for an hour or more every day – if *you* Sit for five minutes every day and *actually* let go and let be: that's possibly better than quite a few of these people may be doing. However long you or other people Sit – it's not a competition, or if it is – it's not practice.

Don't make promises to yourself that you can't keep, or you'll end up not being able to keep promises to yourself about anything. Start with what you can do very easily, and promise yourself that you'll Sit for that length of time every day. It's better to Sit for five or ten minutes a day than for an hour every once in a while. Daily practice is *very* important, and until you can establish a daily practice you'll find it difficult to enter fully into the experience of Sitting. Sitting has to become part of the natural flow and pattern of our lives or it will always be something 'special'. This may seem a strange thing to say in view of the many special things I've said about it, but the *specialness* of Sitting cannot be found outside its *ordinariness*. Until we Sit every day, Sitting will never become *ordinary*, and if it never becomes *ordinary* – it will never be *special*. The *special* quality of Sitting is something that should not be limited to the time in which we Sit. Sitting that has this *special* quality, permeates the rest of our day – giving us access to a more spacious sense of Being. Beyond the formal pattern of our everyday Sitting, it is important to utilise other moments that happen to give themselves to us. During the day it is often possible to enter the momentary spaces between activities, in which we can *stop* – merely to let go and let be. This momentary practice of letting go and letting be, infuses our daily life experience with a sense of openness – we become more able to *see* how we cause our own confusion and frustration.

So, our daily Sitting is our base for other moments of Space during the day. These moments could occur in bus queues, on trains, walking to the shops or lying in the bath. There is no limit to these moments – they're infinite, and once we find ourselves within them, we become open to the Infinite nature of what we are.

The place we choose to Sit is also important – because ultimately although it can be anywhere, relatively, the place and its atmosphere have an effect on us. Not everyone can have a special room set aside for the sole purpose of Sitting and other mystic practices. It is important therefore, to set aside or make

ready some place in your house, flat or bedsit – where you can Sit
and feel it's where you should be. It's not really conducive to Sit
amongst careless heaps of accumulated household parapher-
nalia. If we just Sit anywhere without any sensitivity to our
environment, then we will create an untidy energy within
ourselves. It *is* possible to Sit anywhere and under any prevailing
conditions, but for that we need to have *Ultimate View*. As long
as we only have relative view, some situations are conducive and
others inconducive. If the place where we Sit reflects our
distraction rather than our *Attuned Intent* toward Realisation,
the *atmosphere* of our practice will be restricted in its
conduciveness to Opening.

It is important to respect the practice in which we're engaging,
and also to respect our own intention. If you invite someone back to
your home (because you're strongly attracted to them and you'd
like to get some romantic liaison going with them), then you need to
create conducive circumstances. If this person is very important to
you and you want to succeed in your seduction – it's no use inviting
them back to a scene of squalor in order to share a tin of beans on
burnt toast served up on greasy plates. You don't leave the fire
down so low that you both have to keep your overcoats on and Sit
half-blinded by the stark light bulb dangling unshaded in the middle
of the room. Sure, some of us live on limited resources – but no
matter how poor we are, we can put some care and effort into
making our environment pleasant. The Tibetan refugees in the
Himalayas, no matter how poor they are, always make their home
environment clean and attractive. They paper the packed mud
walls of their dwellings with newspaper, and where possible with
colour supplements or *National Geographic* magazines. They paint
tin cans and use them as plant pots and generally make the best of
whatever little they have. There's always a sense of both space and
colour in Tibetan homes – a feeling of natural nobility. So even if
we're socially deprived and unable to alter our circumstances due to
the policies of corrupt and inhumane regimes, we can still liberate
the expression of our innate human dignity. Living like a slob even
if you happen to be very wealthy is unconducive to the *atmosphere*
of Practice.

In the Tibetan tradition, practitioners employ all manner of complex sensory devices and imagery in order to create conducive circumstances for practice. I'm not necessarily advocating that people should build their own Tibetan temple before they start to Sit, or even that they should have a special room – but some effort should be made in recognition of the nature of the practice in which you wish to involve yourself. Some people reading this book will find themselves moved or enthused by Tantric Awareness-imagery, and others not – so what I am saying is intended to be open-ended in terms of how any individuals might want to apply it in their lives.

Having some focus for your place of Sitting is very useful. Having a picture that inspires us to practise provides an excellent focus. As a reminder of the transient nature of all phenomena and the gossamer texture of our thoughts arising and dissolving in the Vastness of Mind, a photograph of a deep blue sky decorated by a few wispy clouds could provide a focus that is both a Tibetan meditative image and one that is completely acultural. If you are inspired by the lineage of Padmasambhava, there is a picture of him at the end of this chapter that you could copy, and hang on the wall at eye-level when you Sit.

Images such as these are valuable if you become 'scattered' and your mind seems crowded by rampant thoughts that fill out the Space. To be able to open your eyes and gaze non-conceptually on the Awareness-image of Buddha Padmasambhava as a focus, is considered very helpful. This doesn't mean that you should think about the Awareness-image or deliberately generate any kind of attitude towards it; but that you should let the focus of your eyes soften a little and simply *wordlessly gaze* until the buzz of thoughts has calmed a little. If you can make no inspirational connection with a picture of the sky or with the Awareness-image of Buddha Padmasambhava, you could stand a flower in front of you, or anything that might *touch* you in respect of its beauty.

In order to create conducive circumstances you may like to light a candle or a night-light – a stick of incense would also enhance the atmosphere for practice. None of these things are ultimately necessary, but because of the 'ritual' quality of our lives – engaging in *creative ritual* can facilitate an attitude conducive to Openness. There are many aspects to creating a focus for practice according to the Tibetan traditions, but I will not be dealing with them in this particular book. What I have to say here is designed for anyone to use, whether or not they wish to follow one of the Tibetan traditions. This means that whatever inspires you is valid as a focus of inspiration: Jesus Christ, Mary, Odin, Freya, Krishna, a Taoist sage, a Sufi pattern, or an Amerindian medicine shield. There is no need to reject the outer forms of your own tradition in order to engage in the practice of Sitting. I personally find inspiration in the symbolism of many different spiritual paths, but the heart of all inspiration for me is Buddha Padmasambhava. A picture of the sky or some scene of natural grandeur may, for you, prove more inspiring than any of the traditional religious images – but whatever inspires you, it must inspire you to Sit! When you Sit as a daily practice, you may well find that you're able to *feed* and nurture that sense of inspiration from the well spring of your own experience of Sitting. If you continue in this way, then ultimately it won't matter to you what you pin up – a Buddha or Desperate Dan from the *Dandy* comic-strip. But when considering the *Ultimate* and *relative views* of supports for practice (as I have done) it's important not to seduce yourself with the 'thought' of the Ultimate. We may like to imagine that we can operate from an Ultimate perspective, but unless we *really* find ourselves in that View through our Developed Openness – we'll just end up depriving ourselves of support and inspiration.

Any practice functions in terms of time, place and person, and what is practical when those factors are seen in context with each other. Once we have an exact idea of how to enter into practice, we can examine our situation and work out what is possible – we can observe ourselves and become sensitive to what fits with our unique circumstances.

Keep a diary of how you feel from day to day with regard to the *personality* of your practice and get to know yourself more intimately as a practitioner. If you run into difficulties that I don't seem to have covered sufficiently in this book then it would be wise to seek the advice of a Lama or a Teacher familiar with this kind of practice. Whatever experiences you encounter from simply Sitting – treat them lightly and allow your natural humour to be your friend.

Zhu – dissolving

8
Being and Aloneness

It can take a long time to get to know someone.

Sometimes we can know someone for many years and still not really understand them. It can happen that even a life-time isn't long enough, and even though we try as hard as we can – there still seem to be areas we can't touch upon. This is one of the frustrations of being human. People keep areas of themselves hidden from us, and we keep areas of ourselves hidden from them. We find it difficult to be open to people, and although we desperately need to make real human contact, it doesn't seem to happen very often.

Sometimes we meet people to whom we feel close straight away – something inside them and something inside us seems to resonate on the same frequency. When we meet people with whom we feel immediately at home, we may think that there are no surprises left – but our biggest surprise is often just around the corner. I'm sure that most people have either been shocked or delighted when friends have acted 'out of character'. It's then that we're faced with the fact that although we thought that we really knew them well, we must have missed something important. When 'new' facets of someone's personality emerge, we tend to say: 'My friend has changed so much, I can't understand it – there doesn't seem to be much point in seeing each other anymore.' Either that, or : 'Oh, they'll grow out of it – it's just a phase they're going through'. We tend to think that we know the real person, and that they've somehow deviated from what they really are. When previously unperceived facets of people's personalities manifest, the whole picture can change as far as we're concerned and we may or may not be able to remain friends. Imagine some really old friend from your childhood – someone you thought you knew inside out. Imagine them suddenly getting taken over by some freak religious cult. Imagine them turning up on your doorstep, after an absence of a few years, and trying to convert you. Imagine them sloganising at you as if they were some sort of door-to-door vendor, purveying 'nirvana', 'the one true God', double-glazing, stone-cladding, woodchip wallpaper, textured plaster ceilings or some other dubious product. 'Buddhists' can become as much like this as most cultists who imagine they have the sole franchise on 'The Truth'. You may think this friend of yours could never behave like that. But are you sure? Are you even that sure about yourself? People are surprised every day by friends who become born-again Venusians.

If we just meet people briefly from time to time, and if we pass what time we have together in fairly orthodox forms of social exchange – we never really get to know anyone. If we've never talked honestly about what we feel and what is really important to us – no one would ever get to know us well. But who *does* know us? Do we really know ourselves that well? How often do we actually meet ourselves, and how long do we spend in getting to know who we are? Most of us are a complete mystery to ourselves. If we Sit on a regular basis we can get acquainted with who we are. But if we never get round to spending a weekend *together*, or if we never go on holiday *together* – how intimate can we get? It's only when we begin to live *together* that we can break through some of the invisible barriers that prevent us from knowing who we are. So, to get beyond the usual chit-chat, passing courtesies and partial expressions of our true feelings we need to be alone with what we are. We need to take time out and leave behind the distractions that we find in attaching ourselves to familiar patterns. In this way, Chögyam gets to find out what Chögyam *is* when he's not Chögyam-ing.

Once you've made Sitting part of your life, and once you've experienced what that means for you – you'll become interested in finding out where you can take this process of discovery in terms of further *dimensions of experience*. I don't know how long you'll take to get to this point, but if you practise every day, then eventually you'll find yourself asking the kind of question that tends only to have one kind of answer. The answer to this question lies in the expansion and intensification of the experience of practice.

There will probably come a time when you're able to Sit for an hour a day, and once having established that, you may start to wonder what possibilities of experience lie in Sitting for longer periods. An hour a day may come to seem a relatively short period of time in terms of your life, but it may not be practically possible to extend your daily Sitting much beyond that without becoming a recluse. I don't advocate the life of a recluse, not because it is not valid as a path, but because I am writing for people in the Western world who have jobs and commitments that should not necessarily be cast off for the life of a hermit. The View of Dzogchen in particular, is one of integration, and that View is particuarly important for the West at this time. Becoming a real practitioner is *not* necessarily about giving up relationships, home and job in order to disappear into the mountains of some Eastern country – no matter how spiritually romantic that may seem. I'm advocating an escape *into* reality, rather than an escape *from* it.

The problem of how to develop our practice beyond a certain threshold is one that we all face at some point. Some of us may decide to curtail our social lives, or abandon them altogether in favour of intense mystic practice, but that is sometimes not altogether helpful. I'm generally not in favour of extremism – rather, I'm enthusiastic about the possibility of anyone and everyone being able to integrate this kind of practice into their lives. But this still leaves the problem of time, and the fact that there never seems to be quite enough of it. If we want to take our practice further without disengaging from life as she is usually lived in our orbit of society, what can we do? Well, we can either accept our situation and allow our experience of practice to develop at its own rate – or we can engage in periodic retreats.

Accepting our limitations in terms of daily practice is by no means to be underrated as a way of living and growing as a human being. I have seen too many people take on too much in the way of practice only to let the whole thing fall apart at some later stage because they've been living in some fantasy world. It's easy to want to be Great Practitioners – we can all have such desires, obsessions or inspirations, but if we cannot be ourselves and practise at *that* – we may not realise anything at all.

So we must acknowledge how we are in the moment and work with that. If other practitioners we meet are high flyers or make out that they're high flyers – let them get on with it, let them chase their tails round the initiation and teaching circuits until they burn themselves out with their own neuroses. Don't make it your problem. It's like piling up too much food on your plate – it becomes impossible to eat it all, and if you try – you end up with Dharmarrhoea.

Another attitude I've met with runs along these lines: 'If I can't take on the whole shabang, I'll dump it. I'll either be a monk or a nun, or I'll go on trapping my head in the lawn-mower of life.' This isn't a particularly intelligent attitude; it's like saying: 'Either I join the expert ski group or I don't want to ski.' As far as skiing goes, I've seen people fall behind through joining tuition groups beyond their skill, only to be overtaken by those who settle in at a skill group that matched their capacity. This can of course work the other way round, especially in spiritual disciplines, where people can be made to learn their alphabet and recite it every day – even though they can write fairly good poetry. Both teacher and pupil need to be aware of these things and proceed accordingly. A teacher who brings people in at too 'high' or too 'low' a point, is not a skilful teacher. A pupil who demands to start at too 'high' or too 'low' a point cannot really be taught.

In order to break through plateaux of experience that we have come to relate to as barriers to the Expansiveness of our Sitting, we can go on retreat. The Tibetan word *Tsam* which is usually rendered as 'retreat', actually means 'confines'. The idea is that we establish the *confines* in which we practise. Retreat can be solitary or entered into in groups. Retreat can last an hour, a day, a week, a month, a year or three or any of these measures. Retreats can be open or closed – you can either be in touch with the outside world, or completely cut off from it for the extent of your retreat. So with any retreat, you establish what the confines are going to be – and then you abide by that decision.

Sitting with a group of people is a supportive experience and one that will strengthen your individual practice. It may be possible to join a regular weekly meditation group in or around the area where you live. Meditation groups (as long as they haven't become overrun by literalists, sectarians, dogmatists and other such sad people) can be good encouragement to Practise. Some Buddhist groups are practice-orientated and others less so – generally, the less talk and the more practice the better. It's good to be able to discuss the View that accompanies the practice, but discussion groups need to be run well if they are to be helpful. If you find yourself in a group of people with peculiar interpersonal dynamics or whose main aim seems to be indoctrination – you're better off on your own. It's sad to say, but groups and centres *can* just be a stage on which various individuals work out their own personal neuroses under the guise of spiritual ardour. So use your common sense without being either too sceptical or too gullible. People are people wherever they are, and with whatever they may be involved. Rely for your support on the *silence* of the group rather than on the noises it makes over cups of tea. I'm not saying that conversation is the work of the devil, but its quality rather depends on what is being talked about. Dharma gossip and controversy are a sickness that merely disturbs others and creates nothing but bad feeling and narrow-mindedness. It may also pay to remember that all manner of people are attracted to Buddhism, and that it's not possible to judge the View or method of *any* one path by looking at the acts and speech of those that attach themselves to it. So if you meet 'Dharma-nazis' try to learn from the experience rather than being put off by it. The adage of 'baby and bathwater' is as true today and as applicable in this area as it ever has been anywhere.

If your aim is to follow the practices laid out in this book, you may find that your local Buddhist group might not be entirely suitable. This is not in any way to be taken as a value judgement: it's an observation of the fact that there are radical differences of approach and style among the various Buddhist Schools. Groups or centres that emphasise chanting (or the study of Sutric philosophy and psycho-mythology) will be of far less use to you (in your Practice of Shi-ne and the subsequent Methods in this book) than those that emphasise Silent Sitting. For this reason, you may find that a Zen or Theravadin group may be better suited to your needs than a Tibetan group. If for one reason or another these suggestions prove inappropriate, it is always possible to inaugurate a Silent Sitting group yourself – but you need to have the time, space and energy for such commitment. If you *are* interested in facilitating an opportunity for people to Sit – 'Sang-ngak-chö-dzong' can give you some ideas as to how to proceed with that. (See Appendix 3). 'Sang-ngak-chö-dzong' can also give information on courses and the possibility of inviting meditation instructors to give talks. But if you can't find the right group (or any group at all!) close to you: and if you can't entertain the idea of organising a group – it's not the end of the world! You *can* Sit on your own, and rely on support from occasional weekend courses (see Appendix 3).

Weekend meditation courses can be a nourishing experience, from which you can return to your daily life with a renewed sense of commitment to practice, born out of your own new understandings. Spending time with a group of people with shared commitment to practice can have a significant effect on our continued personal practice. The idea of spiritual nourishment becomes more important as we proceed with practice, and as we do so it becomes of value to dedicate ourselves to the thought of nourishing others. When we have recognised the necessity of extending the warmth we are discovering to others, we should allow and encourage ourselves to be continually *moved* by that intention. In this spirit we can dedicate the development of our own practice to the liberation of everyone who has become distracted from their Beginningless Enlightenment. Although ultimately we are alone on this path and have to operate from that *solitary peak* – relatively, we can all help each other. Being able to share experiences with other practitioners on courses, and learn from each other's unique perspectives – is something valuable.

But then there are silent group retreats in which we can engage in more intensive practice. Group retreat can be a powerful experience in which we can support each other through our natural warmth, our Presence and our Stillness. To be *with* others, without verbal communication is to open up to other levels of communication that function in terms of sharing time and space. It's always easier to maintain our practice when we practise with others, and so this kind of group retreat can make for *break-through* experiences that can radically shift the emphasis of our daily Sitting. It's important, however, that we don't grasp at these changes and try to solidify them into possessions or definitions of who we are.

Group retreats are a good basis for solitary retreats. Solitary retreats are by far the most intense kind of practice and certainly the strongest method of transforming our notions of what we are. It's not wise to go into solitary retreat too quickly or the experience may put you off for life! It's not worth going into solitary retreat without the advice of a teacher, and most Buddhist Centres with retreat facilities insist that you have the permission of a teacher in order to enter into retreat. You may find that you need to have an interview with the Spiritual Director of the Centre at which you intend to enter into retreat, so that it can be established that you are properly prepared. This is not very surprising, because in other fields the same principle applies. You need to log up so many hours of flying with an instructor before you can get your flying licence and fly solo. So, to *fly solo* in solitary retreat and for it to be a creative experience – you will need to prepare properly and have some way of processing your experiences in a way which will be beneficial. A teacher can comment on many facets of these experiences in a way that enriches our lives as practitioners.

It may be difficult to find anyone to give you the guidance you need, and so I will lay down some rough guidelines for anyone who feels confident enough of their Sitting practice to engage in solitary retreat. Short retreats can be accommodated in your own home, but longer retreats (which I will not be dealing with in this book) need to be entered into at a retreat centre where your food can be properly organised and where there is the possibility of asking for guidance from a Lama or meditation instructor with the appropriate experience.

I would not recommend that anyone engage in a solitary retreat for longer than one weekend (Friday night through till Monday morning) without seeking advice. Even before attempting a weekend solitary retreat of this kind, I would strongly advise going on a few silent group retreats. Much may be accomplished through quite short retreats, such as 'day' or 'half-day' retreats. A half-day retreat would start after lunch and finish the following morning, the night having been passed sleeping in the retreat-room. A day-retreat would begin an hour or so before going to sleep, continue through the following day and finish an hour or so after waking on the day after. These extra hour periods before and after should be used for starting and completing the retreat with practice. There should be very little in the room to distract you, and you should avoid taking in any reading matter. The practices to be engaged in should be those outlined in this book, interspersed by walking meditation or light exercise. Meditative walking is very slow and deliberate, and as you walk you should find the Presence of your Awareness in the movements of your body. If you're familiar with such methods as Kum-nye or Trul-khor Naljor then these are excellent activities to intersperse between practice sessions. Otherwise, there are many other physical practices from other systems taught in the West – such as Dervish Dance, Tai-chi or Hatha Yoga, etc. There is a particular method from the Tibetan Trul-khor Naljor system in Chapter 13, 'Beyond Emptiness', and this should play an important part in your retreat as well as in your daily practice.

Don't try to Sit beyond your physical capacity to Sit. If you're only used to Sitting for an hour a day, then any length of retreat is bound to put a strain on your legs. So be kind to yourself and don't push yourself beyond your limits. Generally speaking, people have two kinds of limit; a *soft limit* and a *hard limit*. If we don't push ourselves beyond our *soft limit* we will never get anywhere. But if we try to push ourselves beyond our *hard limit* we will damage ourselves and become disenchanted with the whole idea. This is all part of developing our Awareness. It's good to endure a little pain in the legs, but we need to be in touch with the point at which determination stops and masochism starts. So if you enter into retreat prematurely you might never want to try it again – and that would be a shame.

I remember my first three-month solitary retreat. I don't really know whether I was ready for it or not, but the circumstances were quite different from those that would prevail in the West. It was a tremendous culture shock for me, because the Lama under whose guidance I was working treated me in the same way that he would have treated a Tibetan practitioner. It was one of the most distressing experiences of my life (even though I went on to do much longer retreats) and I would have come out long before the end had it not been for the strong relationship I had established with my teacher. Every imaginable thing went through my head as I Sat in my hut high above Mcleod Ganj in the Himalayas. I had to confront so many barbed psychological twists and turns of my own devising that I got to know the patterns of my own stupidity fairly well by the time I emerged. There were fantastic *breakthroughs* and overwhelming relapses into infantile whimpering; but by the time I'd got through it the person who went into retreat had died. A new and *lighter* person came out into the dazzling mountain sunshine after those many weeks of isolation. *He* looked more or less like the one who'd gone in, but his eyes seemed different when *he* saw *himself* in the mirror and his way of seeing the world was reflected in that change. It was almost like amnesia – as if I'd forgotten my previous life. But I hadn't forgotten what went before at all – it was just that it all seemed to have happened several hundred years earlier and *to someone else*.

I've lost my 'old-self' many times since then, and got used to the fact that it's not just in retreat that that happens – it happens with every moment. We mainly try to blur moments together in order to hide from our own Spaciousness. In hiding from our Spaciousness we imagine that the continual process of birth and death will ignore us, but this is a rather sad misapprehension. As long as we continue to pretend that birth and death are forces that affect everything else in the universe apart from us, we can play the endlessly wearying game of imagining that we have a solid, unchanging core. But death and rebirth are the name of the game when it comes to retreats.

Unless we're prepared to *face death* – we're not ready to make a solitary retreat.

One of the things that kept me 'together' (apart from the knowledge that my teacher was *with me* in some way, and that he'd expressed confidence in me) was the *sheer Earth-power* of the wilderness around me. The mountains' brilliant whiteness beyond Cham-ba and the weird glow of the twisting mists that sometimes filled the landscape. The giddying drop just in front of my hut: fifteen paces and then a sheer drop of perhaps a thousand feet. I closed my eyes a few times whilst pacing it out to the count of thirteen. On one of those occasions I must have taken slightly longer paces than usual, because when I opened my eyes – I found myself teetering on the edge. Yes, I got pretty crazy in that first retreat, but I had maybe a lot of stupidity to work through. I had been quite addicted to company and so even to be on my own for a day just walking around in the hills was not exactly an easy experience for me. Isolation was quite terrible for me and this first retreat I did was one crisis after another until I was totally exhausted. After I got to the point where I started rolling around on the floor of my hut yammering and bleating like an animal about to be slaughtered, strangely enough something snapped or opened up and I started laughing – I realised that I was making a big fuss about *Nothing*. It was only really then that I could settle down to the practice of Being.

The mountains were very friendly and nothing ever caused me pain apart from my own rigidity. I felt *at home* with what I could see, hear, smell, taste and touch. Bears and wolves occasionally came to visit me, and sometimes among the noises of the night there'd be something scratching at the door. Nothing worse than that ever happened – the door never got pushed in, which was almost a surprise. It wouldn't have taken a lot to break the rope hinges – half-rotten as they were. It was often bitterly cold, but I had my kerosene burner to boil up the water for my trusty hot-water bottle, and I had some good woollen blankets to pile on top of my sleeping bag. When the sun was up, I'd Sit outside on a large rock overlooking the terrifying gorge. Great white vultures would glide effortlessly in the almost painfully perfect blue. The feeling that everything *was* totally where it was, in that wilderness, seemed to suggest that if I just knew how – I could probably take my teachings from any of the rocks or stones that had been lying there so patiently for the last several thousand years. The wilderness is a great healer and teacher, and practitioners have constantly returned to it to discover the experience of *Being* and *Aloneness*.

PART THREE

Lu-jen – nakedness

9
Naked Presence

Being is a somewhat *Naked State* of existence. Not 'naked' in the shivering goosepimpled sense, but in the sense of a naked flame.

Masters of the Tibetan tradition often speak of Rigpa. Rigpa means Naked-Awareness – stripped of distractedness. The idea of stripping away illusions and preconceptions in order to bare the Essential Reality of *what we are* can seem a chilly prospect. But this fear of experiential hyperthermia is built on the misconception that *warmth* is not something that is natural to us as human beings. Most of us seem gripped by the odd conviction that we have to 'clothe' our Being in 'ways of being' otherwise we'll be frozen out of existence. We seem to lack confidence in our Naked Awareness and appear clouded to the recognition that Awareness *burns* with the *Fire of Being*.

Ideas of Nakedness and the bizarre ways in which we disguise it are useful if we are to approach an understanding of how it is that we distract ourselves from Being and stray interminably in distracted-being.

Our Nakedness is what we are – it describes us. Our continuing activity of hiding our nakedness is our habit of deviating from what we are – it describes how we distract ourselves.

The curious intricacies of social conventions that relate to clothing often have little connection with our physical needs for warmth and protection. Swimming costumes are among the most extraordinary items in our wardrobes – they camouflage parts of our bodies that society deems either 'indecent', 'sexually provocative' or both. But concepts of decency or indecency are completely arbitrary (as the most cursory study of social anthropology will reveal) and have no obvious bearing on *how we actually are*. The ideas that surround clothing betray an absurdly complicated and unhealthy way of relating to our bodies. With these sociopathic attitudes to what constitute public and private parts of our bodies, there is always some tentative and titillating game in progress as to how much or how little of ourselves we can expose.

There's often a considerable degree of fear attached to seeing other people's naked bodies or of them seeing ours. There's also the somewhat fevered fascination with getting to see the prohibited bits – prohibition always arouses enthusiasm. We live in a very back-to-front world in which we fight for peace, punish people who need help and impose censorship in order to avert corruption. I'm quite sure that most swimming costume manufacturers must be aware that partially clothed bodies are far more 'erotic' than completely naked ones. I also think we can be sure that if there was more money to be made from naked swimming, then the cozzies would have long since disappeared.

When I was in my first year at art college I encountered a 'life model' for the first time. Sitting with my 2b pencil in my hand and my sketch pad across my knees, I did little at first but look rather avidly. But it wasn't more than a minute or two before the novelty wore off and the naked woman became a dynamically linked series of shapes and forms that began to fascinate me in their own way – I was after all interested in learning how to draw. So I put pencil to paper and the whole thing changed.

The prurient imaginations of people who suppose that art students are a raunchy bunch of characters who are continually feasting their eyes on sexual delights have very little connection with reality. The sensuality of a Savoy cabbage, a bare breast or a bleached white skull lies in learning to *see* with a pencil – using a pencil to *understand* shape, form and texture.

So having considered your body and the clothes that you wear, you can consider the Naked quality of your Awareness and how it becomes clothed with concepts. Maybe from this you may get a feel for where this explanation is heading.

We started out earlier in this chapter with the idea that we mistrust the Nature of *what we are*, and that we seem to need continual confirmation that we are actually here. The continual activity of seeking assurances of our existence is our penchant for unnecessarily clothing our Naked Awareness in concepts. But our conceptual apparel has something of the quality of 'The Emperor's New Suit of Clothes', and deep down we're never sure when the game's going to be up and we'll be left exposed to our Endlessly Pure Gaze. The 'little children' of our experience often yell out: 'Hey! The King is in the altogether!', but we block them out with the 'crowds' of our rationalisation and stride off with our various bits and pieces dangling free – safe in the non-dangling illusion of distracted-being.

Our mistrust of our own existence is primary in our lives, but it's a veiled mistrust that disguises itself as obduracy, anger, obsessiveness, suspicion and depression.

Our mistrust of our own existence manufactures our struggle with the world, and then struggles with the outcome of that struggle in order that the activity of *struggling* maintains itself.

Unless we practise Sitting, we'll never meet this kind of mistrust face to face, and this kind of explanation will never make a great deal of sense. So it's important to arrive at the level of understanding through our own experience of Practice.

Because we mistrust this whole notion of Being we scan our experience of being alive for proofs of actuality. Shi-ne is a bit of a let-down from this perspective because it doesn't generate the kind of confirmations that we want. So our inclination, more often than not, is to avoid the practice of Shi-ne.

Now, I want to repeat what I've just said (in this last paragraph) – but I want to turn it back to front to provide you with some experientially based reasoning that may strike the right note for you. Let me run it through for you: If we practice Shi-ne and find ourselves within the gap between arising thoughts, our inclination is to fill that gap with thought. We either try to grab the experience of the gap: 'At last a gap! Brilliant!', to retreat from the gap: 'No, this feels bad! I don't want to feel as if I'm nothing!', or to retract our *presence* from the gap: 'Yawn...'. We're either attracted, averse or indifferent to these gaps. But whichever reaction we have, the end result is the same – we fill the gap. Whether we like the gap, hate the gap or ignore the gap. We fill it with thought or drift into unconscious oblivion rather than remain Present in the Space of *what we are*.

We habitually fill spaces of any kind, because they contain no confirmation of our existence – we have no trust in Being. Being is both thought and absence of thought, phenomena and Emptiness, Energy and Spaciousness – but when we begin to practise Shi-ne it soon becomes obvious that we're not at all comfortable with that.

So this is how we are when we Sit – if you have any doubt about it, Sit and find out. That goes for any part of this explanation – if you're not convinced, just Sit and find out for yourself.

Once you've practised in this way you'll know that you're attached to the process of thinking and that you find gaps both difficult to *find*, and difficult to *find yourself* in. The experience of Sitting and doing nothing is also difficult, because when we're not engaging in any specifically recognisable activity – we lack the usual definitions.

Just Sitting means that all we've got left to prove we're alive is our bodily presence and our thought processes. If we get used to the physical dimension of Sitting (which we've looked at in Chapter 4) then our thought processes will be just about all we've got left. Shi-ne puts those processes under the magnifying glass for us, and we learn a few interesting things straight away. We learn that sometimes we'd rather think about anything at all than let go of the thought process. We'd rather think about going to the grocer's, the supermarket or the post office. We'd rather run television commerical jingles or consider the need to buy more toilet rolls. We'd rather think practically anything than not think at all. People are invariably surprised by the utter banality of the thoughts they cling to rather than simply continuing in the process of letting go.

If we've engaged in the practice of Sitting we'll be in a position to ask ourselves how it is that we'd rather think anything or go to sleep than risk the experience of remaining alert in the absence of thought.

The absence of thought obviously threatens us in some way.

What else could it be? At the very least you could say that the absence of thought failed to satisfy our 'needs'. So, our question can push on a stage further: How can we be threatened by 'nothing'? What exactly are these 'needs' that they can't cope with relatively short periods of emptiness?

Anyone who decided to spend a few hours in a sensory deprivation chamber would soon be brought face to face with the nature of their 'needs'. They'd be confronted by feelings of insubstantiality, fear, loneliness, paranoia and bewilderment. They'd also find out exactly what they wanted to do in reaction to those feelings. They'd want to consolidate their sense of themselves; instigate specific defence activities; generate familiar trains of thought and make contact with external objects; devise escape strategies and complicated contingency plans; or attempt to go to sleep. They'd discover that the space of absence in which they'd found themselves failed to provide them with a sense of solidity, unchangeability, individuation, control or definition.

Experiencing total sensory deprivation is obviously a drastic measure, and also one that is not easily available. For those who are unfamiliar with the character of a sensory deprivation chamber, it is basically a large tank full of saline solution kept at blood temperature. A person floats in the tank connected to an oxygen supply – that's it. You see nothing, hear nothing, smell nothing and touch nothing.

Shi-ne is a slower, less experientially violent method of learning everything you could learn in a sensory deprivation chamber. The practice of Shi-ne allows us to make our own discoveries in our own time, and at a pace which allows us to assimilate and integrate our discoveries with our everyday consciousness.

A favourite practice place of mine in the Himalayas was near a waterfall above the Tibetan village of Mcleod Ganj, a former British Hill Station high in the foothills below western Tibet. Not far from the waterfall was a massive flat rock that sat squarely in the middle of the river, surrounded by the continual roaring of the water. The river cascaded down the valley towards the high plains around Dharamsala carrying the icy melt-water of Tibetan glaciers down into the lowlands of Inda. Sitting on the rock I could look out over an uninterrupted expanse of blue sky. I found it an ideal spot in which to practise in good weather; surrounded by the roaring river with the low thunder of the waterfall behind me I could *gaze* out into the endless blue of the sky and allow my definitions to dissolve. To be overwhelmed by the sound of water was actually to be undisturbed by the intrusion of any other kind of sound – the roaring river became a *Roaring Silence*.

When talking about my time in the Himalayas an apprentice mentioned that my Sitting spot had all the qualities of a modified sensory deprivation technique. The technique employs a set of goggles made of two half ping-pong balls padded with cotton wool for comfort and to cut out extraneous light, and joined together with soft elasticated fabric. The idea then is to put on these goggles along with a set of headphones which emit either white noise or 'babbling brook music'. A dim blue light is then set up to colour your vision, and there you are – open to learning some interesting things about yourself. I'm not listing this as an 'official exercise' in this book, but if you care to experiment then I'm sure that you'll find it a valuable experience. You may find such a set-up useful if you live in a flat or a bedsit in a house where it's not possible to get away from the distraction of 'intelligible noise' such as loud conversations or repetitive music.

From these kinds of experiences, we can discover for ourselves that we've all accepted some form of conditioning, indoctrination or programming in which Being has come to have a rigidly fixed definition. Our Sitting practice will show us soon enough that our definition runs something like this: in order to exist we have to know all the time that we exist, and that in order to know that we exist we need constant proof of our existence in terms of solidity, continuity, separateness and permanence.

The discovery of Shi-ne is that our fear of non-existence is both the driving force of our distracted-being, and the *Sparkling through* of Liberated Being. Our mistrust of the nature of *what we are* is actually quite well founded, but we usually aim our suspicion in the wrong direction. We mistrust the *Open Dimension of our Being* rather than suspecting our conceptual criteria for defining existence.

As soon as we follow through with the practice of Shi-ne we discover that the reach and range of our definitions are a barrier. We discover that this barrier is built of feelings of insubstantiality, fear, isolation, agitation and boredom. The Practice of Shi-ne 'tweeks' each one of these feelings. Life 'tweeks' each one of them too – but not quite as definitely. So as long as we insist on maintaining fixed definitions of what we are, the practice of Shi-ne will 'tweek' them either waggishly, wistfully or woefully.

We spend our lives seeking out definitions, so in a sense Shi-ne is a way of taking a holiday from that. The Nature of Existence, *the way things are*, continually both helps and hinders us in our search for definitions in a completely impartial manner. To ascribe partiality to the random functioning of the universe is to invent God and the Devil, and apart from the fact that someone has already thought of that one – it's none of our business. Our problem is that we want to be in charge of the defining process – as if we were unconnected from what defined us.

This is rather tricky stuff: rather than allowing ourselves to be continually redefined and to occasionally be undefined, we demand a domineering kind of control that it is not possible to have.

Sitting threatens our definitions whatever they are, and reveals either impishly or demonically the fact that we believe very strongly in definitions. Sitting displays either daintily or dreadfully that we imagine ourselves to thrive on definitions. We would seem to love to tell people who we are rather than letting them experience us through 'unofficial channels'. We like to say that we're socialists, realists, humanists, buddhists, pragmatists, feminists, masculists, royalists, anarchists, imperialists, communists, conservationalists, racists, nihilists or whatever. Some of us are a little more cunning and demand that we're not any kind of 'ist', but if we demand it too loudly and too often we stand the very real chance of becoming 'anti-ismists'.

In 'New Age' circles people like to tell you that they're Aquarians or that they're Librans, but not satisfied with defining themselves they turn their attentions to you. So you divulge your constellation and they say: 'Ah, yes . . . ', and nod very knowingly – they've got you taped, they've encapsulated you in definitions and you become a 'Bubble-packed freeze-dried, oven-ready instant-serve low-fat high-protein money-off user-friendly sell-by date'. 'So you're a Gemini – yes that explains a lot . . . '. So then you get nervous – you're rumbled – and you counter them with the fact that your Moon is in Scorpio and you have Virgo rising, which of course makes *all* the difference.

Once people learn to define each other sufficiently they feel safe and can begin to relate to each other as sets of definitions. Relating to a set of definitions circumvents the somewhat real pain or pleasure of relating to the unpredictability and inconsistency of a *real person*. I'm reminded at this point of a delightful one-liner occasionally used by my dear friend Dr Flaming Rainbow when he's approached by rabid astrologers as to his birth sign: 'I'm on the cusp between Visa and Access.'

I'm not really ridiculing the ancient and fascinating system of astrology, merely teasing a tendency in some would-be astrologers. The various astrological systems of the world are very useful as tools of discovery, but when they fall into the hands of definitionists they can become vaguely banal. Systems of discovery are only actually helpful if they expose our conditioning and enable us to dismantle it.

The process of Shi-ne leaves us in no doubt that we are conditioned. We discover this in the same sort of way that we discover that water is wet or that ice is cold. If our interest lies in experiencing rather than in defining or theorising then it won't be too searingly important to know why. From the point of view in which intellect dominates and subverts our *Limitless Faculties* this may seem like an outrageous thing to say, because the intellect always wants to know why. But from the experiential point of view, 'knowing why' is rather ornamented – a decorative flourish in addition to 'knowing how'.

'Why?' is an intellectual/philosophical question. It's rather overrated as a means of coming to any profound realisation. The answers to 'Why?' mostly seem to generate more 'Why?s' – there is virtually no end to 'Why?'.

'How?' is a practical/experiential question which empowers us

– gives us direct access to first-hand experience. 'How?' puts the process of discovery in our hands. If we ask someone why they're lighting a fire, they'll probably tell us that they want to be warm. We could then ask them why they wanted to be warm, to which they'd possibly reply that they didn't like being cold. Asking why they didn't like being cold would probably get us no answer at all, or we'd be told to be quiet because we were distracting them from their fire-lighting. Most parents must be reasonably familiar with this style of questioning. Children love to question in this way at a certain stage of their development – it's half curiosity and half the simple desire to maintain the comforting murmur of their parents' voices. When we grow older we learn to extract comforting responses in more sophisticated ways – we become interested in philosophy and enjoy speculating in order to keep up the comforting murmur of our thought processes. But the 'Why?s' of philosophers are often little different to those of little children. The question 'Why?' is often a demand for vicarious experience – a way of playing safe, a way of indulging in experiential laziness. To ask 'How?' is to put ourselves on the threshold of something new. If we ask someone how to light a fire, not only do we come to make a fire ourselves, but we enter the spectrum of varied motivations that constitute the fire-maker's world – *then suddenly we know why.*

'Why?' is the ornament of 'Knowing how'. Having asked 'How?' as our initial question we can then ask why from the ground of our experience. We can ask: 'Why hasn't my fire got going properly?'. This kind of why question is one that works, because it carries an implicit 'How?' within it – 'How can I get my fire going properly?'.

These things are all rather self-evident when it comes to the world we can touch or engage in through our accepted five senses, but our feelings and varying psychological characteristics are not so simple. To ask how we can come to an *Understanding* of what we are and how we can simply *Be* --- Here and Now, takes us into the realm of *explanations* and *instructions* on *Method*, and these are based on experiences that lie beyond our conventional logic.

Nam-pang – flight

10
Fear of Flying

If I'm to say anything about reference points, I'm going to appear to be flying in the face of 'facts' that you may be hanging onto very dearly. I don't think that's going to pose a terrible problem, because I'm fairly confident that with the experience of Sitting you've had so far you're going to be able to fly with me. Even if you don't feel as though you've had any experience worth speaking of, I think that you'll be surprised at what you can take on board in the way of far-flung explanations. Conventional logic won't be quite the barrier it may have been when you first picked up this book.

From the experience of having worked with the exercises in this book, you'll have blurred the tight boundaries of conventional logic and will have the beginnings of a feeling for what lies beyond. But in order for you to fly into conventionally uncharted regions, I'm going to need your co-operation in the way of further Sitting practice.

I'd like you to put this book down every time we part company in terms of understanding – and Sit.

This is the exercise (or series of exercises) that goes with this chapter. You may or may not need to employ this exercise, but I suggest that you Sit at least once a day for half an hour whilst reading this book in order that you have a personal experiential link with what you are reading. This is an experiential book, so to read further without practising will just lead to confusion unless you already have experience or a strong link with what is being expressed.

So, as soon as you feel we've parted company and you can't relate to what I'm saying – check it in the light of your own Sitting experience. There is no point in taking any part of these explanations on trust; it is vitally important to verify this material for yourself. Anything that you accept for whatever reason apart from having first-hand experience will eventually become an obstacle and a problem for you. So, use the method of Shi-ne to discover whether or not any of this is *Real* for you!

To fly in the face of conventional logic seems (from the point of view of conventional logic) to be taking a bit of a risk – you might become a weirdo or a drop-out; but I don't think that is likely. I think that entering into this field of experience will change you internally rather than externally. External changes are more often than not merely an expression of some neurosis.

The practice you have entered into so far will have developed a basis for understanding, so the View we are about to explore should gradually open out for you in a way that will make *Direct Sense*. Also, the View I'm portraying isn't a constructed philosophy – it's a fundamental expression of Being, which means that you already *Know* it; and it needs only to be rediscovered in the experience of Sitting.

Explanations can either be understood on the basis of the immediate recognition that comes from having practised or from the *Sparkling through* of our Beginningless Enlightened Nature.

So, this chapter is a run-up – a sort of springboard, after which I'll talk about referencelessness. This springboard, which is built of ideas designed to undermine our ideas, is intended to enable us to leap into space and plunge into an understanding of the Vastness of what we really are.

At this point I'd like to introduce two terms that may be helpful in relating to the ways in which different kinds of material can be assimilated. These terms are conventional logic and *Realised Reasoning*. Conventional logic is what is regarded in the world as being acceptable. Realised Reasoning is based on experience that lies outside the realm of conventional logic.

There is no way that we can approach the realm of Realised Reasoning with the battering ram of conventional logic. All we can do is ask (if we find ourselves open to asking) how we can arrive at the level of experience from which we'll be able to relate to Realised Reasoning.

The answer to this question is made up of methods, the first of which is the practice of Shi-ne. Once we have had some experience of Sitting we will begin to open to the stream of Realised Reasoning that bases itself on the field of experience we have entered into. Once we are open to Realised Reasoning we become encouraged to bring everything to the level of experience. The further we take our practice of Sitting the more open we become – our faculties become less limited by conventional logic. The barriers dissolve between the boundaries of our understanding and the wider horizons of Realised Reasoning we formerly found frustrating.

This may all be getting to sound rather abstract and difficult to relate to, so I think I'll tell you what it's like to fall out of an aircraft at eighteen thousand feet – I hope that'll give you a clearer picture of what I mean by the terms 'conventional logic' and 'Realised Reasoning'.

If you're a person who enjoys free-fall parachuting, you'll have some singular experiences that other people will not easily be able to relate to or argue with – unless they've tried it themselves. Let's look at what happens. You fall out of the aircraft --- Shazam! There you are in mid-air, engaged in what to many people would be an insane act. The percentage of the world's population who free-fall is far smaller than that of those who practise Shi-ne – it's a pity but it's true. The first experience is pretty much what you'd expect – you fall like a stone! You fall at the rate of twenty-two feet per second.

For the mathematically slow, like myself, this means that you accelerate, and that you continue to accelerate until you reach what is known as 'terminal velocity' which is as fast as any unpropelled object can fall on this planet. Terminal velocity is about one hundred and twenty miles an hour – a fair old lick, and you reach that speed in about seventeen seconds. But something odd happens at terminal velocity – you seem to stop falling. Your stomach catches you up, and then it's as if you were being buffeted by the wind, it's as if you were being suspended by the strength of the wind pushing against you.

Free-fallers generally wear what look like outsize 'Andy Pandy' suits that enable them to turn and circle. By falling 'spread-eagled' and adjusting the position of your arms and legs you're able to circle like an eagle. For a short time you can feel like an eagle – you can observe the curve of the earth, and to some extent enter the eagle's *dimension of perception.*

When at last the earth gets too close you pull the rip-cord, the chute opens and the experience changes. It's still not really like falling, but then after a while as you look downwards something frankly bizarre happens; it's called 'ground rush'. It's very strange, it's a reversal of what anyone would imagine they would be experiencing. The ground seems as if it's coming up to meet you. So you get into your crouched position and roll when you hit the ground – conventional reality recommences.

Now if you were drawn into discussing your free-fall experience with a dyed-in-the-wool conventional rationalist, you'd probably find it quite exasperating. You'd say: 'How can you argue with me about an experience that you've never had?' The rationalist would probably reply that you ought to be able to explain any experience in conventionalist terms to anyone.

You'd probably question the value of trying to do this and suggest that unless he or she were prepared to experience free-fall for themselves, they'd just have to accept what you were saying about it. But they'd only become irritable and antagonistic and say that your description was non-sensical. They'd say that it wasn't possible to feel as though you weren't falling when you obviously were falling. They'd say that you couldn't possible see the ground coming up at you if you were falling towards it. But in terms of your experience their argument would seem rather pointless, tiresome and earthbound. You'd say: 'Try it and see, then there might be some value in discussing it.' But if they were afraid of flying, they'd never find out – they'd never know. They might camouflage their fear of flying by saying that if you could prove these things to them by intellectual argument they'd be willing to try it – but until then, free-falling would just seem like a waste of time with nothing new or strange to experience in it. You'd naturally feel rather sad that they weren't open to the possibility of something beyond their conventional frames of reference – but you might not see any value in cramping your experience into the tight box of conventional logic for their dubious benefit.

The 'tight box' of conventional logic can become an avoidance, an evasion, a way around owning up to the fear of flying. We could make all kinds of highly reasonable excuses for not leaping into space: 'It's my Aunty's Birthday,' 'It's my Grandfather's funeral,' 'My goldfish is looking off-colour,' 'I've got a dental appointment at two-thirty,' 'I've . . .'.

It can actually be something of a relief to cut through all those eloquent escapisms and erudite excuses and admit to our fear of flying. Somehow coming to terms with our reluctance to abandon definitions is a positive step – a move towards working with *how we are*. To acknowledge our fear of flying is to open ourselves to investigating the nature of our fear. From this starting point the fear loosens a little, becomes workable, and the idea of Sitting becomes a positive challenge rather than a negative threat.

Before boarding an aircraft to make the first jump, the instructor will mostly issue the mildly ominous warning that the only person who is going to come back down to the ground in the aircraft is going to be the pilot. It's a one-way ticket – if you go up, you jump!

Working with a Lama has a touch of that quality, and as you can see from the allusion to free-falling: if you never board the aircraft, you never make the jump – you're never in the position either to jump or to be pushed out into mid-air. To face the open sky by leaping from an aircraft, or to face the Open Sky of Mind while Sitting both require that we face the fear of flying.

---

sixth exercise

Sit in a posture of comfort and alertness / find the Presence of your Awareness only in your exhalation / allow your inhalation merely to happen / allow yourself to dissolve your experience into Emptiness with each exhalation / if you find that you have drifted from Presence – simply return to Presence and remain / if thoughts arise allow them to dissolve into Emptiness with each exhalation /

Try this for thirty minutes – see how it goes / if you're used to Sitting for longer – Sit for as long as you would usually Sit / see how it goes /

sixth exercise follow-up

This is the final phase of Shi-ne with form. You've let go of the in-breath, and now you're merely allowing the out-flow of your breath to dissolve thoughts or mental imagery into Emptiness. You may already have had experiences you could describe as *gaps between thoughts*, and you may have reacted to them in the various ways described in the previous chapters. Whatever you've experienced it's quite important (if not crucial) to avoid 'seeking gaps as a quest'. 'Seeking gaps as a quest' is a self-defeating process, because the activity of grasping at *gaps* is not actually possible. *Gaps* are only made possible through *non-grasping*. You may have found that thought or mental imagery which arose with the in-breath simply dissolves into Spaciousness with the out-breath creating a *gap* at the end of each exhalation. If you continue to practise in this way you may find (or you may already have found) that the *gap* at the end of one out-breath, spans several breaths without any *mental event* manifesting. At this point it becomes possible to enter into the practice of Shi-ne without form.

You may find that while Sitting you get disturbed by subtle tendencies to scatteredness or drowsiness. These manifestations of our energy can be subject to adjustment through the simple exercise of involving your head and neck.

If you become a little drowsy, you can work with that by jerking your head upwards three times. You need to use your discretion here – if you jerk your head up too sharply you may hurt your neck, and if you don't make a sufficiently decisive movement the practice will not function particularly well.

Likewise if you feel scattered and unable to settle – jerk your head downwards three times.

Once you've repeated this head-jerk you can return to your practice, but if you notice yourself slipping back into drowsiness or scatteredness again, repeat the exercise. This will be preferable to returning to a type of Shi-ne that is more linked with form.

If, however, you find yourself needing to use this exercise more than three times within a Sitting session, this should be taken as an indication that you should return to a method which relies more on form. It is always useful to remember that our energies fluctuate from day to day and that returning doesn't imply retrogression. It is much more likely that you will undermine the direction of your practice by insisting on using methods that are not geared to how you happen to find yourself in the moment.

These are subtle adjustments that will help with subtle tendencies, but if you find yourself meandering in lengthy thought-stories or nodding off into sleep, return to a more form-based method.

Chö-dzing – clinging to definitions of Being
through attachment to manifestation

11
Sticky Fingers

Being *in* and *of* the world can be a *sticky* business.

There's nothing wrong with our world or with our sense faculties – there is, in fact, nothing 'wrong' with anything. Why then is there this sense of 'wrongness' or 'incompleteness'? What *is* this sense of 'incompleteness', and *where* is it? If we look for it in the world – can we honestly say that the world lacks anything? What should it *have* beyond what it *is*? If we look for it in ourselves – can we honestly say that we lack anything? What should we have beyond what we *are*? So, what is this 'incompleteness'? How does this 'sense' arise if it has no basis?

Being *in* and *of* the world can be a sticky business – that's what we may feel, but is it possible to know why? Many people have propounded philosophies, religiosities and mystical geometries – but the question, as far as most of us are concerned, remains unanswered. We cannot say that there must be 'an answer', neither can we say that there is no 'answer' – all we can say is that we want to *Know* because being *in* and *of* the world is a *sticky* business.

Sometimes the stickiness of the world is very sweet: honey on the razor's edge. We lick the blade and: 'Oh, how sweet it is.' – yet there is the sharpness and the blood.

Some people would say: 'Honey is a wicked and treacherous thing and best avoided if you want to avoid being cut.' This way of thinking sees the razor edge of life as undesirable.

Some people would say: 'Why not find a way of tasting the honey without getting cut?' This is another way of thinking that sees the razor edge of life as undesirable.

Some people would say: 'The razor's edge is all there is – life is nothing but pain, therefore extinction is release.' This is a way of thinking that denies the sweetness of the honey.

Some people would say: 'The honey is all that really matters, if we're cut by the razor's edge then at least we will have tasted the sweetness!' This is a way of thinking that accepts both the honey and the razor's edge, but divides the experience. But the honey and the razor's edge are a single experience – if we manifest a human form we taste the *honey on the razor's edge*. If we live for the honey and see the razor's edge as an occupational hazard our experience of the honey either becomes too sickly sweet and makes us vomit, or we lacerate ourselves on the blade.

What is it to taste the *honey* on the *razor's edge*? It is to accept the unified experience as being *what is*, and thus to be liberated from duality. To reject the experience of either or both in favour of seeking a non-existent alternative is to circle endlessly in distracted-being.

There are *honeyed-moments* when we feel as if we could live for ever; and it's true – *eternity* lives in those moments, but if we try to hang on to eternity it shrinks rapidly into itself and we find nothing left in ourselves or our world but artificial divisions. If we continue to lick the razor's edge when the honey has gone we merely mutilate ourselves. A painful analogy – but, fortunately or unfortunately, life is not always so extreme.

Because is seems so difficult just to Be, without proof of our Being, we relate to our world and the phenomenon of our perception as 'proofs' that we're here – that we really do exist. We seem unable just to Sit back and enjoy the display – we have to touch, and having touched we have to grab, hold, possess and defend. It's as if we've had our hands in the honey jar, and everything we touch gets stuck to us – we have *sticky fingers*.

There's nothing wrong with being *of* the world or *in* the world, but it is a sticky business – we have sticky fingers and need to wash our hands in the Emptiness of Being before we can touch without getting stuck.

Some people would say: 'But the world is so sticky, it's better that we don't touch it in case we get stuck to it.' This is a way of thinking in which the world is imagined to be the problem.

Some people would say: 'But we are so sticky that we must continually wash our hands or we will stick to everything.'

Maybe instead we could try washing our hands whenever we appear to have *sticky fingers*.

I think at this point we should take a look at what these ideas mean in our experience of Sitting. Attaching ourselves to thoughts in order to provide ourselves with proof of our existence, is the process I've referred to in Chapter 2 as 'referentiality'. Referentiality is an unendingly unfulfilling process. The practice of Shi-ne highlights this process for us, and we begin to *see* what we are doing. Reaching out for familiar patterns is what makes our thoughts serve as reference-points. But thoughts, ideas, images, feelings, sensations, people, places and things aren't in themselves reference-points – we merely reduce them to reference-points through our fear of ceasing to exist.

All this takes a deal of digestion – so before I continue, we could take a look at other kinds of reference-points and how we use them.

If you're on a ship and need to navigate – the sun and the stars are very useful as reference-points. So when I talk about letting go of reference-points, I'm not suggesting that we should continuously lose our bearings in the world – but that we should let go of saying to ourselves: 'I'm located here! This is a place that completely affirms me and that means I'm real!' We obviously need to function in the relative world according to relative criteria, but we need to have our Vision extend beyond the relative.

I remember when I was young, looking up at the stars and feeling very friendly about the experience. I knew how to recognize the Great Bear and the Little Bear. I knew how to trace the back leg up from the foot of the Great Bear to find the Pole Star. It was always comforting to recognise my 'friends in the sky', and 'know' that in some way something made sense up there. I've never needed to know how to find my bearings by using the stars, so this information has only ever served as a comforting thought – a way of saying to myself: 'Ah yes, there it is – I'm seeing it. I'm a person who knows about that, and now I've considered that fact – I don't feel quite as lonely or pointless.'

Attaching ourselves to people, thoughts, feelings, situations, and objects when they seem to provide 'existential substantiation' is how we establish reference-points. But reference-points always let us down, because they (like us) are a fleeting facet of a continually changing process. Everything is transient by nature. Some things hang in for so long that they seem eternal, but even our sun will eventually die. The Himalayas are still rising, but other mountain ranges which once were even higher are now eroded into hills. Certain less grandiose phenomena also outlast us – but we may not be able to remain in their proximity, nor they in ours. Even if cherished items remain with us throughout our lives, the value that we accord them can dwindle into contempt. Sometimes (in reverse) the commonplace becomes valuable – but often it's the case that we don't know what we've got till it's gone.

Nothing is stable – but because we want it to be we seek proofs from among the momentary manifestations of stability all around us.

Within the constricted scope of our referential vision – everything is just a little more than it seems. A car is not just a car, a camera is not just a camera and a pair of jeans is not just a pair of jeans. If you were to tell someone from a tribal culture (who knew nothing of technology) about cars, you'd probably be quite simple about it. You'd give a fairly basic picture. You'd talk about transportation, wheels, seats, power source, steering – you'd try to give an idea of how a car functioned and how it was of use. But there would be things that you probably wouldn't mention, such as the function of a car as a status symbol, a phallic symbol, a symbol of adulthood or as a hobby.

There are invariably referential extras attached, which affect the way we relate to everything, and the character of these relationships can often be most inconsistent. When the black paintwork starts to get rubbed away on our Nikon camera and reveals the brass, we're pleased because it looks well used – it looks like a professional's camera rather than a tourist's. But if our Mercedes gets its paintwork scraped in a car-park we're not so pleased – we don't say: 'Wonderful! I can see the metalwork through the paint, now my car looks more professional!' The older and more faded our Levi jeans get, the fonder we are of them – but we're not so delighted about the dilapidation of our other clothes. What is acceptable and what is not acceptable often has little to do with the objects themselves, but a lot to do with the role they inadvertently play in making us feel real.

These things are fairly simple to understand, and we can all have a chuckle about the quirky inconsistencies of status and fashion. But when it comes to the quirkiness and inconsistencies of our relationship with thought – it's not so easy.

Just as the phenomena of the external world are overlaid (by us) with secondary functions, so too are the phenomena of our mental world – but it's only possible to make that discovery through the practice of Shi-ne. When we Sit, we discover that the secondary function of thought is to prove that we exist. Without thoughts, we have no reference-points – there is nothing to prove that we are solid, permanent, separate, continuous and defined.

Shi-ne is *getting used to* that. Shi-ne is just letting go and letting be.

As far as our everyday life goes, seeking reference-points leads us to distort our experiences to suit our need for defining ourselves. Within this context we distract ourselves from Being by our attempts to *be* in a style designed on the basis of our dualistic misconceptions. As long as we take individuation and oceanic experience to be mutually exclusive, we stray from Liberated-Being into unending cycles of distracted-being.

Because we grade what we perceive in terms of reference value, we're only capable of three responses: attraction, aversion and indifference. If what we perceive substantiates our definitions, we're attracted. If our definitions are threatened, we're averse. If what we perceive neither substantiates nor threatens our definitions, we're indifferent – what we can't manipulate referentially we ignore.

We never actually experience anything *as it is* – we only experience according to our need for definitions, and consequently everything is graded as to its suitability as a possible reference-point.

There's nothing wrong with thought, even though some

meditation instructions would have us believe so. Thought is a natural function of Mind just as the other sense faculties are natural to our physical existence – it's our relationship with thought that is in need of an appointment with a marriage guidance counsellor. Our relationship with thoughts is demanding, petulant, possessive, jealous and peevish.

Thought performs a useful function, but when we relate to our thoughts as reference-points they become a problem to us. It is for this reason that the practice of Shi-ne takes us into the condition where thoughts cease to arise – to take a holiday from referentiality.

Finding Mind to be a Referenceless Ocean of Space allows the dualistic knot of panic to untie itself.

Experiencing this Voidness or Emptiness we make a Brilliant Discovery: Being Referenceless is *not* death. If we can remain Present in this condition and not escape into oblivion, we disinhibit our Natural Clarity and *stars* appear in the sky – their Brilliance Reflected in the Referenceless Ocean.

Gya – vastness

12
Ocean of Referencelessness

The oceans of our world are referenceless to seafarers, but the sun in the day and the stars at night (with no intention or design) make navigation possible.

The Ocean of Being is *Referenceless*, but thoughts and phenomena arise in randomness and pattern – a *display* which *ornaments* our Awareness.

In the previous chapter we looked at the currents below the surface of our Ocean of Being – our need to define ourselves. So now we can look at the *glittering surface* of this Ocean and the sun and stars that glint on it – we can look at our relationship with reference-points.

Because of our reactions to the *Sheer Naked Presence of Being*, we play some extraordinary games with ourselves. We act as if there were no connection between *what* we are and *where* we are – between *us* and what we have come to describe as the external world. We imagine that connections are made or broken on the basis of our choices and that we are completely free to insulate ourselves from whatever we regard as uncomfortable. We feel that we can say quite confidently: 'This isn't my bag – isn't my concern, it's got absolutely nothing to do with me!' Or on the other hand: 'I'm going to intervene here! I'll soon alter that! They've got no right to intrude on our property or time in that way!'

It's important that I'm not misunderstood at this point, so I'd like to stress that I am not saying that we have no choice in anything. The character of our energies and the situation in which we find ourselves allow options that are reflective of *what* we are and *where* we are. If I'm thirsty and there's a glass of something that I like Sitting in front of me at just the right temperature – where is the choice?

We're quite capable of directing our energies in a variety of directions, but it's not as if we were alone in this ability. Our choices, plans and their implementation are constantly modified by the continually changing nature of existence. We find ourselves in a *web* of infinite causes and effects, in which everything subtly affects and changes everything else. Any area of interest or involvement we lean towards with our *intent* is in the process of modification.

We could envisage the fabric of existence to be a web of infinite dimensions – a web whose threads are the stuff of the universe. The style or pattern of our living sets up tremors in the web – the tensions of the threads alter, and every part of the web is affected. We can't do anything without affecting everything and, at the same time, being affected *by* everything.

Pattern affects pattern, creating further pattern. Pattern evolves out of chaos and becomes chaos again. Pattern and randomness dance together: ripples in water extend and collide with other extending ripples; a fish leaps to catch an insect; a wild goose takes to the sky; the wind blows and a child throws a pebble into the lake. Nothing in this *Magical Manifestation Web* happens in isolation.

If you've ever tried to bounce on a trampoline with someone else, you'll know something about the inappropriateness of imagining that you can move in isolation. If the trampoline is large enough to accommodate a number of people you have to take the whole situation into account. If you fail to recognise that other people's movements are causing the canvas to stretch and relax in continually varying patterns of tension – you lose your footing. Fortunately life isn't quite as tricky as that unless we *really* go against the grain.

What this is leading to is that we cannot accept, reject or ignore our world as if we were experientially insulated from it. We can't relate to the world on terms we've intellectually devised in *seeming isolation* from what we conceive of as *the external world*.

We are actually part of the Great Ocean. *Fish* and *ocean* go together – a fish without an ocean is no longer a fish, but a stage in a sequence of events that leads to its nestling against a portion of chips, and being liberally sprinkled with salt and vinegar. The practice of Shi-ne is to develop and integrate our sense of *individuation* with *oceanic experience* – to realise that these seeming polarities of experience are aspects of our Beginningless Englightenment.

It is usually only mystics and very young children who experience in this oceanic manner. Coincidentally (as my wife pointed out) Freud also used the term 'oceanic-experience' to describe the way in which young children do not divide themselves from their surroundings. I'm not suggesting that babies are Enlightened, but that there are reflections of Enlightenment throughout the wide spectrum of human experience. From the Tantric viewpoint, every experience is dynamically linked to an aspect of Liberated Energy – of Enlightenment. So, to look at the 'oceanic-experience' of a baby is only to say that this kind of perception is not unknown to human experience outside the field of 'meditation'.

The conventional psychological development of children leads to individuation, but only at the expense of losing oceanic-experience. There's nothing in our early education to encourage us to retain some means of access to oceanic-experience, because society encourages individuation. But the capacity and need for oceanic experience remains (it is after all part of the spectrum of our human potential), though it becomes distorted into various perverse variants of group consciousness such as nationalism, racism, elitism and sectarianism.

Here the two types of consciousness (individuated and oceanic experience) fight it out in the uncomfortable arena of their polarised coexistence. The nature of the fight manifests as our attachment to distorted reflections of our own Enlightenment.

From a conventional point of view, it would seem reasonable to assume that we can either have oceanic or individuated experience – that they're mutually exclusive. This is a way of thinking based on dualistic perception, which can only conceive of the Divisionlessness of these (conventionally polarised) experiences as some kind of compromise or combination. But Meditation Masters don't enter into the baby's field of perception and gurgle at you. Nor do they swing from one type of experiencing to another like some sort of 'spiritual Tarzan' swinging from one perceptual liana to another.

The Experience of Enlightenment goes beyond both oceanic and individuated experience, and enters into *Limitlessness* in which such distinctions are meaningless.

This is difficult to grasp; indeed it cannot be grasped. The very act of grasping distances us from understanding. We're now in the situation we found ourselves in during the previous chapter's free-fall analogy: we're falling yet not falling. Conventional logic has to give up at this point – it can go no further along this road. Conventional logic creates paradox because it is dualistic by nature, yet paradox is a barrier to conventional logic. Conventional logic comes to a halt when it meets a paradox, and there is either a *Spark of Understanding* that *flashes across* – or there is incomprehension.

So we have this idea of dualistic vision, in which our perception and field of perception are split – oceanic experience and individuated experience have become polarised.

In religious terms this polarity has given rise to two views of 'ultimate reality', in which we either 'become one' with the universe or in which we find eternal life as a discreet insulated entity. People have made all kinds of statements on this subject, but largely they either come down on the side of the ultimate loss of individuality or on infinite separateness. There are, however, far wider possibilities. The idea that Jack and Jill go on for ever as changeless isolated units of being is a little narrow and simplistic, while the idea that Jack and Jill are 'dewdrops slipping into the shining sea' is a trifle schmaltzy. So, what else is there?

Jack and Jill obviously die. In daily life they die at every moment, and are reborn at every moment. Beyond physical death the birth and death (or arising and dissolution) of mind-moments continues. The patterns continually change: form emerges from chaos and dissolves back into chaos – chaos and form dance their Beginningless dance. Birth and death follow each other: we wake, we sleep – perchance to dream, perchance to wake up again. But to explore the experiences of rebirth (reincarnation or transmigration) would take us too far from what is possible to experience for ourselves as we begin our Journey into Vastness.

The Experience of Englightenment isn't reserved for some stage beyond death – Enlightenment is possible at any moment. We're not living for an escape into the dubious pleasures of a mythical afterlife or to get blended into the 'cosmic-blancmange', but for Liberation in the moment. So concepts of being that purvey insulation or homogeneity merely arise from extending aspects of our conventional human experience to 'logical conclusions' – the Experience of Enlightenment transcends both.

When we lose touch with oceanic-experience (or when our experience of individuation isn't *informed* by oceanic-experience) we develop fantasy relationships with phenomena.

As soon as we involve ourselves in fantasy relationships with phenomena we enter into judgement (and manipulation) on the basis of wishing to substantiate our sense of individuation. We come to fear oceanic experience as a negation of individuation. But individuation that isn't experienced moment by moment as being born out of oceanic experience infests itself with figments that are either farcical, fierce or futile.

The Intrinsic Spaciousness of our Being is continuously reminding us of our Enlightenment – but from the disconnected perspective of individuation (divorced from oceanic experience) we interpret those reminders as a threat to our existence. This *divorced individuation* creates the unsteady illusion that we have fixed definitions.

The illusion flickers like an old motion picture, and although it's possible to catch glimpses of the white screen – we conveniently blur the flickering frames into each other. We don't wish to suspect that Charlie Chaplin isn't actually there in the cinema. We forget that what we are watching is an intangible image of him that is being projected onto a screen. There is the illusion of solidity, permanence, separation, continuity and definition that we relate to as being real. When we are watching a film we have to pretend that it's real in order to enjoy it – we have to enter into what is known as 'willing suspension of disbelief'. But with our own sense of being, we engage in *actively determined and continuously prolonged withdrawal of disbelief.*

The world of our perception teeters precariously between existence and non-existence. From our conventional filtered vision, the phenomena of our perception are seductive, provocative and highly misleading. Substantiality and insubstantiality dance together. We could be looking at a fan dancer: the ostrich-plumes of Emptiness and phenomena, that somehow *are* the *voluptuousness* of Being – although somehow there *is* something else. But we can only *see* what is really there if we can occasionally dispense with the duality of the fans. The Naked Lady of Emptiness is only occluded fleetingly by the flickering feathers of the ostrich-plume fans – but unless we understand that, and what's more realise that both are equally *naked* and equally *delightful* – we see nothing apart from what we think we might have seen if only we could have hung on to it.

In order to feel solid, permanent, separate, continuous and defined, we have to attach ourselves to facets of the constantly shifting illusion that temporarily display those qualities.

We only need to feel solid permanent, separate, continuous and defined because the experience of divorced individuation requires this illusion in order to survive. We only need to struggle to maintain that illusion because our Beginningless Enlightenment *sparkles through* the fabric of distracted-being and continually undermines the manic games we're playing. We're continually poised on the brink of *Effortless Attention,* but continually distract ourselves in order to sustain our divorced individuation.

These delirious, distressing and dreary deviations from Effortless Attention are 'distracted-being'. 'Distracted-being' is: Being distracted from Being through clinging to fixed definitions. This process of distracted-being is what is commonly referred to as 'ego'.

We're constantly 'under attack' – under the threat of dis-illusionment; so the activity of generating commitment to fleeting apparitions of stability is the character of distracted-being.

Liberated-Being is completely Relaxed in the Flow of whatever *is*.

If all phenomena had a statutory duration of five minutes, and all changed simultaneously everywhere – distracted-being would not be able to maintain itself. As a touch of whimsy, you could say that this would represent a sure proof of the non-existence of a Creator as separate from his creation.

Nothing that comes into existence has the qualities of solidity, permanence, separateness, continuity or definition as fixed features. But *Everything* shares these qualities temporarily – which enables us to generate our illusory vision of 'reality'. But it's just another fan-dance where the ostrich-plumes are either: substantiality and insubstantiality; permanence and impermanence; separateness and indivisibility; continuity and discontinuity; or definition and indefinability.

All are *Ornaments* of the *Sheer Naked Presence of Being*.

---

exercise seven

Sit in a posture of comfort and alertness / find the Presence of your Awareness to be without focus / if you drift from Presence of Awareness – return to Presence of Awareness without comment or judgement / if mental events manifest – remain uninvolved / let go and let be / continue to let go and let be / relax completely /

Try this for between forty minutes and an hour, depending on how long you're able to Sit / if you're currently Sitting for less than an hour – gradually build up until you can Sit for an hour / if you're used to Sitting for longer, then Sit for however long you find comfortable / see how it goes /

---

seventh exercise follow-up

This is the conclusion of the practice of Shi-ne, but not the conclusion of practice. Shi-ne takes us to the experience of time without content – mind without mental events. The purpose of Shi-ne is to take us to this particular Experience of Mind in which we discover that we can be Referenceless. This is the Realisation of Voidness and the knowledge that thoughts or mental events are not in themselves the *fabric of Mind*. *Mind-as-such* is Sheer Brilliant

Emptiness. Our *direction* at this stage of practice is to remain in this *Empty state*, and to enter into what is known as 'Stabilised Shi-ne'.

Stabilised Shi-ne is a condition of Mind in which mental events no longer arise for substantial periods within our Sitting sessions. Once we have reached this stage where we are able to let go and let be, and are able to continue letting go and letting be we will have momentarily exhausted the neurotic desire to generate thoughts in order to establish reference-points.

As soon as we enter into stabilised Shi-ne we face a certain problem which at some point will need to be resolved if our practice is to continue to develop. The problem is called 'sleepy Shi-ne' – a state in which mental events no longer arise, but in which we have lost our Presence. It's at this point that we need to dissolve Shi-ne, and enter into Lha-thong, Lha-thong means 'Further Vision' and is the beginning of our real Journey into Vastness, the Way Beyond emptiness.

Nyam – experience/manifestation

13
Beyond Emptiness

Beyond the Experience of Emptiness is the Experience of how our *Energy* manifests as the Endless Display of our Spacious Being.

Many people imagine that the final goal of practice is to attain a condition of Mind in which thought has been entirely abandoned. It's not really so surprising that people have this idea, because many forms of meditation instructions deal with the *stabilisation of Shi-ne* as being an end result. There's nothing wrong with this idea, and anyone who explains in this way is perfectly correct. The end result is the absence of Nam-tog – arising thoughts. But although this is the end result of Shi-ne, it's not the end of practice or Realisation. There are further stages of practice that deal with the energy that continually manifests as the natural function of the Void, and the reintegration of that Energy with the Presence of our Awareness.

The discovery of Emptiness or Voidness is a stage in the process of Realising our Beginningless Enlightenment. So, if you get too stuck with the idea of abiding in the Space of *Mind without content*, it becomes a spiritual cul-de-sac.

Mind without thought is a condition which is as unnatural as Mind crowded with thought. So why have we 'come all this way' merely to experience another limited state of Being? In order to answer this question we need to explore ourselves a little, and ask ourselves what we take *Mind* to be.

Without meditative experience, our examination or investigation of the mind would be rather limited. If we looked at Mind (in the usual way we look at things) in order to find out what it is – all we'd find would be mental events. We'd be confronted with thoughts: the thoughts that constituted the method of observation and the thoughts subject to observation. If we could only observe Mind in that way, we could only ever uncover an endless series of thoughts. This self-limiting activity would never uncover the *Nature of Mind* – it would just ensnare us in an intellectual kaleidoscope that never stopped revolving. Unfortunately that would be the end of our quest whether we realised it or not. We'd imagine that Mind *was* thought, and that would be the end of our exploration.

If we examined the nature of Mind's phenomena using thought as our tool, we'd be limited by the character of the thought-structures we had at our disposal. Also, we'd be examining thought with thought – and that would become progressively more ludicrous. The thoughts with which we examined thought would have to be examined, and what would examine those thoughts apart from more thoughts which would also need to be examined? Thought cannot ultimately examine itself – it's a closed system. Thought can no more examine itself than a knife cut itself or an eye see itself. The only way that an eye can see itself is in a mirror – and the nature of that mirror (as far as thought goes) is the *Natural Reflective Capacity of Mind* which is beyond thought.

This Natural Reflective Capacity of Mind is discovered through the various forms of practice outlined in this book, which take us beyond the limitations of intellectual speculation. To investigate the nature of thought – we need to use some capacity other than thought. In order to discover what other means we have for investigating the nature of thought we need to detach ourselves from our obsessive relationship with thought. So Shi-ne (the practice of remaining uninvolved with thought) is where we start. In our practice of Shi-ne, we've spent time letting go and letting be – and maybe by now we've been able to witness the fact that *Mind is not thought alone.*

When we first look at Mind, without the practice of *thought-free observation* – all we're able to see is a flat screen of thought. We see Mind as a patchwork or a pastiche of interlocking, overlapping thought. It's as if we were looking at the surface of a lake ruffled by the wind, or the sky churning with dark clouds. From these impressions, we'd have little idea that the surface of the lake could be like a mirror perfectly reflecting the sky. We'd have little idea that behind the clouds lay the infinite, in which the sun shone or the moon and stars glittered against the Vastness of Space. If we rigged up some sort of wind generator in order to examine the lake, we'd just create more disturbance, and all we'd learn is that waves can become more pronounced. We'd gain no idea of the *natural reflective capacity of the lake*. If we set up some gigantic cauldron and issued up yet more vapour into an overcast sky – we'd get no insight at all into the nature of the *sky in which clouds manifest*.

But when we retract our involvement with thought, the turbulence diminishes – the cloud-cover becomes patchy. The wind dies down and we begin to see reflections on the surface of the lake. Occasional gusts may ruffle the surface again, but we now know that water is not always in motion – sometimes it is Still. When we cease to generate thought as an obsessive process, the clouds begin to part – we see the odd shaft of sunlight and the occasional trace of blue. As soon as we realise that the flat screen of thought we initially saw is our construction, we're able to continue to facilitate the process of discovering Emptiness.

Once we've discovered Emptiness and found that we can exist without reference-points, we need to proceed to discover our *natural relationship* with the energy that is the Spontaneous Manifestation of Emptiness.

The Free Nature of Mind is neither a flat screen of thought, nor an Emptiness in which nothing happens – both are partial conditions. But once we've learnt that we can let go of thought, we can open up to a more fluid, frictionless and non-adhesive relationship with thought.

It may come as a surprise to some that 'thought' is not 'the work of the Devil'. Often when meditation is spoken of, the emphasis is on the abolition of thought, and so a lot of people come to the conclusion that thought itself is the enemy. *But thought is a natural function of Mind.* Where nothing arises from Emptiness, there is no Energy and consequently no Clarity.

The reason we continue in our practice in order to arrive at a state without thought is that it provides us with the Space to *unlearn* our neurotic relationship with thought.

If we return to the idea that '*Meditation* isn't, *Getting used to* – is,' we can see that the process, or *Space of unlearning*, is '*Getting used to*' the Referenceless Quality of Being. Letting go of our neurotic involvement with thought can be looked at in a similar way to letting go of a drink problem. If I want to stop being an alcoholic, I might stop drinking for some time. But if I never feel safe to drink again without the fear of returning to alcoholism, then I'm still an alcoholic – a teetotal alcoholic. The time I spend resisting the inclination to get drunk, and the number of days I go through without the sense of deprivation, are an important learning process. I am using that time to prove to myself that I don't need alcohol in order to live. Once I'm sure I don't need to get drunk merely to get by, I can have a drink and see how I feel about it. If my immediate impulse is to get the whole bottle down my throat, I know that I'm still an alcoholic. But if I can leave it at one glass, I'm free to have a drink whenever it's appropriate – to share a glass of wine over a meal with a friend or whenever it seems pleasant. But still, I would have to watch myself carefully – if I even drank a glass a day and looked forward to it a little too eagerly, then I would know that I was still dependent and would have to abstain again for periods of time.

And so it is with thought and all phenomena. When we can enter into a condition without thought and remain Present and Awake in that experience for extended periods of time – we know that our relationship with thought has undergone a radical change.

This is stabilised Shi-ne, and once we've established ourselves in this practice – we can *dissolve Shi-ne* and enter into the practice of *Lha-tong*. The dissolution of Shi-ne can seem to be the destruction of everything we've sat so long to arrive at – but it is a vital part of the process if we are interested in continuing our Journey into Vastness. Unless we dissolve Shi-ne, we stand the chance of becoming addicted to 'absence'. We'd become 'absence-junkies' rather than 'thought-junkies'. It's difficult to remain for long in stabilised Shi-ne without drifting into sleepy Shi-ne. It's very relaxing to dwell in the condition of sleepy Shi-ne, and, from our initial standpoint of never having practised, it could seem like quite an accomplishment.

The danger of sleepy Shi-ne is that (without this warning) we may well take this state to be the end result of practice, and that would be a depressing conclusion. There's nothing terrible about sleepy Shi-ne; it can be a way to wind down a little after a hard day at work, but getting stuck with that condition doesn't actually help us work with our lives to any great extent. I've met a number of people who've taken meditation to this point, and sometimes they've been very irritated indeed on hearing me speak of practices Beyond Emptiness. In fact, on hearing me say that stabilised Shi-ne wasn't the Ultimate Practice, one person decided he'd had enough and left. It's a shame to become fixated on any idea – we should always attempt to remain open to any idea that contradicts our most cherished beliefs. It's also a shame when communication breaks down, but we're all responsible for ourselves, and ultimately no one else can be responsible for us. The idea that stabilised Shi-ne is the conclusion of the path is almost like saying: 'Enlightenment is to become a statue of Buddha.' There seems to be the notion among such people that: 'The longer we Sit in the thought-free state, the more enlightened we'll become.' But when asked: 'What process is at work in this Empty-state that leads towards Complete Enlightenment?' the answer is usually that: 'Such things are ineffable and cannot be expressed in words.' It is true that words are limited and that Enlightened Experience is beyond concept – but if we're speaking of *process*, that can always be described by someone who experienced that process.

Unless our practice continues into the process of integration – we stultify. We need to open ourselves to *Flowing* with whatever arises within the Empty state we've discovered. Unless we're prepared to engage in that practice we will not evolve into full recognition of what we really are. Without this recognition, the general character of our life-experience will not change very much – we will continue to experience unsatisfactoriness, frustration and turmoil.

In order to dissolve Shi-ne, we have to allow thought to re-emerge, but not by re-engaging in the neurotic process of generating reference-points. I've heard it recommended that once the Empty state has been reached, that one should 'insert' an aspect of the Buddhist View such as impermanence – but however worthy such a technique may be at a relative level, it isn't part of the process described here.

From the perspective of Dzogchen, we're not impregnating ourselves with any 'spiritual values' as additives or even catalysts – we're concerning ourselves with *discovery* rather than indoctrination or conditioning, however virtuous. It should be clearly understood that no criticism is implied of the process of evolving a Wholesome View (Buddhist, Christian or otherwise) but, from the Dzogchen View, whether we condition ourselves with Truth or falsehood, we're still engaged in spiritual conditioning. This process of spiritual conditioning will probably lead us to a more healthy attitude and way of living in the world, and from that basis we may well be able to let go of all conditioning. But the method outlined here is one that enables us to discover what is *naturally there* as the *Energy of the Uncreated State*. These two methods – discovery and positive conditioning – are not mutually exclusive, but they *are* different. We can engage in both in accordance with how we happen to find ourselves – but the *primary method* of Realisation is always to go to the *Source of Being* and re-integrate the Presence of our Awareness with whatever manifests as the Efflorescence of Emptiness.

The method described here is a process that leads to the practice and Realisation of Dzogchen (Great Completion) so it doesn't deal with correcting the Natural State by means of incorporating spiritual values, even though they may be altruistic. The Altruistic-Mind of Compassion spontaneously arises from discovering the Spaciousness of Being. The practices described here are for the purpose of discovery – we're not involved with creating or constructing anything at all. We cannot construct or fabricate the Enlightened State, because it has been our *Authentic Nature* from *Beginninglessness*.

When we dissolve Shi-ne and allow the natural energy of Mind to re-emerge from Emptiness we're not creating anything, we're *Simply Allowing*.

As soon as our energy begins to re-emerge we start to experience what are known as 'Nyams'. Nyam means 'Manifestation of Energy', and we only experience these Nyams when we take our practice Beyond Emptiness. Nyams are often mistaken for Realisation itself, because Nyams can be ecstatic. But Nyams can also be rather weird or dreadful. Nyams can manifest in many ways – there are Nyams that are characteristic of each of the senses. This means that we can hear, smell, touch, taste, see or think in delightful or disturbing ways. Nyams are a sign of progress on the Path, but they should never be regarded as Realisations or we would merely become 'seekers of Nyams'. All we can do with Nyams is to allow them freedom to manifest, and find the Presence of our Awareness in their emergence and dissolution.

This kind of experience is often likened to the leaping of fish from the still surface of a lake. When that fabulous glistening fish leaps into existence from nothingness, exploding the *brilliant mirror* surface of the lake – there are immediately three vital considerations.

There is the *Stillness* or Emptiness – which is the discovery of Shi-ne.

There is the *leaping fish* (arising thought or sensation) – which is the discovery of Lha-tong.

There is the Awareness of the *Stillness* and of the *leaping fish* as a non-dual experience – which is the discovery of Nyi-med.

When I say that these are *three* vital considerations, I'm speaking from the perspective of the Path rather than the Fruit. I'm dividing an experience which from the Ultimate Experience is indivisible in order to define a method of practice. These considerations are divided from the standpoint of dualism in order to define that which is not divided in terms of our experience of Practice. The fact that we discern these divisions defines our dualistic condition.

Initially the practice of dissolving Shi-ne, and wordlessly observing the jumping fish from the Still lake is known as Lha-tong. Lha-tong means 'further-Vision'. It's an extraordinarily *vivid* experience, because for the first time thought is no longer experienced as two-dimensional. Mind is no longer a flat screen, and thought arises in a spatial context, allowing us to experience its *colour texture* and *tone*.

With the practice of Lhatong, we find the Presence of our Awareness in the movement of energy that arises from the Spaciousness of our Being. In this way, the movement of arising and dissolving thought and sensations becomes the nature of the Path.

One method of *allowing* the fish to jump is to open our eyes completely. But having opened our eyes, we may well lose ourselves through grasping onto thoughts again. At this point it's very likely that we could become rather frustrated – it could seem as if we were engaged in some game of mystic snakes and ladders. As soon as we arrive at a still, calm, Empty state, we open our eyes and – shazam! We're 5 years old again, and back in the local sweet shop grabbing at everything in sight. It's then that we learn that our sweet tooth for cerebral sweeties has not left us. This can come as a great shock, so it's as well to warn you in advance that this kind of thing is almost certain to occur over and over again. To open our eyes and find the Presence of Awareness in whatever arises, is not easy. This *movement* of thought; this jumping of the fish from the clear Lake of stabilised Shi-ne is called 'Gyu-wa'. Gyu-wa means 'movement', and it is in this *movement* that we have to find the Presence of our Awareness, rather than losing our Presence through attachment to the intellectual content of the *moving* thoughts. We make no comment on the thoughts. We make no judgements as to whether these are beautiful or grotesque fish that are jumping – we just find the Presence of our Awareness in their *movement*.

The natural development of this practice of Lha-tong is into the stage known as 'Nyi-med'. Nyi-med means 'indivisibility', and it is with the practice of Nyi-med that the practitioner goes beyond duality and enters into the practice of Dzogchen. With Nyi-med, there is no difference between the quality of the experiences of Emptiness and Form (Spaciousness and Energy, thought and absence of thought) – they have *One Taste*. The practitioner is not distracted from Presence of Awareness either by mental events or their absence, and continues in that state – which is the *Primordial Condition*.

Whilst engaging in the practice of Lha-tong, problems of lack of Presence or distraction can be worked with, through specific methods that relate directly with the functioning of our energy at the levels of *Mind, Voice* and *Body*. In these following pages there are three exercises which work with these imbalances and they will prove helpful at this stage of practice.

We should not attempt to remain rigidly with one method of practice come what may. I've heard people make many contrary statements, and they probably have some good reason for what they say – but in the context of the practices described in this book it is most valuable to be able to adjust your practice depending on how you happen to be at any one moment. Sticking to one practice all the time doesn't really comply very well with how we are as people. Our energy functions according to fluctuating patterns, and so we need to be flexible in our approach – one set way of practising can never suit us all the time so we should not become attached to any particular practice at the expense of others that may from time to time be more suitable. Whatever our primary practice may be, we need secondary or auxiliary practices which function according to the way we are at any one time. I've outlined the primary practice according to the system of Shi-ne, Lha-tong and Nyi-med – so now, it's important to look at some complementary methods.

I've left these exercises to this point in the book, because it's as well to have developed a degree of Awareness before starting to switch between practices. This is also probably the intention of those who say that you should stick to one practice. In the early stages of practice there can be the tendency to reshuffle the deck if we get bored with how our practice is going, and if we distract ourselves in this kind of way we can just get side-tracked into playing around with techniques as a form of entertainment. If we employ alternatives as soon as we set out on our Journey, it makes it difficult to gain any kind of perspective on how our practice is evolving.

We need to work through the boredom of 'one-method' in

order to learn something very fundamental about the way in which we work. Only then can we open out into having the choice of a variety of techniques. Indeed it is at this point that other techniques start to become important. Once we have some real experience of practice, auxiliary techniques release us to work effectively with however we happen to be.

The auxiliary practices we will be looking at belong to the categories of *Mind Voice* and *Body* and relate to the Three Spheres of Being: Chö-ku, Long-ku and Trul-ku.

Chö-ku is the Sphere of Unconditioned Potentiality – the dimension of Spaciousness (Emptiness or Voidness)

Long-ku is the Sphere of Intangible Appearance – the dimension of energy (the infinite Display of Light and Sound)

Trul-ku is the Sphere of Relative Manifestation – the dimension of materiality and physicality (our body and our world)

With whatever problem of distractedness that arises, we start at the level of Mind. If that proves ineffective, we move to the level of Voice. If that is fruitless, we move to the level of Body. The three exercises that follow are practices of these three levels and should be practised in succession as shown.

exercise eight

Sit in a posture of comfort and alertness / close your eyes and visualise the Tibetan letter Ah as shown opposite / the letter Ah is white, luminous and composed of light / it appears in Space in front of you / its position should be governed by extending your arm in front of you at 45° to the horizontal and visualising it at the distance of your clenched fist / the Ah should normally be about the same size as your fist – but allow it to be whatever size feels most comfortable or whatever size it spontaneously takes / although your eyes are closed, look upward slightly as if you were focusing on the point where your fist would be / hold your arm in front of you for a while until the visualisation becomes reasonably stable / lower your arm and continue to find the

Presence of your Awareness in the appearance of the Ah /

Try this for three five-minute intervals within your Sitting sessions / if you're used to *visualisation* – try this for ten-minute intervals within whatever length of Sitting feels comfortable / at the end of these intervals allow the Ah to dissolve and continue to find the Presence of your Awareness in whatever arises /

exercise eight follow-Up

As this may well have been your first experience of *visualisation*, you could have encountered some difficulties that interfered with the efficacy of this practice. You may have found working with a letter from another culture an alienating experience. You could have found the shape of the Ah too complex or unfamiliar to remember, or you could have found the process a little too exotic and intriguing. For those people who are interested in following the Tibetan Path, it's a good idea to persevere with *visualising* the white letter Ah. The *visualisation* of Mystic Syllables is an aspect of practice taught by every Tibetan Master. If, however, you find such things a complication and don't wish to use the symbols of other cultures, you might find that *visualising* a white translucent sphere of light may suit you better. If you wish to persist with *visualising* the white Ah, it would be a good idea to copy the one given here and look at it intently before beginning the exercise. The act of tracing the shape will help you remember it, especially if you draw it several times. You could paint it in white on a large, dark blue piece of card that could be placed at eye-level where you usually Sit. The more often that you engage in this practice the more familiar you will become with the shape of the Ah, until you will be able to visualise it very easily.

You may find that the Ah moves about a lot at first – if it does, don't worry about it too much – just leave it to settle down on its own. Try to avoid fixing your attention too sharply for too long or you may give yourself a headache. Focus sharply at first, but then relax your focus. If the Ah is not particularly vivid, don't be upset – just allow it to be a vague presence. There's no hurry.

Work with this practice for at least a week before continuing to the Voice method of exercise nine.

exercise nine

Sit in a posture of comfort and alertness / leave your eyes open /

take several very deep breaths / having filled your lungs, *sing* the sound Ah and extend that Sound to the limit of your breath / *sing* the Ah at a good deep pitch – but not so deep that your voice weakens and breaks up / find your most comfortable pitch and settle into it / allow the Ah to attenuate gradually and disappear into Silence / repeat the Ah with each out breath / allow your sense of Being to be flooded by the sound of the Ah / find the Presence of your Awareness in the Dimension of the Sound / whenever distracted – return to the Presence of Awareness in the Dimension of the Sound /

Try this for five-minute intervals within whatever length Sitting session you find comfortable / enter into the practice of singing the Ah whenever you become distracted /

exercise nine follow-up

The syllable Ah is known as the Natural Sound of the Primordial State. Singing the Ah *relaxes* our vocal energy – the resonance permeates our Being and diffuses the tensions that we create through our attempts to establish concrete definitions of what we are. Singing Ah enables us to enter into a more open recognition of the Spaciousness of Being. Ah is known in the Tibetan tradition to be a Neutral Sound, and as such it allows our vocal energy to enter into its natural resonance without any undue effort. The sensation of singing Ah and letting the sound attenuate into silence can be rather like a very deep sigh – it facilitates the dissolution of patterned perception, leaving us feeling clear and relaxed.

Because the energy of the *voice* is more tangible than the apparition of the visualised Ah, we can use the Ah Sound when *visualistion* seems too difficult or fruitless in terms of allowing us to return to Presence of Awareness.

Work on this practice for at least a week before continuing to the Body method of exercise ten.

---

exercise ten

I would rather you didn't attempt this exercise if you have a heart condition / if you are pregnant or in any doubt about your physical condition – please don't attempt this exercise /

Squat down on tip-toe / the balls of your feet should be touching / your heels should be touching / balance yourself by touching the ground in front of you with your fingertips (as in fig. 1) / when you feel balanced – place your hands palms-down on your knees / straighten your arms / push your knees downward a little / spread your knees apart and straighten your back / rather lean back a little than fail to find your back in a vertical position (as in figs. 2 and 3) / when you feel balanced, raise your hands above your head / place the palms of your hands firmly together about an inch above your head / ensure that your fingers are pointing directly upward (as in fig. 4) / simultaneously attempt to push your hands up and your elbows back without separating your hands or allowing your hands to rise further above your head – these two movements should be matched in effort so that they counteract each other / if you put equal effort into both movements, your hands and arms will remain in the same position / increase the effort until your hands and arms begin to judder / make sure that your fingers are still pointing upward and not leaning either forward or backward / now raise yourself until your legs form the same angle as your arms / remain in that position until you collapse / this should not take longer than a minute – unless you're an experienced Hatha Yogin / fall back onto a cushion and Sit – still stressing your arms / remain in that posture until you can no longer hold it / this should not take long / fall back into the 'corpse posture' – (flat on the floor with your arms at your sides) / remain in that posture until your breathing and heart rate have returned to normal / whilst lying down – just let go and let be / whilst at any stage of the practice – just let go and let be / when you Sit up again continue in your Sitting practice / this practice will last no more than a minute or two (for most people) as far as holding the stressed posture goes / the relaxed posture will vary according to your fitness, but should not last beyond three or four minutes / try to avoid lying down for too long or you may well lose the sense of alertness and freshness that comes from this practice / repeat this practice as many times as feels comfortable /

exercise ten follow-up

This Practice of *Body* is called the Thunderbolt posture. It takes its name from the Thunderbolt-wand (Dorje) which accompanies the bell (Drilbu) in Tantric rites. The shape of the Dorje mirrors the shape of the Thunderbolt posture. It symbolises the indestructibility of our Primordial State of Awareness. The Three Spheres of Being are often called 'The Three Thunderbolts', illustrating that the integrated condition of these Spheres is beyond conditioning.

The principle of this practice is *exhaustion*. Through a highly specific method of exhausting ourselves physically, we are able to exhaust our neurotic involvement with thought as the definition of Being. In a state of exhaustion it is very difficult to conceptualise. So through exhaustion it can become easier to enter into a condition where we can drop our frames of reference. In a state of exhaustion we find ourselves far less interested in generating thought merely to identify and fix reference-points.

If you've ever run for a bus (I'm thinking of a London bus without a door, but with a pole you can grab hold of to pull you on board) and you've just about split your gut after a heartbursting sprint through the traffic fumes – you'll have some idea of what I'm talking about when I say 'Exhaustion inhibits conceptuality.' Think about it – you collapse into the nearest

vacant seat with your eyes bulging and your heart performing a drum solo. And it's at that point that the conductor asks you where you want to go! But at that precise moment you hardly know where you are, let alone where you come from and where you could be going.

But there's a problem with exhausting yourself – it makes you tired. The longer it takes us to get exhausted, the longer it takes us to recover from that exhaustion. The longer it takes to recover, the sleepier we become by the time we've recovered. The Thunderbolt posture is the answer to this problem, inasmuch as it exhausts us very very quickly. Because of the speed with which this practice exhausts us, we recover surprisingly quickly. Because of this we're left feeling energised, clear and refreshed. The high-speed quality of this practice is very important – if it takes you too long to become exhausted you have to improve the posture so that it becomes more painful.

The idea of causing ourselves pain obviously isn't going to be particularly appealing. If this idea *is* appealing, then that in itself is a problem of a somewhat complicated order. The idea of arriving at the most painful possible position is that as soon as you've found it – you collapse! We're talking about seconds rather than minutes, and we're not talking about hurting ourselves or damaging our bodies in any way. The kind of pain that I'm talking about is the pain that athletes experience most days of their lives, so we're not discussing anything *too* extraordinary. We're not discussing masochism or self-punishment. This kind of athletic pain can make us realise that we're actually alive in a physical body. This can only be to our advantage, because that is actually where we are. Practice isn't orientated towards forgetting that we have a physical manifestation as well as a body of Energy and Spaciousness. This practice involves our awareness and our honesty with ourselves. If we don't stress our arms enough or work to find the exact position in which our legs like it least – we'll just end up holding the posture for too long! The idea is to spend as little time as possible in the posture, so that our recovery rate is proportionately fast.

Depending on who you are, and what you're like, you'll find different problems with the posture. If you're very stiff and unused to using your body, you may have to squat down with your feet slightly apart – and maybe not in such a high kind of tip-toe. If you're just unfit, you may have no problem at all as long as you're fairly supple and have a sense of balance. If you don't have a developed sense of balance – this posture will help you centre yourself and discover a greater sense of emotional/psychological equilibrium as well. Physical balance and emotional balance are interrelated, so it's helpful to work at this practice every day if possible. Some people may be quite fit and have a great deal of stamina, but little sense of balance – how you are will give you something different with which to work.

The Thunderbolt posture is part of the Trul-khor Naljor system. It has some superficial similarities to Hatha Yoga but it is different in a number of essential respects – especially with regard to the Thunderbolt posture as described here. Attainment of the perfect posture is *not* the principle here – exhaustion *is*. Exhaustion in the quickest possible time is what matters most with the Thunderbolt posture. So if you've got some experience of Hatha Yoga, please don't approach this exercise with the same attitude – especially if you're used to the kind of Hatha Yoga in which you're advised to use force and will-power beyond a reasonable limit. I've seen a number of people damage themselves through Hatha Yoga taught by extremists. Because of this I'd like to stress that this exercise *must* be applied with Awareness rather than the exercise of will. (No criticism is intended here of Hatha Yoga as it is generally practised and taught by qualified instructors of non-extremist schools). Having shown people this exercise on guided retreats over a number of years, I've found it necessary to stress repeatedly that this is *not* an exercise in machismo. You are *not* doing it better if you hold the posture for longer than other people. The principle is *speedy exhaustion*, so it's important to discover the exact point where the angle of your legs will lead to almost instant collapse.

If you're used to practising Hatha Yoga you may be very supple indeed, and if this is the case, you'll need to make the posture very exact. The more supple you are the more you'll have to make this posture *work* – and for this you'll have to use your awareness. The posture can be made more acute by perfecting the symmetry. This can be achieved by placing the soles of your feet flat together in the same way as you press your hands together, and by pushing your knees further apart. You will notice the similarity to the drawing of the Thunderbolt-wand or Dorje at the beginning of this follow-up section. So, whatever your physical capacity or incapacity, it's vital to tailor this posture to work in the best possible way for you. If you're interested in visualisation, there is an internal aspect to this practice which involves visualising yourself as a dark-blue Dorje surrounded by flames. This will intensify the power of the practice, but if you find this too complicated, simply find the Presence of your Awareness in the sensation of the posture.

Not only is this an excellent practice for cutting through distraction, but it's also a superb cure for mild insomnia. If you engage in this practice before getting into bed, you should go to sleep quickly and sleep well. For this you should get into bed as soon as you collapse. If you don't get to sleep in five minutes or so, just repeat the practice and return to bed. If you keep repeating this process it will usually not take more than three repetitions before you fall asleep.

1. Thunderbolt posture – preparatory balancing.

2. Thunderbolt posture – finding the correct spinal posture.
(front view)

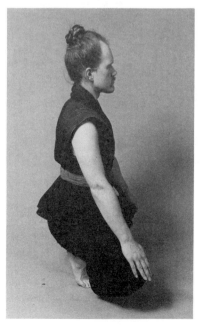

3. Thunderbolt posture – finding the correct spinal posture.
(side view)

4. Thunderbolt posture – positioning the hands and stressing the arms.

5. Thunderbolt posture – stressing the legs: the completed posture.

Rang-rig – self Arisen Awareness

14
Beyond Practice

This is the final passage of our Journey into Vastness, and in one sense it is both the End and the Beginning of a Journey that has no destination beyond Here and Now.

We have spent some time building up a picture, a traveller's guide into what may have seemed an uncharted region – but now it's time to destroy that picture.

We've been looking at the first three of a series of practices known as the Four Naljors. Naljor means 'Unification with the Unconditioned State', and these Four Naljors are the principal means within the Sem-de or Mind-series of Dzogchen. They're also called the Four Ting-nge-dzin (Meditative Absorptions) which comprise Ne-pa (Undisturbed), Mi-yö-wa (Unmoving), Nyam-nyi (Undivided) and Lhundrup (Unchanged). This is a parallel series of terms that are particular to Dzogchen, but in this book I have used the terms that are more commonly known: Shi-ne, Lha-tong, Nyi-med and Lhundrup. The first three terms are used within Tantra, but the last term 'Lhun-drup' applies only to Dzogchen. The first three have been described as a progressive series of practices culminating in the experience of Nyi-med in the previous chapter.

Shi-ne is the method of finding ourselves in the Space of Mind without content whilst maintaining the Presence of our Awareness.

Lha-tong is the method of reintegrating the Presence of our Awareness with the movement of whatever arises from Voidness.

Nyi-med is the recognition of the *One Taste* of Spaciousness and the energy that arises and dissolves into it.

But what of *Lhun-drup*?

Before we can say anything about Lhun-drup, we need to reassess the whole scheme of what has been presented in this book. You may remember the first exercise in this book – if not, it would be useful to read through it again at this point. Go back to it and have a look.

The first exercise is very similar in many respects to the concluding exercises of the previous chapter. This is a deliberate device on my part, and designed to make a certain point.

There is an aphorism from the Zen Tradition that runs something along these lines:

To a Beginner on the Path –
A tree is a tree, a mountain is a mountain.
To one who is treading the Path –
A tree is no longer a tree, a mountain no longer a mountain.
But to one who has Realised the Path –
A tree is once more a tree, a mountain once more a mountain.

We being with Mind as Thought, we discover Mind without Thought and return to Thought as Mind.

Chhimed Rigdzin Rinpoche once asked me a question while we were Sitting together in a small garden in Holland. He pointed up into the branches of the old apple tree in whose shade we sat: 'In your experiencing,' he said, 'which is moving; the leaves or the wind?' He was wearing the impassive and acutely observant expression that I'd come to know quite well over the years. I knew quite well what this meant: his question was intended to rip my understanding apart and expose whether or not there was any Essence to it. He'd asked me questions like this before, and I knew that it was only my immediate answer that interested him. If I took too long thinking about it, he'd no longer be interested in hearing my answer. 'It's my mind that moves Rinpoche.' I replied rather sheepishly, at which he smiled very slightly and said; 'Maybe you hear this question before?' I told him of the Zen aphorism at that point and said that I hadn't heard his question before but that it seemed to have the same flavour. He looked at me very intently for a second and then we both burst out laughing.

Movement within Emptiness characterises the Nature of both Mind and Reality. Realisation is the reintegration of Presence of

Awareness with whatever arises as the Experience of Being.

In a certain sense, it's not completely possible to present the Four Naljors or the Four Ting-nge-dzin in a linear manner because our experience doesn't necessarily completely conform to the linear model. Let's look at what this means. If we're practising Shi-ne, and we experience the arising and dissolution of thought into Emptiness – what can we say about that experience? If we continue with Presence of Awareness, then what is the difference between this state and the state of Nyi-med? The answer could easily be: Nothing at all.

There is no reason at all why the state of Nyi-med shouldn't be Realised without passing through all the intervening stages. There is no reason why it's not possible to move from Shi-ne into Lha-tong without having to pass through stabilised Shi-ne. Fundamentally, stabilised Shi-ne is more difficult to arrive at than Lha-tong or Nyi-med for some people. But without significant experience of stabilised Shi-ne, the Lha-tong and Nyi-med experiences within Shi-ne are mostly like lightning in a day-time sky.

Because our Enlightenment continually *Sparkles through* the unenlightenment that we continually fabricate from the Ground of Being, anyone with or without meditative experience can have flashes of Lha-tong or Nyi-med experience. Often illness or near-death experiences can open us to such illuminating insights. Enlightenment *is* our natural state, and so it's not surprising that it manifests from time to time. Unenlightenment is a constant activity that we engage in, one that we have to work at all the time – so when life-circumstances intervene (short-circuiting this continual effort) we experience *glimpses* of Realisation. The *glimpses* of Realisation can radically change people's lives, but it's a hit or miss affair to hope that life's going to do it for us 'when the time is ripe'. We have to co-operate with the *Sparkling-through* of our Enlightenment by disengaging from referentiality, and continuing with Presence of Awareness.

So it's not possible to say that the Naljors are a linear process, unless our experience also happens to evolve in a linear way. But although the process is not necessarily a linear one, it has to be described in that way. This kind of description operates in the same way that a series of words operates within a sentence. From the relative perspective we cannot start with the *meaning*; we have to start with the first word of the sentence and proceed to the second, third, fourth and so on. At the end of the sentence the *meaning* becomes apparent, and then the linearity of the words ceases to have any importance. Once we've read the sentence we know its *meaning*. Once we know the *meaning* we can, if we wish, return to the individual *words* in any particular order according to what we feel is appropriate.

Lhun-drup is our Spontaneous Self-Perfectedness, and is the fourth Naljor. Lhun-drup is the *Knowledge* that is *there* at the end of the sentence. If we forget, or get distracted from the *meaning* of the sentence – we may have to take a look at the words again.

Lhun-drup is the integration of the experience of Nyi-med with every aspect of our Being. We move Beyond Practice. There is *no method* with Lhun-drup apart from *Continuing* in the Non-dual Presence of Awareness with the efflorescence of every moment.

PART FOUR

Tri-wa – questions

15
A Question of Questions

Both this book, and my previous book *Rainbow of Liberated Energy* are based on transcripts of courses I have given since 1979. These transcripts contain some lengthy question and answer sessions which for the most part have been condensed into straight text. But from that transcribed material, much was left over in the way of themes that didn't clearly fit into the plan of this or other books in the series. Some of these sessions had a certain 'live' quality that made them of more interest if left in dialogue form, and these are represented here. The themes explored complement the main body of the text; they appear at the end of the book in order not to complicate the earlier chapters. You may find it helpful to compare these dialogues with the pattern of your own understandings. Being able to observe 'where other people are coming from' in terms of their comprehension and incomprehension will enable you to understand more about the habit-structure of your own ideas and frames of reference.

Questions are an integral part of the Teaching process. Questions portray individual styles of confusion and incomprehension in limitless variety, and in so doing give rise to limitless patterns of explanation.

Every style of incomprehension is a distorted reflection of Enlightenment. This means that the greater the number of different styles of confusion, the greater the number of ways to present explanations of *what is Real*. Every style of distracted-being is dynamically linked to limitless Enlightened Mind, and the energy of the *dynamic linkage* is individually our greatest opportunity for Realisation. *Understanding* the particular pattern of confusion from which questions arise opens out the *quality* of Enlightenment (of which that particular confusion is a distorted reflection). Once this Opening occurs, the Enlightenment Qualities can be reflected in the form of *explanations*. Teaching only really happens when the teacher *mirrors* our Enlightenment in such a way that we see its connection with our personally distracted frame of perception.

Teaching only exists because of confusion and perplexity. Without the manifestation of perplexity – explanations that dissolve perplexity would never arise. So questions are very important. Without people's questions my capacity to explain would be markedly reduced and my explanations would be far less applicable. For a teaching to be successful, everyone concerned has to participate fully – everyone has to take responsibility in terms of opening up the area to be explored. Without this degree of involvement nothing of any consequence unfolds, or at least this has been my experience. The great Tibetan Masters usually communicate directly, imparting teachings at many different levels without the need for questions. Their words cut across personally individuated boundaries and the confusions created by ambiguity and the misleading connotations of words. But I am not such a teacher, and so I rely heavily on question and answer sessions in order to bring out understandings that people can integrate with their lives.

I remember being invited back on numerous occasions to teach at a Buddhist group in England. I had already spoken on as many topics as would be appropriate for a group of no fixed tradition, and so I threw the session open for questions. The group was a general Buddhist group with little or no knowledge of Tibetan Buddhism, and so further information in technical areas specific to my own tradition would not have been that helpful to them. But having suggested that they ask questions, I was confronted by several rows of blank faces – my suggestion had obviously thrown them into bewilderment, because no one seemed to have anything to ask.

In this situation (and wondering how I could best be of use to them) I thought that I should ask *them* a few questions. I asked them what they would like me to talk about, to which they answered that they would very much like me to continue telling them more about Tibetan Buddhism. So I said: 'What you're asking me, is that I should give you answers to questions that have never occurred to you.' This response puzzled them, so I reminded them that from there on in I could only discuss technical aspects of practices they were not likely to become engaged in as a general group. They saw the logistics of the problem, but the problem remained: a group of people Sitting in a church hall with an hour or two to while away, somehow expecting me to say something illuminating – but I had nothing to say.

I tried another tack, and said: 'Are there no problems in your lives with which you are trying to work or reconcile in the light of your practice?' This launched a barrage of questions that took up the rest of the evening, and we all ended up learning something useful. It became obvious during the question and answer session that they had imagined that it was only kosher to ask questions that lay within a 'Buddhist' framework. They generally seemed to have the idea that questions that were to do with 'ordinary life' wouldn't concern someone like me. They had evidently formed the notion that day-to-day situations have scant connection with Buddhism. Of course, dealing with real-life issues soon led back to Buddhism – but then that *is* what it's about after all.

When my apprentices tell me that they have no questions, a frequent response I give is: 'Unless that means you're En-lightened, either practice more, study more, or live a bit more life. Any of these will generate the confusion necessary to prompt you into asking questions again.'

My apprentices have often expressed their appreciation of other people's questions in terms of the different styles of answer they get in response. This appreciation has been comprehensive – 'new' people's questions invariably provoke a lot of interest, and often open up radically new angles of approach. Usually, the more these questions apply to the lives of the questioners, the more value they find in the answers. Questions that come from 'spiritually uneducated' minds can often elicit far more interesting answers than those that come from people who want intricate information couched in technical Buddhist language.

I would like to thank all those people who consented to the publication of their exchanges with me.

Sampa – intent

16
Attuned Intent

Questioner I've always been very interested and impressed by Buddhism and what it has to tell us about reality; I can't imagine a superior outlook on life – but I can't find time for meditation. I want to meditate and frequently promise myself I will get going with daily meditation, but then when I do get going – it gets interrupted and I let weeks or months slip by. Can you suggest a remedy for my predicament?

Ngakpa Chögyam How much do you want to practice?

Questioner It's very important to me.

Ngakpa Chögyam That's very interesting. I wonder why that is? (pause) You want to do something very much, it's very important to you, but you don't do it. I think that when you want to meditate more than you want to use your free time in other ways, you'll find less difficulty. I must apologise if that sounds a little blunt, but it's a simple statement of the manner in which motivation functions. You could look at it another way – you could say: 'I want to get thinner, but I keep eating too much and do no exercise.' My response would be the same: 'You obviously like eating and not exercising more than you'd like to be thinner.' I'm not making a value judgement here – just saying: 'Enjoy the roundness of your belly as much as the taste of your food, or enjoy your moderation and exercise as much as your envisioned thinness.'

Questioner But isn't it important to meditate?

Ngakpa Chögyam Of course, very important – but that's just *me* telling you that. What do *you* think? How important do you think it is?

Questioner   All the books say . . .

Ngakpa Chögyam   Yes; all the books say it – but what do *you* say?

Questioner   I'm confused.

Ngakpa Chögyam   Splendid! That's a good start. The next step is to accept that with a certain sense of humour. None of us likes confusion, but as long as we cling to our dualistic vision – we will always translate *not knowing* as 'confusion'. We don't like confusion, because within the *space of confusion* the definitions have become vague and intangible, and that makes us feel insecure. Accepting or *relaxing* in that insecurity is in itself a practice – this is what is known as the *wisdom of insecurity*.

Questioner   Are you saying that ignorance is all right?

Ngakpa Chögyam   Ignorance in the sense of *not knowing*, and recognising our condition of *not knowing* isn't just 'all right' – it's quite an accomplishment! Ignorance in the sense of ignoring – being indifferent or not wanting to know is quite another matter.

Questioner   You mean the 'ignorance' symbolised by the pig on the Tibetan Wheel of Life isn't 'not knowing', but not wanting to know?

Ngakpa Chögyam   Yes, but even more than that, it is ignoring – actively shutting out Knowledge.

Questioner   Then ignorance is an activity?

Ngakpa Chögyam   Exactly. It's part of the motor that turns the wheel of life, or rather the wheel of cyclic existence. In the middle of the wheel you'll find a green circle (green is the colour of activity) and within the circle are three animals that chase each other – biting each other's tails. Each animal represents a fundamental aspect of our distracted motivation. The cockerel represents attraction, the snake – aversion, and the pig – indifference or ignorance.

Questioner They're usually referred to as lust, hatred and ignorance, or is there some difference?

Ngakpa Chögyam We have our problem of words again. There is no difference, it's just that I don't find that style of translation helpful – it seems to tie these three distracted potentialities in with the 'seven deadly sins'. The whole atmosphere of this Teaching is different – so to use these emotive words with their unhelpful array of connotations can be misleading. I prefer the terms: attraction, aversion and indifference. These are hopefully more neutral terms, that allow us to examine them as parts of the motor that turns the wheel of indirect experience. So the real meaning of the pig is: not wanting to know rather than *Simply not knowing*. Do you understand? Do you see the difference?

Questioner Yes, thank you – that is very helpful, I had never thought of 'not knowing' in a positive way before.

Ngakpa Chögyam So, if you don't know – and *know* that you don't know, you can set about finding out. If you don't know that you don't know, where do you start? So what do you think will help you get started into this daily Sitting practice? (pause) What do you think will motivate you?

Questioner (pause) I don't know.

Ngakpa Chögyam To be motivated, you have to develop your understanding of what the process of Shi-ne helps you to discover. To develop motivation you have to take a serious (or *wholly humorous*) look at your life. Not wanting to Sit is not feeling motivated to change. Not feeling motivated to change is either being afraid of change or seeing no reason to change. If we have a good understanding of Buddhism through reading, reflecting and listening – through checking these Teachings against our own experience, *motivation* naturally develops. But take your time, be Kind to yourself. Be honest and question your present motivations accurately – allow your Attuned-Intent to grow. This is your experiment, so you don't have to complicate it with guilt and frustration. You'll enter into practice when it makes sense at an experiential level. If we want to meditate because we think it's a religious observance, then *Real motivation* may never arise from that. Accept yourself as you are now, and start from there. How does that sound?

Questioner   It sounds like a great relief!

Questioner   Could you say something about keeping up a daily practice of meditation. I mean – what would be the best way of keeping continuity, of not letting it slip?

Ngakpa Chögyam   Well, the best way I know of Sitting every day is to Sit every day. The longer you maintain the practice of Sitting every day, the longer it will continue – it's a bit like that with Sitting. This probably sounds absurd, and in some ways it is – it could sound as if I'm not saying anything at all. But I'm not being awkward or obtuse – just stating something absurdly simple – so simple that it could be missed completely. We're all here because we have an interest. We've come here to find out about, and practise Shi-ne – so we all have some enthusiasm or energy in connection with this practice. The experience of being here and Sitting together, is something that I appreciate very much – and maybe for you it's something you can develop when you leave this place. If the motivation is there, if we've looked at our conflicting emotions and come through with the *active wish* to practice, then we should avoid dissipating that energy by generating 'conflicting priorities'. If practice is a strong priority, we should avoid weakening it by letting our other priorities contend with it. So we should just Sit. When we get home we should Sit. We should Sit again tomorrow morning and continue Sitting in that way. Every time we Sit should be the first time, and every moment we live should be the last moment. Remember to make friends with death, and let present sensations flow like sand slipping through your fingers.

If you want to keep up a daily practice, you should make very sure that you really do want to Sit every day – that it *is* very important to you. Try to ensure that you make time and space available in your life for Sitting, and avoid setting yourself up for failure. Don't aim to Sit for too long every day – keep a small promised time and don't increase it until you feel that you really need more Sitting time to develop your practice. You can always Sit beyond your promised time if you feel you can, but never Sit for less than your promised time. Even if your promised time is only five minutes, it is far better to Sit for five minutes a day than the odd half an hour here and there. Only make promises to yourself that you know that you can keep, otherwise you'll never have confidence in yourself and you'll find that you won't be able to make promises to yourself. Being able to make promises to yourself is quite important, it's a way of giving your life real direction and enabling something positive to happen – especially if you link your promises to the wish for the Liberation of everyone everywhere.

In this way you can make Sitting part of your life, and once it becomes part of your life, Clarity will begin to develop. When you start to gain a little Clarity there will be a much stronger motivation to practice. Once you see the value of practice in your life, you'll be motivated to make further discoveries – and then maintaining motivation will no longer be a problem. Motivation has to propel you into practice – but there it must stop. If you fill your Sitting Space with the desire for progress you'll stifle your developing Awareness. So, letting go of motivation is also important. When we Sit we should Sit without purpose – without hope or fear.

Questioner   What about the motivation to liberate all sentient beings from the round of suffering?

Ngakpa Chögyam   That is a very powerful motivating energy once we can tune in to it, but in order to *generate Kindness-Mind* – to have *genuinely Attuned-Intent* – we need to have some awareness of our interconnectedness. If we don't have (or if we're not conscious of having) Kindness-Mind, we can't simply adopt it as an attitude because meditation Masters tell us 'it's a good idea'. Kindness-Mind *is* our Innate Nature and needs to be discovered. We can *imitate* Enlightenment by cultivating kindness-thought and kindness-activity, and this will open us to the discovery of our Beginningless Kindness-Mind. But we'll need to Sit and let go of all constructs before we can really experience that. Genuine Kindness-Mind is *truly effective motivation*, but if we aren't able to feel it that strongly – if it doesn't permeate our View, how can it motivate us? Remembering to generate Kindness-Mind, or *insinuating* it into our mixed motivation is a remarkable means of making sure that Kindness-Mind has the chance to *develop*. In this way it can *become* a more dominant factor within the pack of mongrel motivations that usually fill our Silences with their barking.

Questioner   And when I Sit . . .

Ngakpa Chögyam   When you Sit – you *just Sit*. You may generate Kindness-Mind before you Sit, but when you Sit – you *just Sit*. To consider the Liberation of all beings as the driving force of motivation will keep your motivation not only aerodynamic, but will ensure it's pointed in 'the right direction'. Aquisitiveness-mentality can also be aerodynamic in some respects, but we end up flying into high-intensity narrowness and frustration. Kindness-Mind helps us in our attitude towards Sitting. But when we *are* Sitting, there should be no motivation whatsoever. Motivation gets you to the cushion or stool, but then it's served its purpose. Your car takes you to the seaside, but if you want to go for a swim – you have to leave it behind.

Questioner   Could you say a little more about Attuned-Intent, I'm finding this idea very helpful.

Ngakpa Chögyam   Delighted. Attuned-Intent is motivation with-out a 'drag-factor'. Attuned-Intent is streamlined – aerodynamic. Attuned-Intent gives us access to incredible power and capacity for accomplishment of whatever needs to be accomplished. This is why generating kindness-thought and kindness-action is so important. Kindness-intention cuts against the gravitational pull of divorced-individuation. Divorced-individuation is what keeps us earthbound. In order to accelerate into the *unimaginable*, we have to let go of the ballast – jettison the habits of view that create drag factors.

Questioner   I'm not sure what you mean by 'drag factors', could you say a little more about that?

Ngakpa Chögyam   When our motivation is mixed, it can be said to have 'drag factors'. To give an example: if I want to help someone who is in need of help, but I also want to be seen as a good person (which means that I want to be appreciated, thanked and praised), then I'll be of less help than I could have been. I'll have made the situation complicated – it won't run smoothly, and I'll be distracted from my helping by my desire for recognition. When motivations conflict there is a considerable drag factor, and when there's a drag factor our goals become much harder to reach. But this can also work the other way around, which is why I speak of insinuating Kindness-Intention into our unskilful motivation in order to undermine the process of distraction. But in terms of reaching a goal we could look at it this way: Say that I want to save money in order to go to the Himalayas. But say I also want to acquire new clothes and other items that take my fancy. This will keep me eating into my savings, and it's going to be a long time if ever before I get to go out and be amongst those mountains. This is what I call 'the drag factor' – it's the thing that slows us down. Mixed and conflicting motivations produce a drag factor and inhibit our development and growth as human beings. As long as there's a drag factor we experience frustration and the unsatisfactory outcome of our wishes or intentions whatever they might be. Attuned-Intent is unmixed motivation, motivation without conflict – single-pointed motivation.

Nying-je – kindness-Mind

17
Kindness-Mind

Questioner   Could you say something about compassion?

Ngakpa Chögyam   Yes, of course – what would you like me to say?

Questioner   Well it's regarded as being extremely important, it's always stressed in all the Buddhist Teachings.

Ngakpa Chögyam   Yes . . . it is certainly very often stressed – although I wouldn't say it's *always* stressed. But what is your question? What are you asking me?

Questioner   Isn't it important to stress compassion?

Ngakpa Chögyam   Certainly – if that is the Teaching that's necessary at the time. But what is it that you don't understand about compassion? What are you actually asking me?

Questioner   Whether compassion plays a part in what you teach?

Ngakpa Chögyam   Certainly. (pause) Have you received Teachings on compassion before?

Questioner   Yes, on many occasions. I studied the *Bodhicaryavatara* for two years in India, and (interrupted)

Ngakpa Chögyam   So you already know a great deal about this subject. Where is your uncertainty? What are you unclear about?

Questioner   It's not that I'm unclear (interrupted)

Ngakpa Chögyam Good, but I don't see that you're being entirely clear with me – what is the question behind your question?

Questioner I don't understand.

Ngakpa Chögyam Let's put it this way: I don't think that you're being entirely honest with me. You've looked rather irritated with my answers – they've obviously been most unsatisfactory! (laughter) But you can't expect to be satisfied by my answers when your questions mask some hidden agenda. There's a question behind your questions, and until you ask it – you'll continue to imagine that I'm being evasive. (laughter) What you really want to know is: why I haven't brought the subject of compassion into this course of instruction on Shi-ne meditation. Is that an accurate rendition of what's on your mind?

Questioner Yes it is.

Ngakpa Chögyam (pause) I'm sorry if that's made you feel angry.

Questioner I'm not angry!

Ngakpa Chögyam (pause) Could you repeat what you've just said?

Questioner I'm not – OK. I *am* angry. The Dharma is about compassion and you're just playing word games with me.

Ngakpa Chögyam Yes. You're quite right, but the word game was your idea – I've just gone along with it. The problem is that you're no longer enjoying the game. I've been playing this game of yours with you in order to show you that it's your game, and that you made up the rules for it. Your rules are that you are able to hide behind your questions, but I never agreed to play by your rules, so there's nothing to make yourself angry about. If you started by asking me your question in a direct way there would be no game – I'd just be answering your question.

Questioner (pause) I'm sorry. I suppose I didn't want to seem critical, but I felt that there was no reference to compassion in what you'd said, and I've been taught that compassion is of great importance.

Ngakpa Chögyam Yes. Compassion is absolutely crucial. Realisation of Emptiness is absolutelely crucial. I've been talking about the practice of Shi-ne and how to develop the experience of remaining uninvolved with arising thoughts. This practice leads to the discovery of our Unconditioned State, which is the very source of compassion. Kindness-Mind is the spontaneously arising energy of our Beginningless Enlightenment. The frustration you've experienced is keyed into my failure to conform to patterns of teaching with which you've become familiar. If someone had been giving a course on aerodynamics (and you'd attended it because of your strong wish to build a car that would break the land speed record) you may have been disappointed that engines weren't mentioned. If car engines are your favourite aspect of striving to build the world's fastest car, you might argue that the engine is the heart of the car. But just because the engine means so much to you, and simply because you've studied with a whole string of brilliant engine experts, is no reason why every course of study on how to break the land speed record should necessarily include the engine as the core-curriculum. There are obviously two highly important factors that influence the top speed of a car: its engine and its aerodynamics. A powerful engine mounted in a square box might move very quickly, but it might be very unstable at high speed and never travel as fast as it could. Ultimately these two factors have to be considered together, but if you have a limited period of time, it's more appropriate to study in a specialised way. If you already know a lot about engines, but very little about aerodynamics, then it would obviously be more appropriate to go into the area where you lack knowledge. If a course is listed as being a course on aerodynamics, then you shouldn't be surprised that engines don't get much of a mention. The fact that engines weren't mentioned, doesn't mean that the lecturer considers them irrelevant, unimportant or even that he or she knew nothing about them. But this course isn't as black and white as that. We're here to help each other Realise our Beginningless Enlightenment rather than break the land speed record. So there is room for everybody's questions whether pertinent, interrelated or side-issues – but that has to come from you.

The fact that I've cut across various expectations and pre-conceptions in what I've said is neither intentional nor unintentional. If everything I said conformed to the expectations or preconceptions of the group, what would any of us have gained? The purpose of our being here, is to Realise the nature of what we are. We may well have other purposes in mind, or conceive the same purpose within radically different frames of reference. But if our frames of reference are threatened, then it's worth remembering that having our frames of reference threatened is the name of the game. We aren't here to consolidate our ideas and religious convictions, no matter how worthy – but to expand our view into such Vastness that any attachment to familiar form evaporates into Space.

Questioner   (pause) Yes, thank you, I can see that. I accept what you're saying.

Ngakpa Chögyam   But I still want to answer your question. What about asking it in a way that will resolve something for you?

Questioner   Thank you, yes, I'd like to do that. I think I've been tying myself into a bit of a knot over this. I think that what I want to ask is based on the need for developing compassion as the basis for realising voidness. Your instruction on Shi-ne turns that the other way around, which is contrary to the Teachings I've heard before. That's what has been confusing me.

Ngakpa Chögyam   This is really quite an important question and something that needs to be explained. Thank you for asking – I hope this will clear up this area for everyone. I appreciate your courage in coming out, rather than remaining silent and going away with misconceptions. The problem in one sense is part of the problem of dualism in general. What we have here is the contentious issue that Realisation can be discovered by methods that contradict each other – methods that are the reverse or mirror image of each other. If we don't understand that these methods are mirror reflections of each other, we polarise them, and interpret their respective angles as antagonistic to each other. This kind of paradox is common in Buddhism, and it points to something absolutely crucial. If Enlightenment 'made sense' from a relative standpoint, it would be a relative state of being. The fact that it's not possible to speak in relative terms about Ultimate experience without using paradoxes, is what defines the relative view as dualistic, and the Ultimate View as beyond dualism. The practice of generating compassion as 'the basis for Realising Voidness' doesn't contradict the practice of Realising Voidness in order to discover the spontaneous compassion that springs from that Realisation. If we generate Kindness-Mind we imitate Enlightenment-Mind, and in imitating Enlightenment-Mind we expand and dissolve our distracted frames of reference which facilitate the Realisation of Voidness. If we *let go* and *let be* through the practice of the Four Naljors we discover that Kindness-Mind is the spontaneous expression that is liberated by that *Unfolding*.　　There is no reason at all (none whatsoever) why anyone shouldn't follow both practices – indeed, I would strongly advocate it. The main point is that you should understand the principles of these methods – you should understand how they function. Once you comprehend their individual characteristics, once you understand the ways in which these methods work – you stand the chance of being able to engage in them and Realise something. If not you'll just get into all kinds of knottedness. The Wisdom of Voidness and the Infinite Compassionate Activity that arises from it are not actually divisible, but from our dualistic perspective – we divide them. Having divided Wisdom and Compassion in this way, we

devise means of Realising *either* through the Practice of
manifesting the *other*. This means that we either manifest
Wisdom-Mind through non-attachment to referentiality, or we
manifest Kindness-Mind through contemplative thinking and
processes of active-imagination. The Realisation of both
practices is that Wisdom and Compassion are indivisible – Do
you understand?

Questioner   Yes, thank you – everything suddenly fits into
place. (laughter)

Ngakpa Chögyam   (laughter) Ah yes, the cosmic jig-saw rides
again.

Questioner   Is compassion the same thing as love?

Ngakpa Chögyam   They're aspects of the same energy. Love
and compassion as words or terms, are framed by specific
meanings which make them different in a relative sense. But love
and compassion as aspects of the energy of Enlightenment are
divisionless. Love in the conventional sense of the word is
different to the conventional sense of the word compassion, but
from the View-point of Realised Reasoning – they're undivided.
Both *love* and *compassion* mean the *Experience of
Divisionlessness*. It's not possible to experience either love or
compassion if our sense of ourselves exists separately from our
experience of others. When *your* pain and pleasure are to some
extent *my* pain and pleasure, then you can call that love. If we
extend that outwards to encompass all living beings, then we call
that compassion or Kindness-Mind. Kindness-Mind is Divisionless-Mind, and Divisionless-Mind is Enlightenment. Both
Love and *Compassion* are free from the inhibitions and
constrictions of self-orientation. Selfishness springs from a sense
of dividedness, of being separate from the rest of the universe.
Selfishness is our distorted sense of hyper-individuation, in
which we imagine we can act on behalf of ourselves alone. We

don't often seem to connect with the idea that if we love selectively or conditionally, it can all turn rather sour. For real love to exist, Kindness-Mind needs to pervade our perception. If we Discover Kindness-Mind within ourselves, then love can flower in radiant profusion. But if we contrive a narrow clinging possessiveness for one person (to the exclusion of others), we cripple our capacity to manifest Kindness-Mind.

Questioner If you feel compassion for someone who has malicious intentions, don't you just leave yourself open to attack? How can you feel compassion for an enemy without becoming a victim?

Ngakpa Chögyam Kindness-Mind isn't 'simplistic pie-in-the-sky idiot-grin-mind'. If someone doesn't have your best interests at heart, you need to remain aware of their intentions. This doesn't mean that you can't wish them well – just that you don't wish them well at your expense. Until you lose the 'victim-concept' – you have to work within the scope of your limitations. Generating Kindness-Mind towards people who may wish to victimise you is actually the very best means of protecting yourself. To feel compassion for someone who wants to do you down, you need to try to *understand why* they want to hurt you. You also need to work out why it could be that they've come to feel ill-disposed towards you. One thing you can be fairly sure about is that they're only doing whatever it is that they're doing because they want to create the causes for happiness. The fact that what makes them happy makes you sad is often overlooked because they have divided themselves from you and are unable to *feel* for *you*. If anyone seems to be out to put one on you, you can be sure that they've got some pretty efficient rationalisations on the go. What's more, you can be fairly confident that they feel quite justified in their motivations and whatever schemes their rationale suggests. If you sincerely try to understand the pattern of their motivation, it becomes easier to feel compassion. Kindness-Mind doesn't necessarily mean saying: 'Hey look! I'm going to lie on the ground so that you can stomp all over me.'

Kindness-Mind doesn't really constitute allowing or encouraging people to abuse you. If you encourage abuse it only entrenches people in the belief that their behaviour is somehow 'in order'. It's not really compassionate to facilitate the development of distorted view in others, even if it gives us the dubious buzz of feeling like martyrs. Compassion includes _us_ – we need to love and look after ourselves. If we have no love for ourselves, it's not possible to have compassion for others. If our love for ourselves is so exclusive that we are only free to hate whoever it is who's after our guts, then they're never likely to have a _change of heart_. But if we try to understand – if we keep an _Open Heart_, we might change the whole situation. We might be in a position to do some 'enemy' a kindness, and if that can _flow_ easily from us – we could transform emnity into harmony. But we need to be _Open Hearted_ – our Kindness-Mind has to be non-exclusive, otherwise we're not likely to feel we have the capacity to be charitable.

Questioner   Taking precautions and feeling compassion aren't incompatible then?

Ngakpa Chögyam   Right. You've got your common sense, you've even got your uncommon sense. We've got our everyday intelligence and we need to allow that to function in the same way that our metabolism or blood circulation function. There's no particular value in a contrived naïvety that imagines everyone is mainly good, purely because it chooses to ignore their manifest negative complexes. Trying to understand where a person is coming from, naturally informs your dealings with them. If you haven't really got a clue why someone wants to stick one on you, you're unlikely to be able to side-step an attack. If you've developed enough experience of practice to have developed your clarity, other people's motivation also becomes increasingly transparent. When people's motivation becomes transparent they cease to be able to surprise you. If people are transparent to us, compassion is a natural reflex.

Questioner   What would you say to the idea that compassion is wasted on some people, because they would only mistake it as weakness?

Ngakpa Chögyam   To mistake compassion for weakness is to be in a very pitiable state of mind. How could you *not* feel compassion for people who are so far removed from access to natural human warmth? That compassion can be considered to be weakness is no reflection on compassion. You could mistake an eagle for a bluebottle fly, but it would make no difference to the eagle. Only a bluebottle fly pretending to be an eagle would be worried. Compassion which is concerned about being seen as weakness is maybe not really compassion at all. It's only possible to take advantage of weakness, but not of compassion. With compassion, with *Great Kindness-Mind* – there's no concept of being taken for a ride, because you're joy-riding anyway! Kindness-Mind, rather than being in any way weak, is actually enormously powerful because it flows from the *Indestructible Nature of our Being*.

Questioner   Can you feel compassion for someone who is totally evil?

Ngakpa Chögyam   (laughter) It's difficult to answer that question because of the way you've asked it. If you were to see it as I see it, you may as well have asked: 'Can you feel compassion for some "thing" that has never existed.' From my point of view it's not possible to answer that question because I would be discussing someone without Beginningless Enlightenment – what do you mean by 'totally evil'?

Questioner   Someone who's cold, ruthless and vicious. A man who exploits others without pity. A man who enjoys cruelty.

Ngakpa Chögyam   That sounds a little more hopeful. (laughter) That's not quite what I'd call 'totally evil', (laughter) I'd call that very isolated, frightened and insecure – someone to be pitied. It's a matter of understanding that person's motivation. Why do you think such a person would want to be vicious, exploitative and cruel?

Questioner   I don't know – that's just it, I don't know.

Ngakpa Chögyam   Have you never been angry, arrogant or done anything spiteful?

Questioner   Well, as a child – and, well yes – but I don't like myself when I feel like that.

Ngakpa Chögyam   So you do understand a little. I mean, it's not as if there were people like Hitler and people like us without any connection. If any of us were in the 'right' place at the 'right' time, and in the 'right' frame of mind for becoming some sort of Hitler, Stalin or Caligula clone – we'd understand even more about what the choices were. But it would be difficult to have an over-view at that point – we couldn't stand outside what was happening and understand what we were becoming through our choices. But think about what you just said: 'I don't like myself when I feel like that.' Part of your answer lies in that. You don't like yourself when you feel evil because you don't understand that feeling, from the perspective of being who you usually are. So if we act spitefully, it's important to attempt to understand that manifestation of ourselves. If we just hate ourselves for how we act, that acts as a wall between us and our understanding of what we are. The dislike for ourselves that we generate is really only a way of hiding from ourselves and obscuring the root fear, isolation and insecurity that arise out of misconceiving the Spaciousness of our Being. We're usually afraid of what we don't understand, so it's rather important for us to face the distortions of our Being in the practice of Shi-ne. If we have no *sympathy* for ourselves – if we fear our own negative feelings and wish to disown them, how can we have compassion for others? If our own 'evil' feelings frighten us, we need to stare into them and gain *Knowledge* of the nature of their arising. We cannot possibly understand an 'evil' person if we remain a mystery to ourselves. If we have no knowledge of ourselves then poor old Hitler won't even get a look in. This is why Sitting is so important. We have to confront what we are and acknowledge it, before Kindness-Mind can arise and *flood the world with our unrestrained warmth.*

Mon – crazy

18

The Sanity Clause

Questioner   I've heard people say that there is a risk of going insane through meditation, what do you think about that?

Ngakpa Chögyam   Ah yes – the sanity clause!

Questioner   (laughter) the sanity clause?

Ngakpa Chögyam   (laughter) Yes, the sanity clause! (laughter) There was a Marx Brothers film: *A Night at the Opera* I think it was called. I don't remember much about it – but among the rapid succession of wisecracks and outrageous puns, was a delightful sketch about signing a contract. Groucho reads it out, and there's a whole string of insane legalese concerning: 'the person of the first part being known as the person of the first part, and the person of the second part being known as the person of the second part.' After Groucho gets past the person of the fifth part he interjects: 'Then there's the sanity clause.' To which Chiko retorts in fluent Italio-American: 'Ah y'no foola me, I no believe in a Santa-di-Claus!'

Questioner   (laughter) So there's no need to worry about . . . no chance of going mad?

Ngakpa Chögyam   Certainly (laughter) there's every chance. If you practice enough, you're sure to go mad – there's no need to worry about that! (laughter) what do you mean by 'going mad'?

Questioner   (laughter) Like going doolaly.

Ngakpa Chögyam   Well, Dulal was the place they sent British soldiers in India when the heat had got to them and they got a bit out of hand. But let's get to the bottom of what you mean. Are you talking about acting in ways that you are afraid people wouldn't understand?

Questioner   I'm not really sure anymore. I'm not sure what I mean – maybe 'losing control' is what I'm worried about.

Ngakpa Chögyam   What is the 'control' that you think you might lose?

Questioner   Well, control of myself I suppose.

Ngakpa Chögyam   So who has control of yourself?

Questioner   I (laughter) hang on – what's happening here . . .

Ngakpa Chögyam   You were about to tell me that the 'yourself' could lose 'control' of 'yourself'.

Questioner   (laughter) Yes, I was, but there seems to be something wrong with that.

Ngakpa Chögyam   There certainly does. (laughter)

Questioner   It doesn't make sense put like that. (laughter)

Ngakpa Chögyam   Can you think of any other way of putting it?

Questioner   (pause) No. Not without making it sound as if I was talking about being split into two independent parts.

Ngakpa Chögyam   That's what's meant by the word 'dualism' or 'duality'. That kind of thinking is part of how we see the world – you've made an interesting discovery there. It's this dualistic split that is the root of our insanity. Our *basic sanity* (as Trungpa

Rinpoche calls it) is not divided against itself, and the practice of Sitting facilitates the dissolution of that sense of dividedness. So let's look at this idea of 'losing control' again. We could talk about three fields that could possibly come under 'your control' – the physical, sensory and mental fields. I can't imagine that you're worried about the loss of physical control – I mean; you're not worried about Shi-ne leading to incontinence, so what about sensory loss?

Questioner   (laughter) No, (laughter) neither of those, apart from how they'd be affected by my mind. I suppose it's the fear of losing my mind that comes up sometimes.

Ngakpa Chögyam   But the practice of Sitting is about discovering the nature of Mind – discovering the Real Mind and losing the habit-mind. All you can lose is the habit of being you.

Questioner   Maybe that's what I'm worried about . . . what is it I'm worried about? (laughter)

Ngakpa Chögyam   Nothing (laughter) You're worried about losing your unenlightenment.

Questioner   Yes, I see that. But in a way, couldn't that be taken as a dualistic statement?

Ngakpa Chögyam   Sure – language is dualistic, and we're talking about Realisation from the illusory perspective of non-realisation. But let's compare our dualistic statements and see what comes out of that. When you said that *you* were worried about losing *your* mind – which one was worried, you or your mind? Which one is real?

Questioner   My . . . no – my . . . can't they both be real? (pause) or maybe they're both unreal. (laughter)

Ngakpa Chögyam   Splendid! Now you're sounding good and

crazy. (laughter) It's the division that's unreal, and not knowing 'it's the division that's unreal' is what makes it a dualistic statement. When I said that you were worried about losing your unenlightenment, that was a response based on the dualistic context of what you were saying. The word 'unenlightenment' indicates some state of not experiencing what you are. You can't possibly lose the experience of not experiencing a state you're not experiencing. That state doesn't actually exist. You can't lose something that's not there – all you can do is *Realise* it's not there. That's what Enlightenment is. (laughter)

Questioner   You mean that Enlightenment is just realising that I'm not unenlightened?

Ngakpa Chögyam   (laughter) What else could it be? (laughter)

Questioner   And that happens in Sitting practice?

Ngakpa Chögyam   It happens all the time – Sitting practice is just a way of facilitating *Sparkle*. The Sparkle of Enlightenment is always there – it's the Ground of Being. But you see, we're all so insane that we call our unenlightenment 'sanity' and fear that our Enlightenment is 'insanity'. That's the sanity clause in our distracted human contract. And yet although we all continually sign this contract in every moment, we also have the impulse to break it. That impulse to break our distracted contract *Sparkles through* no matter how law-abiding we are. We're all here participating in this retreat because we feel that there's some other way to be. In order to Realise Beginningless Enlightened Mind, we have to go *crazy*. To use a dualistic metaphor: We have to leap over the wall of the funny-farm and join the inmates in order to become truly *sane*. But once we're 'there', we discover that – *there* is where we've been all along. From the Ultimate perspective there is no sane world, no funny-farm and no fear of either sanity or insanity.

Questioner   What makes a Crazy Wisdom person different from someone on a psychiatric ward?

Ngakpa Chögyam Ultimately, nothing. (laughter) But relatively, a Crazy Wisdom person may sometimes appear crazy to our unenlightened perception – but there's the question of their being able to keep their life together from the relative perspective, or at least having the capacity to do so. I may think I'm Enlightened, but if I can't act *as if* I'm sane when it's expedient or necessary – then I'm a crazy person rather than a Crazy Wisdom person. I think that this is a somewhat important point to get hold of. Some people may have the romantic notion that psychiatric wards are full of over-the-top geniuses. I'm sorry to have to disappoint anyone, but I'm afraid it's not really like that – I wish it was. Certainly there are aspects of psychotic and psychopathic states that echo the Enlightened State; and certainly there have been great practitioners whose experiences on the Path have been pretty *wild*. I've had some fairly terrifying waking nightmares during the practice of Chod in the Himalayas in which I completely lost track of what was real and what was unreal. When the realities of other dimensions of experience open up, you need to hang onto your hat, but there is a basic difference. The living nightmares of Chod practitioners are deliberately cultivated in order to cut attachment – that is what the word 'Chod' means: 'Cutting'. Basically, if you can't adapt yourself to circumstances – you have a problem. If other people find your inability to adapt appropriately is a problem to them – you've got an even greater problem. If, moreoever, you are also unhappy with the responses you get in reply to your behaviour, then whatever else you might be – you're no Crazy Wisdom Master. It's a question of *fluidity* – of not being stuck in any 'set' of perceptual frameworks. A Realised Master could live and work with other people completely unnoticed. It's a matter of versatility, ease of communication and appropriateness of response.

I have a story that might possibly illuminate this a little, although it's not a story of Realised-Appropriateness – just an attempt at everyday appropriateness. During my time among the

Himalayas, I became close friends with Lama Sonam Zangpo, whom I knew by his personal name of Tsering la. His English, although much much better than my Tibetan, was not so easy to follow unless you listened carefully. He also found it difficult to understand people if they spoke too quickly or used language that was too sophisticated. I travelled to Tso Pema with him on one occasion, accompanied by an Englishman who had hired the car in which we were travelling. During the six-hour journey, I found myself in the unusual position of having to translate this gentleman's speedy and complicated English into a slow and simplified form, so that Lama Sonam Zangpo could understand what he was trying to say. This had the effect of making the English gentleman rather irritable after a while, because everything he said had the same effect on Lama Sonam Zangpo. The Lama would just turn to me after everything that was addressed to him in order that I could rephrase it, which meant that everything that was said had to go through me. I tried to explain to our gentleman companion that he would have to speak more slowly, and simplify the structure of his language. This didn't seem to help matters, because he confessed to being unwilling to sound like an imbecile even if I was prepared to do so. The problem was never resolved, and in the end he gave up all attempts to communicate.

The point that this is supposed to illustrate is that although I was perfectly capable of saying: 'Tsering la, I've had this frightfully good idea – what about you and me taking a jaunt up to Tso Pema together? What d'you say?' it would have sounded like a crazy string of incoherence to him. I would have sounded like a madman. It was more appropriate for me to say: 'Tsering la, you – me, we go Tso Pema, yes?' accompanied by all the attendant gesticulations, but that of course made me sound like a madman to our English travelling companion. So, what I am saying is that effective communication is more important than acting in accordance with any particular set of value-judgements. I'm not just talking about language, but about behaviour at all levels. For example: just because you have no inhibitions doesn't mean that it's appropriate to exhibit your freedom and antagonise others through it. So, one important distinction between a psychiatric patient and a Crazy Wisdom Master is appropriateness of activity. This doesn't mean that such people should be entirely conventional or seem from our limited perspective to be continually appropriate, but there must be the capacity for such a Master to appear 'perfectly normal' at any given moment.

Questioner   Would you say that Shi-ne could not under any circumstances lead to psychiatric problems?

Ngakpa Chögyam   Yes. (pause) You look as though you'd like a longer answer. (laughter)

Questioner   (laughter) Well yes and no, your answer just created a kind of gap after the thinking that had gone into the question. (laughter)

Ngakpa Chögyam   Shi-ne is simply not doing anything. The worst thing that can happen (from the perspective of Realisation) is that you could lose Presence and get attached to the state of sleepy Shi-ne. From the perspective of relative relaxation, however, you could be said to have found a way of resting. I think that it might be useful for you, and maybe everyone, to look at the field of conventional psychiatry – if only to get a clearer picture of what constitutes mental illness from that perspective. I don't entirely agree or disagree with it, but I think that it makes a number of valuable observations that could be more popularly disseminated. If you know nothing of psychiatric disorders and how they usually manifest, your fears of Shi-ne leading to psychiatric problems will be generated by lack of information. Once you've cleared away your uninformed fears, you'll be left with your *basic fear*. This basic fear is that of losing our conditioned definitions of who we are.

Questioner   Then is Shi-ne useful for people in disturbed states of mind?

Ngakpa Chögyam   As a general principle, I'd have to say no. Practices such as Shi-ne are too threatening. I would like to say that you should be a 'stable and well-adjusted person' according to current conventional criteria in order to practise Shi-ne. This doesn't mean that you have to be uncompromisingly happy or positive, just that you're relatively strong, self-reliant and that you've got some emotional resources to fall back on. If you've got no strength or stability of any kind then you can just end up making room for complicated extensions of your own already convoluted intensity. It's quite often the case that schizoid personalities feel drawn towards religion, especially the more esoteric Eastern religions. I've seen a number of very unhappy and disturbed people who would have made far better use of some form of humanistic psychotherapy. Obviously there is room for the development of Tibetan Buddhist psychotherapy and the use of Tibetan medicine in this area. There is obviously a great deal of work that could be done to help people in more effective and wholesome ways, but people have got to learn to co-operate with each other and learn from each other's systems. For people with disturbed backgrounds, or histories of instability – involvement with esoteric disciplines can often exacerbate their problems and complicate their existent neuroses. The great Lamas could work with *anyone*, and in fact aided quite deranged people to become quite extraordinary practitioners. But not everyone with such problems can have such protracted contact with such Masters. From a Tantric perspective, *any* state of mind is dynamically linked to the Enlightened State, and as such can be transmuted or self-liberated. But it takes a Realised Master to work with psychosis in a meditative context.

Questioner   Can a spiritual environment be helpful to someone with mental illness?

Ngakpa Chögyam   Well, it would depend on the cause of the mental illness. Mental problems are a spectrum within which the categories are somewhat arbitrary. It's hard to say. Obviously a spiritual environment led by a Realised Master would be beneficial for anyone, but sometimes such communities have their share of people working out all manner of less extreme personal problems. Contact with people of this type could do more harm than good to anyone in a sensitive condition. To work with people who suffer with psychiatric problems, you have to be able to put your own problems on one side. It's absolutely vital to be Open and Kind. I've met a number of people in 'spiritual communities' who would not really be up to this kind of demand. What is important is that there should be sustained warmth, and readily available human contact. This is something which at present cannot be guaranteed in psychiatric hospitals, so the alternative is to rely on sedation. I would certainly like to see something develop along the lines of Buddhist psychiatric hospices where people could work through their intense intricacies without resorting to drugs that suppress the symptoms but do nothing about the cause.

Questioner Thank you

Ngakpa Chögyam Thank *you* – I'm glad you brought this question up. How many of you are still worried about 'going mad'? (pause) Good, let's hope that we can all get crazy enough to liberate others from their more distressing variations of 'sanity'.

Gom – meditation

19
Practice

Questioner   You spoke of the initial discomfort we would have to go through when we began to Sit regularly. Could you say something about what gets you through that?

Ngakpa Chögyam   Well. There are various answers to this question. It rather depends on what motivates us. There's curiosity: many people find the subject of understanding Mind highly fascinating, but that motivation often leads people into the intellect. Sutric Buddhism contains enough material to absorb the intellect for several lifetimes.

Questioner   So that's a blind alley?

Ngakpa Chögyam   No, but it certainly can be. Any Path can be a blind alley if we heap so many rubbish bins across it that they become impossible to climb over. Intellect can definitely be a springboard. The Buddhist analysis of *what is,* is intellectually brilliant and has the capacity to allow us access to the Vastness beyond intellect.

Questioner   Some people seem more curious about the magical side; I would think that was even more of a blind alley.

Ngakpa Chögyam   A blind alley is a blind alley. Fascination with Tibetan magic *does* serve as a motivation to engage in practice, but often people with this type of motivation are more interested in reading about mysteries than *Staring into their own Mystery*. There have been a fair number of books about the magic and mystery aspects of Tibet – some have been factual and some not so factual. There obviously has to be something more to motivate us than fascination and curiosity. Because fascination is such a fickle motivator, some teachers cut through the tales of the spiritually exotic and stress the everyday realities of being alive. This approach inhibits the tendency many of us have to entrap ourselves in a personal Tibetan Fairyland. If there's too much 'magic and mystery' in our lives, we tend to magnify the inconsequential out of all proportion, in order to attribute 'meaning' to the otherwise 'commonplace' nature of our lives. But the problem with cutting through the wondrous aspects of the Tradition is that the sense of excitement can get squashed – and with it a certain sparkle that's actually very valuable. There obviously has to be some balance between remembering to put the rubbish out for collection, and allowing our enthusiasm for a world (apparently beyond our reach) to initiate a sense of wonderment.

Questioner   Isn't it better to live in the real world?

Ngakpa Chögyam   (laughter) What or where is the real world? The real world contains both the Tibetan mystic engaged in the development of *psychic heat*, and the need to remove the tide mark from the bath before someone else uses it. This could be understood as the *Middle Way*, a primary concept of the Buddhist Path. But let's get back to what gets us through the initial discomfort of Sitting. What is there apart from curiosity and fascination?

Questioner   Faith?

Ngakpa Chögyam   Mmmmmm. Faith is a tricky little number. It depends what you mean by faith. I understand faith to mean some sort of compromise between *Knowing* and not-knowing. I'm not deprecating people who have faith – it's a powerful force for good in many people's lives – but it's not for the likes of us. (laughter) Certainly faith can help people to be kind to each other, and it gives people a sense of purpose and fulfilment – I would never try to undermine that. It is said that faith can move mountains, but with loss of faith the mountains invariably slip back again, and if we're not prepared for that eventuality we can end up getting crushed in the psycho/emotional avalanche. Faith is a powerful motivator, but the experience of faith isn't a stable condition. If we meet great Tibetan Masters and we're spontaneously taken by faith in their Enlightenment – we may well believe every word they say. But if we haven't integrated the meaning of these words at the level of our own experience it can become problematic. At some later point, our faith could take a knock (as faith often does) and then the whole fabric of what we believe could fall apart. Whatever we take on board as a belief-system can cease to have any relevance in our lives if our faith is threatened or destroyed. If we merely believe in Karma, we may later disbelieve in Karma. If we merely believe in the teachings we hear and are never able to actualise them – we'll lack direct experience of how these teachings function at the level of our own experience. If this is the nature of our view then we'll probably always manipulate our belief to suit the ends of our distracted-being. You see, it doesn't matter whether what we believe is false or true, if we believe rather than *Know*. Why do we decide to believe? We could say that our belief is based on a spark or synapse between the Truth of the Teaching and our Beginningless Enlightened Nature – but we could be wrong. It is generally better either to Know or not to know. The *Don't-Know Mind* is always open, the belief-mind tends to be closed.

Questioner I think I've got a bit lost; could you explain the difference between Knowing the Truth and believing the Truth, and what difference that makes?

Ngakpa Chögyam Exactly. The answer lies in the difference it makes. If you Know, you act in one kind of way – but if you believe, you tend to act in another. If you Know and someone disagrees with you, it doesn't worry you. But if you believe, it often does worry you. Sometimes it can worry people so much that they have to burn each other at the stake or torture each other because of differences in belief. No such problems exist with knowledge. Knowledge is Knowledge – knowing is knowing. There is not more than one knowing. If there are two knowings, one of them is not-knowing.

If two people with opposed 'knowings' come together, the one with the belief will want to convert the other. If the other shows no willingness to be converted, the believer may become hostile or think of the other as a heretic and have him or her excommunicated. As far as the one who Knows is concerned, there is no problem – he or she may have a method by which the believer could Know, but if the believer is not interested then that is the end of the matter.

If two people who make the same 'statement of truth' speak to people, the one who believes will only have one way of explaining and will become frustrated if met with disbelief. The believer will always be threatened by disbelievers. The Knower will have many ways of explaining because he or she knows, and when there is knowledge there is an infinite fund of explanations according to the disposition of the person who has no belief or Knowledge. The Knowledge of someone who knows is not shaken by contrary views. There is no compulsion to express Knowledge – it is expressed when the need arises, and so is usually appropriate. But with belief there is often the compulsion to express that belief whether it is appropriate or not. So this is the point: the Truth whether believed or Known may be the same, but the believer and the Knower act in different ways. We could maybe talk about two people who have a saw. Both are aware that you can cut wood with the saw, but the person who knows, is free to take a violin bow and play a beautiful eerie tune on the saw. The person who merely believes in the saw will say: 'Damned heretic, don't you know that the saw is for wood-cutting alone!' Not a perfect analogy perhaps (but then analogies never are) but do you understand?

Questioner Yes, I think I've got that.

Ngakpa Chögyam So you see, if we merely believe and carry on in this way, we'll probably end up as the kind of people whose social gossip sounds like: 'lama karma dharma.' rather than the usual: 'Rhubarb rhubarb rhubarb.' Belief or faith can often manifest in this way, and occasionally when it does: Karma gets to sound more like 'karma-cola'. As a foundation, faith is rather unreliable as an endeavour towards Realisation. It can engender considerable kindess, but it can also engender bigotry and sectarianism. In general, it's better either to Know or not to know. Mostly when people are presented with ideas, many assume that they should either express belief or disbelief – but there is a more open option, we can say: 'I don't know – I have no experience upon which to base an opinion.' We could even say: 'Well, hot dang! I have a strong feeling for this idea – so maybe I'll test it out in my life as a working hypothesis until I come to *Know* it, or see it as a fabrication of distracted-being.'

Questioner   Does that mean there is no one I can trust?

Ngakpa Chögyam   You've got it. (laughter) We have no ultimate guarantee that anyone's words are infallible – but we can develop confidence based on experience. There's a Zen saying that runs: 'To be a true practitioner you must have great confidence and great doubt!' This means that if we test a teacher's advice and instruction in the laboratory of our personal experience and find it concordant, time and time again – we can begin to free ourselves of the tight constraints of our conventional logic. It's this kind of *confidence* that enables us to Sit through the initial discomfort of Shi-ne. If what I'm saying makes sense in some way, if the explanations I've given have *co-incided* with the *Sparkling through* of your own Enlightenment in a way that makes real sense in your life – then maybe that will give you a start.

Questioner   Can I clarify that for myself a little? I've understood you to say . . . there's no one to trust, and yet the inspiration to practise comes from a relationship with a teacher.

Ngakpa Chögyam   That's right. At first, the teacher is the last person you should trust. But at the last, the teacher can become the only person there is to trust! (laughter)

Questioner   (laughter) Pardon?

Ngakpa Chögyam   You're welcome. (laughter) The meaning of this may need some elaboration. (laughter) What I'm saying is that you shouldn't trust teachers because people call them teachers. Only you can call a person a teacher through your own perception and experience. Someone may well be a great teacher, but if you cannot recognise that quality – then for you that's how it is. That doesn't mean that they're not a great teacher – just that they're not a great teacher for you. Fundamentally no one can call themselves a teacher – only you can call someone a teacher by recognising that that is what they are for you. You can't accept someone as a teacher purely because other people accept them. Neither can you discount a teacher on the basis of other people's non-acceptance. On the other hand you can't call yourself an apprentice, student or pupil – only a teacher can do that. It's a matter of mutual recognition. You have to recognise the quality of the teacher in someone and they have to recognise the quality of the apprentice in you. The relationship has to be based on personal research – it must begin with *Great Doubt*. *Great Doubt* is not cynical scepticism, *Great Doubt* is being open to change, but keeping your integrity. If you feel that you cannot accept what you're being told, you must express that. Without *Great Doubt* we cannot learn or discover *Great Confidence*. If you begin to practise, and the teacher seems to *Know* the field you're exploring under his or her guidance, you gain confidence. The only way you can really check teachers thoroughly is by putting their instructions into practice, and then asking questions based on your experience. If we don't practise we'll only be able to ask philosophical questions, and it'll always be a matter of faith whether or not we can accept the answers. The more we practise, the more the teacher is revealed. The more we practise the more experiential our questions become, and the more obvious it will become whether the teacher is genuine. Of course it also works the other way round – If we don't practise, the teacher will *Know* from our questions what kind of apprentices we are. So – Great Confidence and Great Doubt: we need them both or the whole thing can be unreal. There's no one you can trust immediately, but *trust* can develop from your experience.

Questioner What if there is no teacher, or if you can't find a teacher?

Ngakpa Chögyam (laughter) There's always a teacher! Your own Beginningless Enlightenment is your teacher.

Questioner But how do I find that teacher?

Ngakpa Chögyam You find that teacher reflected in the *mirror* of the phenomenal world. You find that teacher when you Sit – you Sit and the teacher manifests. But at a more relative level, if you cannot find a teacher who has the capacity to *Reflect* your Enlightenment back to you – you just have to practise to the limit of whatever inspiration seems to arise in you. You may get stuck.

Questioner Is it indispensable to have a teacher?

Ngakpa Chögyam No. It's not indispensable. I wouldn't like to say it's indispensable. That wouldn't take into account the fact that people have individual capacities and predispositions. There is no rule that can always be applied at the relative level. I would say that virtually everyone would benefit greatly from working with a teacher. But there are also people who may well find problems in working with teachers. There are individuals who through past life experience have no need of a teacher – there are many conditions and circumstances as you can imagine.

Questioner Could you elaborate on what you said about people causing themselves problems with teachers?

Ngakpa Chögyam Well. There are many things I could say

about teacher–apprentice relationships and the problems that can sometimes arise. Fundamentally your own Beginningless Enlightenment is your best teacher, and anyone who can reflect that for you can help you on your Path. Basically if we approach teachers because we wish to have our Beginningless Enlightenment reflected – that is the basis of a good teacher–apprentice relationship. If we want our teacher to be some sort of god, mother or father figure, we're in trouble. I've been through that one myself. Working with a teacher isn't always comfortable. If we want it to be comfortable – we're bound to find certain aspects of that relationship problematic. Some teachers, masters or gurus aren't always quite as Realised as they're made out to be, so you need to have your critical faculties sharpened in the initial stages – especially before you make any kind of commitment. But also with your critical faculties; don't make them so sharp that you cut your own throat or impale yourself on them. The intellect can supply us with excuses and justification for avoiding anything, good or bad. So don't make a commitment to a teacher just because you're lonely. The teacher is invaluable on the Path, but we must be *in touch* with what we need from such a person. Trungpa Rinpoche describes the teacher as a 'dangerous friend'. We need to know how far we're prepared to go with this person, whether what we want is holding hands, kissing, heavy petting – or whether we want the earth to move.

Questioner   What do you do to get you through the difficult times in meditation before you have a teacher to work with?

Ngakpa Chögyam   You find inspiration wherever you can – in books, pictures, people, dreaming and waking. We need to be open to inspiration, and remember to nurture our enthusiasm. The *fabric of life* and our relationship with what we perceive is our constant teacher – we can all learn from this teacher endlessly. We can learn from others – we're not alone in treading the Path. Everyone has Beginningless Enlightenment as their intrinsic nature, and that cannot help but Sparkle through from time to time. To *See* that *Sparkle* as it manifests in ourselves and others can be a great inspiration, but we need to be open to being *moved* by that.

Questioner Is it important to find a teacher as soon as possible?

Ngakpa Chögyam Yes and no. I don't think it's good to attempt such a relationship too soon. You don't get married to the first person you get sweet on. If you're hungry, you don't necessarily eat at the first restaurant you pass. Maybe you read the menu outside and then decide to move on. Maybe you go inside but because the place is packed with posers you decide to try some place else. Maybe you go in and Sit down but they take too long to serve you and so you leave. Maybe you can't afford the prices and have to try and find somewhere cheaper. I'm not strictly talking about making value-judgements, but about suitability. Many Masters are charismatic, but there has to be some sort of connection beyond that – something has to correspond with your experience. Many Masters will take anyone on as an apprentice, simply because they'd never wish to dampen people's enthusiasm. But some Masters are known to turn people away simply because fostering a relationship with some individuals would be detrimental to their growth. Lama Namkhai Norbu Rinpoche once recounted the story of how a certain very wild and fierce Master use to drive most people away by rolling boulders down the mountain as soon as they became visible! From one perspective, there's no useful purpose to be served in trying to teach someone who would be ideally taught by someone else. These two methods of accepting or rejecting apprentices may seem in conflict with each other – but there is no right or wrong in this, both function according to an individual principle. Masters who accept all comers simply allow prospective apprentices to self-select – if the relationship isn't right the apprentice just moves on when that becomes obvious. It is better, however, if the aspiring apprentice is *active* rather than passive in the choice of teacher. It's important to work with a teacher for some time before making a definite commitment.

Questioner   But it *is* important to stick to one teacher, isn't it?

Ngakpa Chögyam   Not always. If your association with teachers works out in that way, then it's very good – but if it doesn't, that wouldn't be the end of practice. When the time comes to work with one teacher alone as a Tsa-wai Lama (Root Teacher) it will become very clear – incredibly obvious, but that is very much part of Tantra, and we're not really discussing the practice of Tantra at this point. As far as the practice of Sitting goes, what's important is that you're able to go and speak occasionally with people who have experience. It doesn't matter how many teachings on View you hear from different Buddhist Masters – it can only be of benefit.

Questioner   But isn't that just 'spiritual shopping'.

Ngakpa Chögyam   Yes.

Questioner   But isn't that bad?

Ngakpa Chögyam   (laughter) Not necessarily. (laughter) You have to shop around a little at the start in order to find out where you belong. I mean, it's no good becoming a Kentucky-fried Buddhist just because there's a Kentucky-fried Buddhist Centre just around the corner. I think that 'spiritual shopping' is very necessary. What is unhelpful or indeed positively detrimental is spiritual bigamy or spiritual adultery. Whose phrase is this : 'spiritual shopping'?

Questioner   I can't quite remember – no, I don't know.

Ngakpa Chögyam   Mmmmmmmmm. I don't intend to be critical – it depends largely in what context this analogy was being used. Anyhow, I'd like to crack this nut and find out what's inside it. I think that what we're really talking about is adolescence and maturity. When we're young it's healthy to frolic a bit – to have a series of lovers. But when we're pushing forty and still act in that adolescent way, it means that we lack maturity. There's nothing wrong with adolescent experimental restlessness in an adolescent, but for an adult it becomes a barrier to personal growth and maturity. In adulthood we need to learn how to sustain long-term relationships. Do you see the parallel?

Questioner　I do.

Ngakpa Chögyam　When we're young on the Spiritual Path we need to experiment and change – we need to try things out a bit. But when we grow up and have a little more experience, we can settle down and form a relationship with one teacher. It doesn't matter what age we are – we often need to go through a spiritual adolescence, and that is not a problem – it's a healthy part of our growth. It's only unhelpful to shop around when you're married. If you keep getting married and keep getting divorced – that's a problem. If you make marriage promises but keep having affairs on the side – that's a problem. Don't get me wrong on this, I don't intend this analogy to be taken too literally. I'm not an advocate of life-long marriage – divorce can be a stage in growth as well. I'm mainly talking about continually making and breaking relationships one after another. So, when you're spiritually young and doing your spiritual shopping, don't make promises or commitments you're liable to break. Does that make some kind of sense?

Questioner　Yes. Thank you for explaining that, it makes it a lot less intense.

Questioner　What happens if you get nothing from meditation?

Ngakpa Chögyam　If you continue to discover nothing of value in your Sitting then it's unlikely that you'll be able to sustain the motivation to Sit for very long. It's for this reason that I stress the examination of our initial experiences in such detail. (interrupted)

Questioner   But what if it just makes you feel bad?

Ngakpa Chögyam   Shi-ne doesn't make you feel bad, neither does the examination of how you are – Shi-ne merely exposes *what is there*. It's vital to recognise the experiences that occur when we Sit, and learn to acknowledge them as the fertile field of our development. We must expect discomfort, irritation, boredom, anxiety and melancholy. These feelings aren't 'produced' by Shi-ne like pulling a rabbit, lizard or seven-pound broad bean out of a hat – they're *discovered* through the process of Shi-ne. Our negative feelings are part of how we happen to be, and won't disappear merely because we say: 'Oh no, this Shi-ne makes me feel bad – I'm going to cut it out of my life for good and all!' We could possibly stop practising Shi-ne and say: 'Gosh, I'm glad I don't do that awful Shi-ne anymore – life is so much more pleasant without it,' but our negative feelings would still be there. Because negative feelings are generated by our perceptual patterning, we'll experience them whatever we do. Shi-ne just puts us in a position in which we can find out why we have such feelings.

Questioner   Can I ask about itching? I feel that itching can be a problem. I'm never sure if I should relieve the itch or whether that's just another distraction. I mean, should I try to control that?

Ngakpa Chögyam   The best thing to do if you itch is scratch. You can move slowly, and be mindful of the process of scratching. There's no need for any of us to be spiritually embarrassed about the fact that we have bodies. The problem arises when we keep itching and can't seem to stop – first we scratch here, then we scratch there, then we go back to the first itch again and scratch it a bit more. If this goes on all the time when we Sit, but doesn't seem to happen when we're not Sitting – we could become a little bit suspicious about that, we could be involving ourselves in some devious form of entertainment. I itch therefore I am. If I feel the need to have a scratch, then I need to be aware if it's a real need or a diversionary tactic. If I'm scratching all the time, maybe I could think: 'Mmmmmm – about time I changed the cat's flea collar!' So, the answer here is like most other answers as far as practice is concerned: Awareness. Awareness first, Awareness last, Awareness at any other time or in between times – Awareness. Awareness gives *you* confidence, makes *you* autonomous and makes *me* superfluous!

Questioner   Makes you superfluous?

Ngakpa Chögyam   Yes, that's my intention – to make myself dispensable, to enable you to have no more need of me.

Questioner   You mentioned earlier, that we didn't have to be spiritually embarrassed about having bodies, and I thought that was interesting in view of the emphasis on Voidness in Buddhism, which seems to deny the value of having a body and being in the world.

Ngakpa Chögyam   Yes, there is that tendency in Buddhism in general, but it's a patriarchal bias – I don't see it as something intrinsic to Buddhism. You must remember that Emptiness is initially stressed a great deal because, while we *do* have contact with substance-reality, very few of us have awareness of the *substanceless essence of substance*. The aim is to Realise Emptiness in order to relate genuinely with the transience of phenomena. The patriarchal line tries to tell us that because substance is transient, it is of no spiritual worth. But phenomena are the efflorescence of Emptiness, and so to denigrate the world of form is to deny that quality of Emptiness that gives birth to form. This is like praising the mother whilst disparaging her children. The word 'spirituality' actually gives the game away a little with the idea that Enlightenment means leaving the world and becoming a 'spirit'. This is a patriarchal distortion. The patriarchy has always denied the earth, and that tendency wherever its found needs to be exposed and seen for what it is.

Questioner I thought that it was absolutely primary to Buddhism to describe the nature of existence as suffering?

Ngakpa Chögyam Well now, that needs to be examined a little bit more carefully. It's *not* the nature of existence itself that has the quality of suffering – it's our experience of existence that is characterised as suffering. But 'suffering' is such a dreadfully emotive word. I prefer to use the word unsatisfactoriness. Sure, I know many people in the world suffer dreadfully and I have no intention at all of underplaying that – there *is* terrible pain in the world, and we should all do whatever we can to change that. But not everybody experiences the world as being such a terrible place. I know quite a lot of people who seem to enjoy life to a modest degree, and if you told them that the chief characteristic of life was 'suffering' – they'd think you were a depressive or a pessimist. They'd probably say: 'Yes, I've had a few bad times, but in general it's been all right – in fact on a few occasions I've had a whale of a time.' I don't think, however, that most people would say that their lives were completely satisfactory. There's always something that could be better, wider, longer, shorter, narrower, darker, lighter, or more highly paid – but that's our perception, not the world. *The world just is as it is.*

Questioner You're saying that this denial of the earth and the body is a patriarchal distortion?

Ngakpa Chögyam Yes. Space is the *Great Mother*, but Earth is also our Mother. Water, Fire and Wind are also our Mothers. This is the Transmission of the Mother-Essence Lineage.

Questioner When you were talking about the Referenceless Ocean of Being, you said that the analogy of 'the dewdrop slipping into the shining sea' was rather schmalzy. I found that surprising, because it has always seemed such a beautiful poetic statement about the Ultimate. Can you expand on why you consider it schmalzy?

Ngakpa Chögyam (laughter) I'm sorry. (laughter) If you find it beautiful (and I'm quite sure a great many people do) I've got no argument with that. But once you've taken away the beauty, what does it mean?

Questioner I thought it was supposed to express something ineffable.

Ngakpa Chögyam (laughter) Right! It is pretty ineffable, but maybe silence is better on ineffable subjects. If a sentiment is a finger pointing at the moon, what has beauty got to do with it? Truth may well be beautiful, but is beauty always Truth?

Questioner (laughter) I think I see what you're getting at, all dogs are animals but not all animals are dogs.

Ngakpa Chögyam The very same. What makes me describe this as schmalzy is not the beauty of the words, but some kind of inherent sentimentality. I mean, you could transpose the words of this little saying on the same lines, and it might not appear to mean quite as much: 'A gobbit of phlegm slides into the cosmic spitoon.' (laughter) How does that sound? (laughter)

Questioner (laughter) Not very meaningful. (laughter) Thank you, I see what you mean.

Je-thob – post meditation

20
Everyday Life

Questioner   How can I bring the practices of Tibetan Buddhism into my everyday life?

Ngakpa Chögyam   By letting go of the sharp divisions between the times when you're Sitting and the times when you're not Sitting. Sitting is a little bit like going into retreat – it's a period of time when we completely let go of all involvement. Sitting is a space in our lives where we can nurture our mindfulness; but mindfulness should manifest continuously. His Holiness Dudjom Rinpoche once said of our initial experiences of Rigpa (the Naked Awareness of Being) that it is rather like a baby thrown ruthlessly into that battlefield of arising phenomena. This means that we have to nurture this experience through integrating it gently with everyday life – we can't just plunge back into our conventional existence if we're aiming at integration. So to integrate practice into everyday life, we should allow the Spaciousness we discover in our Sitting to *overflow* into our 'ordinary life experience'. To make a metaphor : we must dismantle the dam that holds back the Great Ocean of Being from flooding our existence. We can start by allowing the post-Practice period to be a time when we remain completely *with* whatever we are doing.

Questioner   Is there a method . . .

Ngakpa Chögyam   (laughter) No, there is no method. (laughter)

Questioner   (laughter) No, of course not.

Ngakpa Chögyam   There is just Being. If there is a method, then . . .

Questioner   Quite. (laughter)

Ngakpa Chögyam   But maybe I could say something about the post-practice period. If you want to develop the post-practice experience, you'll need to make sure that you leave time for it. If you Sit for an hour, make sure that you have at least 15-30 minutes for the post-practice period. When you get up from your Sitting session, stand up slowly and mindfully. Massage any pain or stiffness in your legs and ankles, and continue to find the Presence of your Awareness in whatever sensation arises – but avoid conceptualising about the process. Find the Presence of your Awareness in every nuance of your movements but don't become too 'internalised' – just Be where you are. You could get up and make a cup of tea or do the washing up – but whatever you do, simply Be with what you are doing, and if you're distracted – return to Awareness. It's best to be on your own in the post-Practice period, so that you can integrate Presence of Awareness at each moment without too much external distraction. When your post-practice period time is up, don't let that end suddenly either. In the same way that you moved carefully from Sitting into movement – move gradually from the post-practice period into whatever it is that has to happen next. In fact, there's really no need to end the post-practice session at all. We all continually lose Presence, but whenever our Presence re-emerges and we realise that we've drifted off – we can remain *in* or *with* that Presence. This is the practice of everyday life – continually returning to Presence whenever distracted from Presence, and continuing with Awareness to remain in Absolute Presence. The real practice of integration is to return to Awareness whenever we are distracted from Awareness. This is in fact the practice of Dzogchen – the most direct practice of Enlightenment, so maybe we can't practise like this. (laughter) But maybe we can. But whatever our level of practice, we can try to be mindful of whatever it is we're doing.

Questioner 2   That seems almost too simple.

Ngakpa Chögyam   Yes, (laughter) almost. (pause) You're

wearing the expression of someone expecting an answer to a question – what would you like me to add?

Questioner 2   Well, I feel as if there is nothing for me to get hold of in that, as if there should be something more.

Ngakpa Chögyam   Like a mantra, visualisation or breathing technique?

Questioner 2   Well no but . . .

Ngakpa Chögyam   Like something that would enable you to 'be' in a particular style, rather than just Being?

Questioner 2   Oh, I see what you mean.

Ngakpa Chögyam   The *method* is a method of *no-method*. The *method* is *Just Being*. If we find that we can't continue in that state of *Just Being*, then we can try to be mindful.

Questioner 2   And if we can't be mindful?

Ngakpa Chögyam   Then we trip over things, which is life's way of reminding us to be Mindful. From a Tantric perspective we could say that the Khandros observe our lack of Mindfulness and give us an ankle tap which sends us sprawling onto the ground. But if we can't be mindful, then maybe we can try to acknowledge what is going on around us as being a teaching.

Questioner 3   Could you say a little more about that – about seeing life as a teaching?

Ngakpa Chögyam   Well – we can let the world speak to us. We can *listen* to the world – we can *see* what the phenomenal world is *mirroring*. We can see impermanence, sickness, old age and death all around us. It's a free teaching. It's performing all the time, and all we have to do is observe it and take it in. We can understand from just looking at what is going on all around us, that this is what life is. Sometimes it's happy, sometimes it's sad, and sometimes it can't quite seem to make up its mind. But what is 'it'? It is our perception – sometimes it's attracted, sometimes it's averse and sometimes it's indifferent. And what is it that we're attracted, averse and indifferent to? To *what is*. Maybe from this we could work out that it would be more appropriate to mirror this *what is* in our perception, so that when someone asks us what we think of *what is*, we could reply: '*What is*, is *what is*.' I suppose that that may seem a little unhelpful, and maybe in some ways it is – that is why we practise, and that is why there are so many different kinds of practice. In order to acknowledge *what is*, we need to learn how to *see what is*. I had a very interesting English teacher when I was young. His name was (I suppose he's dead by now) Mr Preece, and he would sometimes set us amusing, though complicated exercises. One of these was concerned with how many repetitions of a word you could use, and still have it make sense – so I worked out this one: 'That that is, is. That that is not, is not. That that is not is not, is not is not – is not that it? – That is!' (laughter) Yes it was quite an amusing word game, and I suppose that sometimes the explanations of Mind can get to sound a bit like that. But there's a difference – one is a game and the other is for real. As soon as we deal with areas beyond conventional comprehension, words become stretched to capacity, and we either follow them or we don't. But we can always learn from life. We can walk down the street and let it be a contemplation on the nature of existence. We can allow our *Intrinsic Warmth* to arise in response to the sadness we see. We can allow ourselves to feel *open* and *loving* towards the people we see passing us. Walking down the street can be a powerful experience if we actually take in what is going on.

Questioner   There is so little time for us here in the West with job and family and so many demands. How is it possible to find peace and tranquillity in our lives?

Ngakpa Chögyam Do you think that the East and the West are so different?

Questioner In India there must be much less pressure than here.

Ngakpa Chögyam They also have jobs and families. But what about the pressures; what kind of pressures are you talking about? You don't have to answer too personally if you'd rather not.

Questioner No, it's not so personal. It's the pressure of society to achieve and to perform, and for your children to achieve and have status.

Ngakpa Chöygam That sounds pretty much like India to me. But have you no choice as to whether you want to accept the dictates of this pressure.

Questioner It's expected.

Ngakpa Chögyam Well yes, maybe – but what is the penalty if you don't do what's expected?

Questioner You mean we should all drop out?

Ngakpa Chögyam No, that's the other end of the scale – I don't see the situation as having to be that polarised. I think that you can drop out if you like or be an executive if you like – there's no problem with what you do, but how you feel about what you do. I think that there's no need to be a typical drop-out or a typical executive, but I think that the penalty of being non-typical can sometimes be isolation. If you interest yourself in anything outside 'the norm', you'll be going against the general trend. But I think that if you've been interested enough to come along here tonight, and interested enough to come along on many other occasions, that you must have some freedom and independence from 'the norm' already. Everyone here is really free enough to be an individual and write their own script for how they'll live their lives. Some of the choices we make in our lives are bound to set us apart from one social group or another. My choice not to smoke puts me in a position where I have to excuse myself from smoky environments. It's not really possible to direct our lives creatively if we're governed by what is expected of us. What happens when people close to us expect opposite things from us? What do we do then? It's really not possible to please all the people all the time. We can maybe please half the people all the time and all the people half the time but . . . but you can be in my dream if I can be in yours – I think Bob Dylan said that. So, choices have to be made – directions have to be taken, and we have to accept the whole situation in terms of the person we are becoming.

Questioner   But if I lived in a place where spiritual values were important and honoured, there would be less conflict. The pace of life in India must make it much easier to meditate.

Ngakpa Chögyam   That depends on who you are, and on the character of your experiencing. What do you think my life is like here in the West?

Questioner   But you gained your Enlightenment in the East.

Ngakpa Chögyam   Hummmm. Well, I certainly spent a lot of time practising in the Himalayas and from that I gained something very real – but as to Enlightenment, that's another matter. I'm a practitioner and speak from a practitioner's experience. I spend several hours in formal practice every day. Enlightenment is our Beginningless Nature – we're all practising in order to Realise that. We all have flashes of our Beginningless Enlightenment from time to time. For some of us that experience is more frequent – for others less frequent, but we all practice to increase the frequency and intensity of the *Sparkling through* which is our Innate Enlightenment. Maybe this answers your question to some extent – it's not the environment that makes the difference, it's the state of mind. I've got no complaints about the

West or the East, but I can see that there seems to be a sense of spiritual romance about the East – and that is a fantasy balloon that needs to be punctured. The idea that India is a peaceful place is a little misleading. Sure, there are peaceful tracts of the Himalayas that have a wonderful atmosphere for practice, but then if you go to the highlands of Scotland or wherever – you'll find equally wonderful places. But in India, wherever there are people, there's usually also quite a lot of noise and bustle. I remember Sitting in a quiet place in the woods above Mcleod Ganj. A more tranquil spot you couldn't hope to find – but it wasn't long before a conspicuous party of Indian tourists arrived to have a picnic about two hundred yards away from me. Now our idea of a picnic may be to go off to some remote and idyllic spot to immerse ourselves in the beauty or grandeur of the scenery. But the popular Indian alternative is rather different. It gives them more pleasure to turn a woodland glen into an open-air night-club! I'm making no serious value-judgement here, each to their own, but I know which kind of picnic I'd find more appealing. I think that the industrial environment in which many of us live, gives us more of a taste for the beauty of nature than our rather more festive Indian friends who often love nothing better than to have half a dozen radios wound up to capacity and emitting the most fiendish row – have you ever heard Hindi film music? (laughter) When I first went to India, I had some fantasy notion of swanning around in a starry-eyed Sergeant Pepper frame of mind entranced by gracious glissandos of Sitar music. I imagined that just by being in India I would somehow become transformed by the power of its great spiritual heritage. (laughter) But it didn't quite work out like that. (laughter) I'm sure it was my fault. (laughter)

One thing that being in India certainly did for me just by being there, was to push my nose hard up against the reality of death. And it wasn't just the sight of a Ganges hippo that did that, it was the sheer closeness to death of everything. It was the way that in that heat and humidity, buildings would be showing signs of decay before they were even finished. Sorry, I should explain about the Ganges hippo. When human bodies have been immersed in water for long enough to swell up and become almost unrecognisable as human beings and some speak of them as Ganges hippos. But India is also full of life. Dr Bertie Beecham, a lecturing colleague of my wife, recently went back to India for a holiday. He'd been brought up there, but had moved here many years ago having married a Welsh lady. During dinner with us one evening, I asked him how he'd enjoyed his holiday in India. He laughed and jovially replied: 'I call it the land of yells, bells and smells!' He was quick to point out that the yells were not always raucous, the bells not always shrill and the smells not always unpleasant – in fact it was part of a poem he had written on his return.

No – India is hardly a peaceful place, although I am very fond of India and her people for all that. But I can't say it was a 'better' place for practice than here. The best place for practice *has* to be wherever you live; otherwise the path we're discussing would merely be a cultural manifestation. The practice of Sitting is transcultural – it deals with the human condition in all its diversity. The tall pointed hats with long ear-flaps worn by Tibetan Lamas represent 'retreat caves' – and the symbolism is that ultimately your retreat is wherever you are. In the noisiest place you could imagine – there is silence. Sound manifests within Silent Space, and the function of practice is to discover Silent Mind. When Mind is Silent, there is *Endless Silent Space in which Sounds Sing Infinitely separate Songs*. Even if you were to find yourself a retreat cave high in the Himalayas, or Sit in a soundproof room – you'd start to hear the sounds of your own body. There'd be fluids gurgling, the sound of your breathing and the background hiss of your ears. These sounds would eventually distract and disturb you as much as any other sounds, simply because you'd never have come to terms with the dissonance of your own subconscious noise. Your body sounds would seem as offensive as the din of London traffic.

People often say they'd like to meditate, but that there never seems to be enough peace and quiet. They say: 'If only I could go and live in the country, I'd be able to settle into a meditative life-style.' I'm sorry to say that this is just another fanciful idea – the countryside is as full of noises that would be distracting as anywhere else. The sound of a pneumatic drill in the street below your bedroom window or the sound of several thousand crickets; which would be more distracting? Sure, the crickets aren't there all year round, but then neither is the pneumatic drill. I gave a course once at Caroline Sherwood's 'Meditation Room' in Dorchester, and the most profound meditative experience anyone had was when a road resurfacing machine passed by below! I heard it coming and just as it started to annoy the people Sitting I said 'Just find the Presence of your Awareness in the dimension of the sound.' And they did. It was a wonderful sound! The sound of rooks roosting can be very intrusive – much more so than the hum of distant traffic. The 'natural world' has romantic associations for us, but ultimately it comes down to concept – it's a matter of our attraction, aversion and indifference to what these various sounds represent – rather than to the energy of the sound itself. To imagine that a 'peaceful place' makes meditation easier is ultimately nonsensical.

Questioner So we would be better off accepting whatever situation we find ourselves in.

Ngakpa Chögyam Exactly. Wherever you are is exactly where *you are*, and where can you be apart from where you are? If you have to alter your location to Realise you're not unenlightened, it means that the method you've chosen is limited by circumstantial conditions. But if we take the relative view there are a few things I could say that might apply to how we happen to find ourselves, in relation to daily practice. If we have extensive experience in practice, we can Sit anywhere and integrate the Presence of our Awareness with whatever arises as a sense-perception. But when we are new to practice we need to treat ourselves a little more gently and take account of the fact that we can easily become distracted. Now this may sound as if I'm contradicting what I said before, and to some extent I am – because Ultimate View and relative view often appear to conflict. My first comments dealt with the fact that there is no such thing as a distracting influence –

this is the Ultimate View. We distract ourselves – we cannot blame the noises as they have no volition or distracting intention in themselves. I made this point in order to discredit the idea that we have to find some peaceful tranquil spot before we can Sit. But from a relative point of view, you *do* have to find a situation where you're not intruded upon by noises that have a regular or intelligible pattern. What I mean by this is that if there's someone next door, and they cranked up their radio on some manic fast-talking commercial music show, it can be very difficult to keep yourself from 'tuning in' to it. If the couple next door are having a shrill acrimonious row and your walls aren't particularly thick, trying to *let go* and *let be* can be tricky. The problems lie in the 'intelligible quality' of the sound rather than its volume. Traffic hum or the critching of crickets are 'unintelligible' sounds, and we should be able to get along with that kind of sound in most of its manifestations. With unintelligible sounds there's not so much for our intellect to latch on to. Because these sounds aren't deliberately fabricated by intellect (and because they have no discernible intellectual content), intellect doesn't key into them unless we overlay them with our concepts of liking or disliking. Our intellectual faculties lock like velcro-fastening into intellectually produced sound unless we have considerable meditative stability. So if you have to battle to keep your attention *off* intellectual noise, it can become a bit like trying to swim with a few fur coats on.

Questioner Can it ever be dangerous to meditate in everyday situations – I'm thinking about how it would be if I was driving a car. That could be dangerous couldn't it?

Ngakpa Chögyam It largely depends on what you mean by meditation. If you find the Presence of your Awareness in the process of driving, you'll be the safest driver on the road! If your mind is wandering, if your attention is not *in* what you are doing – if you're hang-gliding in your imagination when you're driving, that could certainly be very dangerous. Have you ever seen those stickers in the back of cars that say things like: 'I'd rather be wind-surfing!' ? I think that the meditative version could run: 'I'd rather be precisely where I am!' Because often – we're off somewhere else, even when we are wind-surfing. If your meditation is something like a trance-state in which you enter some other world and cut off to the 'outside world', then yes, that would be lethal. But that's not the kind of meditation I've been talking about. I've been explaining the practice of maintaining our Presence of Awareness – Being completely *with* whatever we're doing. In this way driving your car *is* the practice. The idea that the Four Naljors cut you off from the 'outside world' dies hard, and so I must emphasise that whatever methods of meditation are taught in other systems – these Naljors are *not* about turning inward. There is *no* inward or outward bias in these practices – just Being in order to heal the dividedness of inner and outer.

Questioner   How does that fit in with the Vajrayana (Tantric) idea of everything we perceive being the mandala of the deity (Awareness-Being) and everything we hear being the mantra (Awareness-spell) of the deity?

Ngakpa Chögyam   This is probably a bit technical for some of us here, does everyone understand the question? (pause) Well, (laughter) I'll answer it in brief – it would take a few weekends to explain this in simple terms, and in a way that would be better. Still for those of you who have had initiations, which is (pause) Oh I see, *all* of you. Well in that case you should find something to catch hold of in this. Basically Tantra or Vajrayana is based on visionary experience. It functions according to the principle of Transmutation. Tantra involves finding the Presence of our Awareness within the Sphere of Energy. So, we're working with *sound* and *light*, which are dimensions of *energy*. What you called 'deity' is a Spontaneously Liberated Appearance – a *Wisdom-Quality* of our own Enlightened Nature. What you called 'mantra' is the Spontaneously Liberated *Resonance* of 'deity' or Awareness-Being – the sonic reflex of our Enlightenment Energy. When we integrate that *visionary experience* with everyday life, we recognise our world as the *dimension of awareness* – radiating from the *visionary nature* of what we are. The sound quality of our environment is the resonance of that *visionary nature* in the *dimension of sound energy*. But this is a very difficult subject to discuss in so short a period of time. Every concept I've used needs to be expanded and simplified. Unfortunately we're just about to leave this place and go our separate ways. But what can I say about entering into *visionary experience* whilst driving a car? (laughter) In view of the fact that we're all going to be doing that in ten minutes I'd better say something hadn't I (laughter) I don't really think it's such a good idea – I'd like to see you all again one day, in your present bodies! (laughter)

With *visualisation* we're re-creating our world and ourselves in the same way that everything arises out of Space. With *visualisation* we're practising to find ourselves beyond karmic-vision, through using the self-same process by which karmic-vision arises, but without attachment. The Appearance and Resonance of Awareness-Being *is* the method of transmutation. We dissolve our karmic-vision into Emptiness and *spontaneously* arise or recreate ourselves and our world according to the Tantric Transmission we've received. This process of recreation takes place initially in the visionary sphere (the Sphere of Intangible Appearance – Long-ku / Sambhogakaya). Once we've Realised ourselves in that *dimension* we can work towards an integration of that experience with everyday life (the Sphere of Relative Manifestation – Truk-ku / Nirmanakaya). The integration of visionary experience with everyday life completes the practice (of the reversal of the three Spheres of Being in which after dissolving all appearances into Emptiness, we arise again in the Liberated form of Awareness-Being and Realise the Essential Unity of the Three Spheres of Being – Chö-ku, Long-ku and Trul-ku). Entering the Visionary Dimension of Experience in everyday life is a great accomplishment. It depends on the level of our experience and capacity if it's not just going to be a day-dream. We need to Realise Emptiness before we can approach this. Practising Tantra means entering the Sphere of Energy!

APPENDIX 1:

The Life and Lives of Chhimed Rigdzin Rinpoche

These interwoven narratives (in the form of mystical-hagiographic, biographic and autobiographic material) relate to the life of H. E. Khordong Terchen Tulku Chhimed Rigdzin Rinpoche, and his previous lives as Incarnations of the Great Tantric Master Nuden Dorje.

The beginning of this Timeless unfoldment of Enlightened Activity towards the Liberation of others, takes us back into a previous time-cycle. History in Tibetan Buddhist understanding is undifferentiated from Mystic Visionary Experiences, and this can often confuse people who assume from their cultural orientation that there is one set way of looking at the past. We could speak of history in the West as being the history of the world of substance – the Old Testament and the 'mythologies' of the Norse and Greek deities are exceptions to this, but they no longer form part of one coherent system of history. We could contrast this substantial view of history with the Visionary history of Mystic Experience, and to the Western frame of reference they would be very obviously different. But from the Tibetan point of view the Realities are undivided – the Visionary and substantial histories flow into each other, they are interwoven. Visionary history only becomes mythology when we lose contact with the Visionary Sphere of Experience, so to comprehend the meaning of this history will be difficult if we are not able to *move* slightly from our fixed cultural perspective. If we are able to let go of our commonly accepted ideas of what is real, then this *Spiritually Relevant* stream of sequences will provide inspiration and wonderment for anyone open enough to let it *move* them.

Time in Tibetan Buddhist history is calculated in aeons – great time-cycles. In each time-cycle, *Knowingness* manifests and *reflects* the Beginningless Enlightenment of all sentient beings. In our current time-cycle, Buddha Sakymuni (Completely Awakened Sage of the Sakya clan) appeared in the land now known as Nepal in order to Reflect our Beginningless Enlightenment. During the previous time-cycle, Buddha Rinchen Nyingpo (Jewel Essence) appeared and Transmitted Wisdom to four Awareness-Beings. These were known as; Ö-pa-me (Boundless Light), Chenrezi (Great Compassion), Chana Dorje (Thunderbolt Wielder) and Nuden Dorje (Undeposed Powerful Thunderbolt). They committed themselves through the Inspiration of Rinchen Nyingpo to act continuously for the Liberation of all sentient beings (the vow of Chang-chub-sem).

In our current time-cycle, Nuden Dorje first took rebirth as Shariputra, the foremost disciple of Buddha Sakyamuni. He then took rebirth as Dorje Hum-dze, one of the eight Great Tantric Adepts. Dorje Hum-dze (Humkara) received the Lineage of Buddha Garab Dorje who first Transmitted the Teaching of Dzogchen, and meditated in the Diamond Cave of Guru Padmasambhava. He received also the Transmission of Chu-len (extracting the Essence) from the Dzogchen Adept Gaga Siddhi in a secret cave in the Karakoram Mountains on the border of Afghanistan. The method of Chu-len involves living on the Essence of the Elements rather than eating food and Realising the Fulfilment of this Practice, Dorje Hum-dze became invisible.

When Guru Padmasambhava took the Teaching of Tantra to Tibet, Nuden Dorje took rebirth there as Do-wang Khye-chung Lotsa, one of the twenty-five closest disciples of Guru Padmasambhava. He received many transmissions of Wisdom from him at Chim-phu, Thamdrug, and Zhi-trö De-dro in the company of the Great Sky Dancing Lady Yeshe Tsogyel. He remained close to Guru Padmasambhava all the time he was in Tibet right up to his departure into other dimensions. Khye-chung Lotsa was a Great Master and had the power to attract the birds of the air by mudras (mystic hand gestures).

By this means he was able to teach beings at many levels of existence the Nature of Reality and enable them to achieve Realisation. This aspect of Chhimed Rigdzin Rinpoche came across very strongly to me in a letter he sent me in 1979 where he wrote: 'As I write I am watching the birds that have come from Siberia to the local river and are now returning home. They have very large wings and as they fly towards their home in the evening the sound is like the noise you hear at the time of storm. It is fantastic to watch them.'

Nuden Dorje next took rebirth as Gyalwa Thondup, the principal pupil of Ma-chig Labdron the famous female Lama and Realised Adept who developed the practice known as Chod (Cutting attachment to the corporeal form).

He then took a series of rebirths as: Namgyal Gonpo who was the son of Rigdzin Go-dem (founder of the Chang-ter – Northern Treasury of Mystic Discovery): Mahasiddha Sang-gye Palzang; Mahasiddha Tong-chö Repa; Mahasiddha Bum-pa; Tertön Chenpo Dudul Dorje and Tak-sham Nuden Dorje.

In the nineteenth century he took rebirth as two individuals at the same time, as had been instructed by Buddha Padmasambhava. These two rebirths were: Nuden Dorje Drophang Lingpa of the O-chung Family in Nyi-khok, and Dudjom Lingpa of the Cha-kyong family who lived near the immense Kokonor Lake in Northern Tibet. These were both very Great Masters who taught profusely and were powerful in their influence for the benefit of all beings. Nuden Dorje Drophang Lingpa discovered twenty-three volumes of Terma (Rediscovered Mystic Treasure), and also other Terma of many different types. He discovered the magical implements which embody the Energy of Dorje Trölo. (These are the large Dorje and Phurba that have come down to Chhimed Rigdzin Rinpoche today and give him the name of Khordong Terchen Nuden Dorje Drophang Lingpa Trölo Tsal.) He also discovered the amazing Do-dom Thong-ba Ton-den, a Terma box made of stone that is almost two feet in circumference. This box carries the impressions left by the hands of the great Wisdom Khandro (Sky Dancer) Yeshe Tsogyel; and a mark left by Guru Padmasambhava's index finger. This incarnation of Nuden Dorje had extraordinary magical powers – he could fly, remain below water or vanish completely. He lived to the age of 63 and on the day of his death a great rainbow appeared in the sky emanating from the hill where he died. The second incarnation, Do-dul Dorje, died at the very early age of 5. The third incarnation, Kalden Lingpa lived to be 37 years old, and discovered two very important volumes of Terma and a magical box.

Khordon Terchen Tulku Chhimed Rigdzin Rinpoche, the fourth incarnation of Nuden Dorje Drophang Lingpa and one of the greatest living Masters of the Nyingmapa School, was born on the full moon day of the fifth month of the Water-dog year (1922). He was first recognised by the Realised Master, Tulku Tsurlo. He was later recognised by the following nine high Lamas: Zhichen Ögyen Chemchog, Tertön Sogyal, Avam Tertön, Do Kyentse, H. H. Sakya Trichen, Jogchen Pema Rigdzin, H. H. Minling Trichen, Panchen Ertini, and H. H. the Thirteenth Dalai Lama. Three very special Tang-rils (divinations) were performed in which various names were written on paper and placed inside dough balls. At each of these tang-rils the only name to remain floating in the water bowl was the name of Chhimed Rigdzin Rinpoche. There was therefore no doubt at all in anyone's mind that this was the true Incarnation of the Great Nuden Dorje Drophang Lingpa. These Tang-rils were performed in three highly auspicious places to guarantee their complete efficacy: in front of the Jowo statue (the most ancient statue in Tibet), in the Jo-khang Temple in Lhasa, and before the assembly of Lamas engaged in powerful Protector Rites at the Khordong Gompa (Gompa means: Place of Meditation).

When Chhimed Rigdzin Rinpoche was 4 years old, he was enthroned at Khordong Gompa as the holder of the Lineage of Nuden Dorje Drophang Lingpa. H. H. Dudjom Rinpoche, who left his body early in January 1987, was the lineage holder of the other line of incarnations that came from Nuden Dorje (that originated with Dudjom Lingpa of Chakyong), which now leaves Chhimed Rigdzin Rinpoche as the only living incarnation of

Nuden Dorje fully trained in Tibet. Chhimed Rigdzin Rinpoche was also recognised as the incarnation of Kye-chung Lotsa's *Body*, Nanam Dorje Dudjom's *Speech*, and Guru Padmasambhava's *Mind*.

Nuden Dorje Drophang Lingpa built a number of important Gompas according to the Instruction of Guru Padmasambhava, and according to the predictions of both the Great Fifth Dalai Lama and Rigdzin Pema Thinley. His pupils built twelve other Gompas in Eastern Tibet, and these were the charges given to the 4-year-old Chhimed Rigdzin Rinpoche at his enthronement. It was a heavy responsibility for one so young, but he handled everything with ease and confidence.

At the age of 9 he took a stone in his right hand and squeezed it, thereby altering its shape. Chhimed Rigdzin Rinpoche says of himself as a young incarnation: 'I was rough and naughty, and at times my Teacher used to have to lock me inside my room!' But due to his magical abilities he was always able to escape without breaking the door or the lock. At the age of 10 he discovered two important volumes of Terma and an iron Terma box. There are numerous miraculous occurrences to be recounted from his childhood, but Rinpoche has asked me not to enumerate them as they would seem: '… flamboyant and exaggeratory.'

After his tenth year, he went on his first pilgrimage to Lhasa, where he took many important empowerments from Rigdzin Chenpo Nyam-ne Dorje and many other High Lamas. After two years of empowerments, instructions and practice, he returned to his Gompa of Khordong to complete his training with Tulku Tsurlo. He also trained under Ba-ne Tulku Ögyen Tendzin, Khenpo Sang-thar, Khenpo Lodro, Tulku Chö-kyi Gyaltsen, Khordong Khenpo Lo-tö Jigme, and other Great Masters of the time. He studied philosophy, logic, grammar, mandala, astrology, and especially Tantra under the direction of Tulku Tsurlo.

After the completion of his training, Tulku Tsurlo gave him seven important instructions and predictions that would guide his life. These are the words he received: 'You must leave Khordong Gompa at the age of 18 and become a wandering

practitioner in the mountainous lands of Bhutan, Sikkim, Nepal –
after which, you should go into three and a half years solitary
retreat in Tso Pema [Rewalsar in Himachal Pradesh India]. You
should not defend yourself in any way when at the age of 28 you
are attacked by a robber. You will fly in the sky at the age of 37.
You should, before the age of 60, take steps to save one of your
eyes from losing its power. You should return to Khordong to
return all the initiations you have received at a time when your
knowledge and wisdom are needed. You will live to be 84 years
old. You may possibly live to be 125 years old but that is not so
certain, depending as it does on many other factors.' The
prophesy that Chhimed Rigdzin Rinpoche could live to be 125
years old was also made by thirteen other Great Lamas, so his
pupils all wish very strongly that this prophesy will be fulfilled.

At this juncture in Chhimed Rigdzin Rinpoche's life he
continues in his own words. The words are unusually personal
and touching, full of power and yet so completely human that we
are able to understand quite clearly that Enlightenment doesn't
necessarily completely remove the difficulties of manifesting a
human form.

Till now, the first five instructions have been proved. The
third instruction was proved when I flew by aeroplane to Italy
at the invitation of the Tibetologist Giuseppe Tucci.

I have observed all these instructions as I was asked and now
at this age of 65 years I am awaiting to observe the last two. In
order to observe the instructions of my most venerable
Teacher Tulku Tsurlo, I left my Gompa at the age of eighteen
years. It was at eleven o'clock on the full moon night of the first
month of the earth rabbit year (1939) that I set out from there.
After crossing the cold Nyi-chu river, I turned back one last
time on my Gompa. It was very colourful. It was sad for me as
I was looking, and suddenly as I stood there all the good
memories came flooding in me: the fellow practitioners,
teachers, my childhood, disciples and all those years I spent in
study and spiritual training. It was my Lama's instruction to
leave my Gompa and so I was leaving; but it was not a wishful

departure with a happy heart. My heart was heavy and determined to fulfil the instructions of my Lama. Since then I have followed his instructions most sincerely and with great care until this day.

In the year of 1984, and at the age of sixty-two years, I received an important letter. It was from Ra-yab Bon-trul Rigdzin Pal-zor, who had remained in charge of Shik-chong, one of my Gompas. The letter came through Ven Tulku Thöndup who went to Tibet to visit his Gompa of Dodrupchen. Several other letters also came to me, and their message was all the same. They requested me to come back to my Gompa in order to give them the Chang-ter, Ter-sar and and many other Transmissions of which I am the holder. They requested me to come back to Tibet in order to give spiritual guidance to the remaining practitioners who had been without direction for so long. These letters came from: Khenpo Thubten Lodrö my chief disciple at Shik-chong Gompa; Wonbo Sonam Ösel who had been left in charge of Khordong Gompa; Yidrang Geku proctor of Khordong Gompa and Sherab Dorje my brother. I received these last named letters through Ven. Dodrupchen Rinpoche of Chöten Gompa in Sikkim. These fervent requests reminded me of my Lama's fifth instruction which I had promised to carry out.

After contemplation, I decided to visit my homeland and my Gompa, because in the Lineage of Teaching practised at my Gompas, I am the only Lineage Holder left alive on this earth. My son Ögyen Chenchö Lama and I were given the Chinese visas easily and flew from Calcutta to Beijing. From Beijing we flew to Cheng-du, and from there by road to Khar-nya Chu through Ta-chin-lo, Ta-ngo, and Kan-ze. Wherever we went we were given warm and friendly reception by the Tungko (Chinese) officials. We were hosted at dinners and taken to visit Chinese Buddhist Temples in Beijing and Cheng-du which we were pleased to see were in good shape and had never been destroyed. During our stay in Beijing I met H. H. Panchen Lama for two hours and discussed the current situation of Buddhism in Tibet and was satisfied that things had changed. I

talked to him regarding my Gompa and its restoration, and he
assured me all possible help through the Tungko Government
in his capacity as Fu-tushi (Deputy Chairman of Buddhists).

From Khar-nya Chu we travelled as far as we could by jeep
but reached a weak wooden bridge so we had to leave the
vehicles there. Across the wooden bridge a large crowd of my
own people from Khordong had assembled to receive me and
they took us from there on horseback. The ride took six hours
which was hard because after many years I am unaccustomed
to horse-riding. On the way we were met by many people who
had gathered along the route to offer us tea and nourishments.
We stopped at Dewa-nang, a place where Nuden Dorje had
been reborn and from there I saw my Gompa again for the first
time since the full moon night when I was eighteen. I couldn't
hold my tears and was unable to utter a word. All the
memories came at that moment, and I realised that I would not
be able to see the shrine that once stood there. What I saw of
my Gompa was just a ruined area. Only supporting columns
remained of what was once a most gorgeous Gompa. It was
then that I realised the value of my Lama's instruction. He had
foreseen the end of Buddhism in Tibet as it had been till then,
and wanted to save the Essential Transmission which should
not be lost. The destruction of a building is not the destruction
of a Lineage of Transmission. I had left Tibet at the age of
eighteen years along with my Termas (rediscovered Spiritual
Texts laid down for future discovery by Buddha
Padmasambhava) of my Lineage, and now I was bringing
them back to be practised once more.

As soon as we reached the Gompa we did the needed rites for
ten days, after which I gave Initiations for a further twenty-
two days. Then I went to Ser-ta district and gave Initiations for
fifty-two days. On this journey we also visited Shik-chong and
Ba-ne Gompas and saw that they had also been badly
damaged.

I returned to India on the fifth of December with a heavy
heart, but with renewed determination to return to help my
people according to the instruction of my Lama. So now my

first and most important work is to prepare to return to Tibet in order to teach the people of my country so that the teaching will not be lost. This is the most meaningful activity for me to undertake.

Many remarkable and inspiring reports have followed Chhimed Rigdzin Rinpoche's visit to Tibet, and some I feel it important to recount, as these miracles were not only witnessed by over a thousand East Tibetans, but by the Chinese officials who were so taken aback that a marked difference in attitude has followed his visit. Prior to his visit the Chinese Government did not allow the recognition of incarnations or the ordination of anyone under 18 years of age. However, during his visit, Chhimed Rigdzin Rinpoche recognised and declared sixty-nine incarnations and enthroned twelve of them with the approval and recognition of the Chinese authorities. Now the bar on monastic ordination below 18 years has been lifted and young children can be ordained.

On the 19th day of the seventh month of the Wood-ox year (6 July 1985) Chhimed Rigdzin Rinpoche consecrated a Great Chörten at Ser-ta, during which 20,000 monastic practitioners and Ngakpas together with over a hundred Incarnations and Khenpos and 15,000 lay people gathered in the largest valley of Kham Ser-ta Gor-gon Thang. The rite started at half-past ten in the morning in which Chhimed Rigdzin Rinpoche invoked the Lineage power of Guru Padmasambhava, Yeshe Tsogyel, Khye-chung Lotsa, Nuden Dorje, Tulku Tsurlo Apang Tertön and His Holiness Dudjom Rinpoche (the Supreme Head of the Nyingma School and Chhimed Rigdzin Rinpoche's Tsa-wai Lama). After this invocation an enormous rainbow appeared across the Ser-ta River and arced across the entire valey of Gor-gon Thang and remained glimmering in the sky until half-past four in the afternoon. While he was performing the consecration of the Chörten, a translucent white ring encircled him and the Chörten. Within this ring of light three Thig-les (rainbow-coloured Spheres) appeared, and it is reported that people saw many different things within these Spheres. Most people reported that they saw five white vultures (embodiments of the Five Wisdom-Sisters – the Yeshe Khandros) wheeling around the Chörten as if dancing in flight. At the moment the five vultures appeared Chhimed Rigdzin Rinpoche threw a Katag (white blessing scarf) into the air and it remained suspended in mid-air above the Chörten for twenty-four hours.

Throughout his life he has been known for his magical abilities and power over the weather. In Tibet he averted many hailstorms that would have ruined harvests and also in India he has caused similar changes in the weather. When he came to Wales in the Spring of 1986 and stayed at 'Sang-ngak-chö-dzong' Tibetan Tantric Periphery, he interrupted several days of continuous rain in order that the people who had come to see him and share a seaside picnic would not be disappointed. But no sooner was the picnic over and we were back in the cars than the torrential downpour recommenced. Rinpoche repeated this Inspiring Display of Attainment in the car on our way back to London when the rain was driving down so hard that the driver couldn't see properly. No sooner had Dr Steve Glascoe mentioned the lack of visibility than it was cleared with a wave of Rinpoche's hand. When asked about these phenomena, Rinpoche denies his own capacity, saying that these things are only possible due to the Power of Guru Padmasambhava's Lineage of Realisation and the Great Confidence of the people who witness these things. The appearance in print of these astonishing incidents is due entirely to my insistent requests that such information should be made known.

When Chhimed Rigdzin Rinpoche returns to Tibet in 1988/89, it will be to a life of hardship and difficulty in the fulfilment of his Lama's instructions and in his own wish to be of help to his people. He is determined to return to Tibet for good, rather than accept an easy retirement when he leaves his post at Santiniketan University. Chhimed Rigdzin Rinpoche is not asking for any help for himself – he has already given away most of what he has in order to rebuild the Gompas under his charge and to house his disciples.

Because Chhimed Rigdzin Rinpoche's task is far greater than

his resources, the work will take many years to complete, even with the partial funding from the Chinese authorities. So I am asking, on behalf of Chhimed Rigdzin Rinpoche, that if anyone is interested in giving their help they should send whatever money they can to the address given in appendix 3. Because this work will take so many years to complete, your contribution will be of great value whenever you read this and feel moved to make a donation. However little you are able to help, you will be part of an effort to preserve a vital system of human transformation motivated by the altruistic wish to liberate all beings from confusion.

Since living in India, Western people have continuously sought out this Great Lama's instruction. He has always given freely and unstintingly of his time and energy without regard for a private life of any kind. The teaching that he has carried out has always had to occupy his spare time and vacations from his post as Professor of Tibetology and Buddhist Sanskrit at the University of Santiniketan. Because so much of his time has been devoted to supporting his family, he has not become as widely known in the West as some of the other great Lamas, and so he has no network of support in the West apart from a small number of pupils. If Tibet is to become once more the seat of advanced mystic attainment that it was, substantial help must be forthcoming. Chhimed Rigdzin Rinpoche's future work is crucial and historically significant in as much as what is lost now will be lost for ever. He is the last Lineage Holder of teaching and meditation systems that the world cannot afford to lose. The survival of this great lineage is of great value to all people of the world because although we may not all wish to make use of it, the fact that such lineages of wisdom exist and are available is one of the hopes of humanity. So to all those who are concerned with Liberation and value the spread of peace, harmony, kindness and freedom in the world: please help to ensure the continuity of this priceless part of our global inheritance – its message belongs to all of us.

Sang-ngak-chö-dzong

'Sang-ngak-chö-dzong' means: Secret Awareness-spell Fortress. This name was given to Ngakpa Chögyam by H. H. Dudjom Rinpoche, Supreme Head of the Nyingma School. The name was given as an inspiration and direction for the loose assocation of practitioners under Ngakpa Chögyam's guidance and instruction. There is, as Ngakpa Chögyam recounts, some humour in the name – a deliberate pun on his name vis – 'Sang-ngak(pa)-chö(gyam)-dzong', although the humour is lost if you don't happen to be a linguist. Tibetans often reduce terms and names to their initial syllables – as in Ngakpa Chögyam's name, which is a contraction of Chö-ying Gyam-tso: meaning Ocean of Space. The essential humour of Ngakpa Chögyam's radical presentation of the Teachings however, is a more obvious aspect to the approach to life and Practice that characterises those associated with 'Sang-ngak-chö-dzong'.

This name conceals many layers of meaning, but one that has become central is the idea of a Secret Fortress. ' For a Fortress to be Secret, it must be invisible. It must have no boundaries of exclusiveness – it must be an Internal Fortress of Practice rather than an external institution.' It is for this reason that there is no plan for a centre. There is a long term plan for a retreat place with land where people can pitch tents and where retreat huts can be built, but it would be a facility rather than a focus.

Humour, together with the idea of a 'secret fortress' and the emphasis away from Centres, gave rise to our own loose translation of 'Sang-ngak-chö-dzong' as: 'Tibetan Tantric Periphery'. The idea of a periphery rather than a centre, is that everyone must ultimately find their own 'center' within themselves, rather than in an institution, establishment or organisation. ' That we are a Periphery, isn't strictly meant as a criticism of Centres because in many ways they do fulfill some very valuable purposes. But in Tibet there was always an alternative to the monastic institutions – a Tradition of house-holding Lamas and nomadic Practitioners who were free of certain constraints.' It is this style of house-holding and wandering Practice that Ngakpa Chögyam has set out to encourage. With this approach – everyone's home is their Centre and Ngakpa Chögyam spends a lot of his time (when he is not writing or counselling) travelling to Teach in many different places.

Courses, Guided Retreats and Information

If having read *Journey into Vastness* you would like to take your interest further, courses and guided retreats are held several times a year which use this book as 'core material' and further evolve the themes within it.

Ngakpa Chögyam also gives experiential counselling courses based on his previous book *Rainbow of Liberated Energy* – a manual of working with emotions through the colour and element symbolism of Tibetan Tantra. He guides an 'Apprenticeship Programme' and travels on invitation to other countries. For those who have attended courses given by Ngakpa Chögyam, who are interested in developing a closer association with Ngakpa Chögyam the 'Apprenticeship Programme' facilitates personal contact with him through correspondence, interviews and Apprentice Retreats.

For further information on establishing Sitting Groups, and 'Sang-ngak-chö-dzong' activities, enquiries (enclosing a large stamped addressed envelope or envelope and international reply coupons sufficient to cover the weight of a dozen A4 sheets) should be addressed to:

The Secretary,
'Sang-ngak-chö-dzong'
Tibetan Tantric Periphery,

5 Court Close
Whitchurch
Cardiff CF4 1JR
Wales, United Kingdom
Telephone: 0222-620332